Messianic Imagination

Messianic Imagination

Politics, Theology, and Literature

EDITED BY
Joseph R. Wiebe,
Paul G. Doerksen,
Maxwell Kennel, AND
Grant Poettcker

FOREWORD BY
Stanley Hauerwas

CASCADE *Books* • Eugene, Oregon

MESSIANIC IMAGINATION
Politics, Theology, and Literature

Copyright © 2025 Wipf and Stock Publishers. All rights reserved. Except for brief quotations in critical publications or reviews, no part of this book may be reproduced in any manner without prior written permission from the publisher. Write: Permissions, Wipf and Stock Publishers, 199 W. 8th Ave., Suite 3, Eugene, OR 97401.

Cascade Books
An Imprint of Wipf and Stock Publishers
199 W. 8th Ave., Suite 3
Eugene, OR 97401

www.wipfandstock.com

PAPERBACK ISBN: 978-1-6667-6132-0
HARDCOVER ISBN: 978-1-6667-6133-7
EBOOK ISBN: 978-1-6667-6134-4

Cataloguing-in-Publication data:

Names: Wiebe, Joseph R., editor. | Doerksen, Paul G., 1960–, editor. | Kennel, Maxwell, editor. | Poettcker, Grant, editor. | Hauerwas, Stanley, 1940–, foreword.

Title: Messianic imagination : politics, theology, and literature / edited by Joseph R. Wiebe, Paul G. Doerksen, Maxwell Kennel, and Grant Poettcker ; foreword by Stanley Hauerwas.

Description: Eugene, OR : Cascade Books, 2025 | Includes bibliographical references and index(es).

Identifiers: ISBN 978-1-6667-6132-0 (paperback) | ISBN 978-1-6667-6133-7 (hardcover) | ISBN 978-1-6667-6134-4 (ebook)

Subjects: LCSH: Christianity and politics. | Political theology. | Christian ethics.

Classification: BR115.P7 .M51 2025 (paperback) | BR115.P7 (ebook)

VERSION NUMBER 10/29/25

Scripture quotations cited as NRSV are from The New Oxford Annotated Bible, Third Edition, 2001.

Scripture quotations cited as NIV are from New International Version, Zondervan, 2011.

John Terpstra poems are published with permission from Gaspereau Press.

Contents

Contributors | vii
Foreword: An Interview with Stanley Hauerwas | ix
Acknowledgments | xiii
Introduction | xv

Poems—JOHN TERPSTRA | 1
    Ceremony 1
    Topographies of Easter 3
    Conviction 5

Engaging Messianic Politics

1 Mediating Divine Love in the Messianic Imagination | 9
    —GREGORY D. WIEBE & JOSEPH R. WIEBE

2 Wrestling with Apocalyptic Eschatology and the Task of Political Theology | 26
    —MATTHEW THIESSEN

3 The Price of Christian Messianism | 37
    —PHILIP G. ZIEGLER

4 Do Nations Have Souls? An Augustinian Inquiry with a Canadian | 50
    —ERIC GREGORY

5 *Regnum Christi*, Apocalyptic, and the Everyday: Engaging the Work of Travis Kroeker | 64
    —GERALD McKENNY

6 Critique of Possessive Desire | 77
   —Maxwell Kennel

Extending Apocalyptic Theology

7 Decolonizing Grace | 93
   —Nancy Elizabeth Bedford

8 Is a Messianic Theology of Science Possible? A Sketch | 106
   —Douglas Harink

9 Miracles and Matter: Toward a Messianic Theology of Creation | 122
   —Justin D. Klassen

10 The Speed of Christian Patience | 136
   —Paul G. Doerksen

11 Labor of Love: Simone Weil's Kenotic Spirituality of Work | 150
   —Rachel Matheson

12 Paul's Apocalyptic Doctrine of Justification | 163
   —Stephen Westerholm

Exploring Literary Revelations

13 Apocalyptic Reversal and the Struggle for Honor | 177
   —Bruce K. Ward

14 Sex Unburdened: Augustine, Foucault, and the Transfiguration of Desire | 193
   —Sarah Stewart-Kroeker

15 Unveiling Beauty: Seeking the Messianic Measure in Elaine Scarry and Dostoevsky's *The Idiot* | 208
   —Grant Poettcker

16 Kissing, Killing, and the Epistemological Significance of Faith: A Reading of *Othello* and *Sapientia* | 223
   —Chris K. Huebner

17 Enough: Casey Plett on Everyday Trouble and Love | 234
   —Grace Kehler

Major Publications of P. Travis Kroeker | 247
Subject Index | 251
Scripture Index | 255

Contributors

Nancy Elizabeth Bedford, Garrett Evangelical Theological Seminary

Paul G. Doerksen, Canadian Mennonite University

Eric Gregory, Princeton University

Douglas Harink, The King's University

Chris K. Huebner, Canadian Mennonite University

Grace Kehler, McMaster University

Maxwell Kennel, Hamilton Mennonite Church and Pandora Press

Justin D. Klassen, Bellarmine University

Rachel Matheson, McMaster University

Gerald McKenny, University of Notre Dame

Grant Poettcker, Briercrest College

Sarah Stewart-Kroeker, Princeton Theological Seminary

John Terpstra, poet

Matthew Thiessen, McMaster University

Bruce K. Ward, Thorneloe University

Stephen Westerholm, McMaster University

Gregory D. Wiebe, Canadian Mennonite University

Joseph R. Wiebe, University of Alberta

Philip G. Ziegler, University of Aberdeen

Foreword

An Interview with Stanley Hauerwas

> *The following conversation between Stanley Hauerwas and Joseph R. Wiebe took place over Zoom on October 14, 2024. It has been edited for concision.*

STANLEY HAUERWAS: I was trying to remember the first time I met Travis. It was during the American Academy of Religion [AAR] about forty years ago at the Mennonite scholars and friends panel, and Travis was giving a paper on Augustine. I went with James McClendon and thought it was one of the most knowledgeable accounts of Augustine I had ever heard. Afterwards McLendon asked me what I thought. I told him I loved it. He said he hated it. He didn't think Mennonites ought to be reading Augustine because he was Constantinian. But that was something that never bothered Travis. You know we were both students of James Gustafson but he had a better relationship with Jim than I had. Travis was closer to the later Gustafson and I think was more sympathetic. I had a more antagonistic relationship with Jim so I was supportive of what he was trying to do.

JOSEPH R. WIEBE: So, you had different relationships with Gustafson, but you and Travis were both supportive of his work.

SH: Gustafson didn't want followers. He wasn't trying to get his students to do what he did. What he wanted was for his students to have the kind of independent mind he had.

JW: What makes Travis's mind different from yours?

SH: What you need to know about Travis is how the radical reformation, Anabaptism, is always in the background of his thinking. His critique of modernity is firmly rooted in that tradition. He's an Anabaptist with insight. That means he's an Anabaptist who can learn from Augustine.

JW: OK, so you met at AAR, but you both seemed to have found more of a disciplinary home at the Society of Christian Ethics [SCE]. Is that fair to say?

SH: I don't know if either of us would ever call SCE home. Maybe at times once. But there are people who want to make a distinction between theology and Christian ethics. People like to do ethics because it seems more relevant. But Travis is theological all the way down.

JW: That makes it difficult to find a disciplinary setting for the work that you both do—even between religious studies and Christian ethics?

SH: Christian ethics seems to focus everything now on social justice. It's not that I'm against social justice or anything like that, that would be ridiculous. It's that for Travis it's not abstract from radical Anabaptism. I never thought Travis got the recognition he deserved, not that it was his fault.

JW: Why do you think that is? I mean, he always takes his interlocutors seriously, he always talks about texts and theology as if they matter . . .

SH: He doesn't make it easy on you. Travis writes with a wide knowledge of the philosophical tradition and assumes you know you ought to know it. It just isn't all that common. He engages literature that a lot of folks in Christian ethics don't know what to do with. And there's a strong constructive aspect to Travis's work. My colleague Paul Griffiths would say that there is theology done in a speculative mode and then there is theology done in conversation with other people. I do more of the latter. I think Travis does it both ways.

JW: How do you account for that difference in how you do theology? What difference does it make?

SH: Travis can read texts slowly. He can get an understanding of texts that I can't because I read them too fast. And as a student of ours, you know

I want you to read fast. Travis gets his students to spend more time with texts. It's a gift.

JW: Well, you're both committed to supporting your students. And friendship seems to be a big part of how you both do your work.

SH: I think so.

JW: You talk about friendship, Travis talks about eros . . .

SH: That's because he reads Plato. He talks more about the soul than I do. I've never been pious or had much to do with sentimentality. But neither does Travis. I never did like using the language of transcendence because it was too abstract. There were people who wanted to talk about needing a transcendent purpose in life and that was good enough. Travis and I both were against that idea. He just found a way to talk about it. Does he talk at all about Charles Taylor and John Milbank?

JW: Yeah, on Augustinianism . . .

SH: It would be interesting to hear what he thinks about how they talk about transcendence and Plato.

JW: I've heard people criticize Travis for being "a little too gnostic."

SH: Well, some people have a tendency to overemphasize. I don't know if someone can be a little gnostic. But Travis is able to talk about the soul without sentimentality, as an abstract thing from the body. I always say that for Aquinas, the body is the best image of the soul. Travis reads Plato through Augustine so he uses language of desire. I think my work would've been fuller if I had been able to talk about that. When he talks about the soul and transcendence it's part of a critique of modernity that isn't overly determined by liberalism. That's another way you could state the difference between me and Travis. My work is unintelligible without [Alasdair] MacIntyre. You don't need MacIntyre to read Travis. Alasdair and I were both preoccupied with liberalism in a way that Travis isn't.

JW: Why do you think that is?

SH: Because Travis is Canadian. Canadians have as one of their conceits that they can tell themselves they're not American.

JW: [*laughs*] Yeah, well, I think there might be some self-deception going on in that narrative.

SH: [*laughs*] I'm sure there is. How is Travis's work received by Mennonites?

JW: Well. He has a strong relationship with folks at Canadian Mennonite University. He has also been at the annual Mennonite Studies conference at the University of Winnipeg several times.

SH: Why is that? Is that a Mennonite Brethren conference?

JW: It connects many of the Mennonite communities. Travis has been connected to it through the former chair of Mennonite Studies, Royden Loewen. But many people there have heard and received his work. And it's generated a lot of response from younger scholars. What do you think is important for them to know? How should these academics go forward with Travis's work?

SH: What's important is to emphasize the Kingship of Christ. You know, I think of you, and Alex Sider, Chris Huebner, and Peter Dula . . .

JW: That's very generous of you to group me with those names . . .

SH: OK, well the important thing is to have work that is unintelligible without Christ at the center. To do theology like it matters for the world. Travis did that out of Anabaptism, but he did that work with broad philosophical knowledge. That insight is there. And you can't do theology without philosophy. But I don't need to tell you that.

Acknowledgments

BRINGING TOGETHER THESE ESSAYS, conversation, and poetry has been a labor of admiration and respect for P. Travis Kroeker, and so we are deeply grateful to all who made this volume possible. Maxwell Kennel got the ball rolling and invited us to envision a collaborative approach to produce a tribute that could yet stand on its own as a contribution to delineating a messianic imagination. Gary Dunfield at Gasperau Press Ltd generously allowed us to reprint John Terpstra's poems. Maureen Epp's copy editing ensured each aspect of this contribution was of the highest quality. Support for the process was made possible by the Canadian Mennonite University's Social Science and Humanities Research Council Institutional Grant funding, Briercrest College and Seminary's Competitive Research Fund, the University of Alberta Augustana, and The Chester Ronning Centre for the Study of Religion and Public Life.

Introduction

Polemical, Vocational, and Existential Appreciations
(Joseph R. Wiebe)

IF ONE WANTS, IT is possible to draw a line in the sand between theology and religious studies; nevertheless, both fields invoke existential reflection. The difference between them might have less to do with methods, epistemologies, or ontologies than with the extent to which scholars in these respective fields are able to incorporate the personal. Every once in a while, there are academic conversations that remind us that our work does not consist in entirely disembodied arguments. Among the gifts of Travis Kroeker's writing are those moments offering a reminder that what we're studying in our disciplines, what we're putting under scrutiny, is ourselves. I introduce Kroeker's work here by focusing on one such dialogical moment. It calls attention to important themes he returns to in his other essays as well as in his unique approach to philosophical theology. It also demonstrates a passion for a particular kind of academic work that has helped others find their calling in scholarship.

The exchange between Travis Kroeker and Donald Wiebe—published in *Studies of Religion*, with a diplomatically stated editor's note that both authors "enjoy writing in a lively fashion"—is paradigmatic of how personal scholarship can turn out to be. What is far more revealing than reading Kroeker and Wiebe's dispute as one over proper methods in the study of religion is noting how these authors register what's at stake in their disagreement. Looking at it dramatically demonstrates both Kroeker's contribution to his field and his teaching philosophy, to use academic parlance. It feels more fitting to say that in this exchange we can see how Kroeker has invested himself in his writing in a way that helps us find him there.

Wiebe published *The Irony of Theology and the Nature of Religious Thought* in 1990. The next year, Abraham Khan organized a book panel for the Canadian Society for the Study of Religion at Queen's University. Panelists included Lorne Dawson and Tom Settle, whose papers were published in *Method and Theory in the Study of Religion* along with Wiebe's reply. Kroeker's response came two years later.

In "The Ironic Cage of Positivism and the Nature of Philosophical Theology," Kroeker criticizes Wiebe's account of the relation between theology and religious thought. Friends, readers, and students of Travis Kroeker will recognize the basic claims and critiques in his essay. All his major themes and commitments to his vocation are there, right near the beginning of his career as an assistant professor at McMaster University. "True thinking," he writes, is "the loving attunement of the soul to the order of being."[1] True thinking is "existential thinking," which is "rational reflection on the spiritual substance and order of existence in the world" (95). Scholarship fails when it refuses to engage with ancient wisdom. Methodologically, this is a refusal to carefully examine ancient texts, opting instead for a reliance on secondary sources to give only "the appearance of scholarship" (97). Learning how to truly think—training in critical philosophical theology—is more than merely learning to "repeat other people's thoughts and opinions" (102). Pedagogically, this is soul formation. Education is "the search for the true measure by which to make critical judgements based on existential knowledge of the order of reality" (99). This search cannot be reduced to research trajectories, though it can be described that way pragmatically. It is "a crucial existential issue concerning what is real, true, good, beautiful and the difference between a good life and a bad life" (102). The goal is to open the soul to the true and the good. Only with this right "relation to the transcendent" can a soul mediate what is true and good and thereby make critical judgments (100). Opening the soul involves imagination (101) and insights are attained dialectically (100), both of which mean neither the search (i.e., method) nor the truth (i.e., knowledge) can be possessed. What Kroeker is arguing for, what he's trying to get Wiebe and both their readers to see, is that critical philosophical theology is the vocation and struggle of learning how to love.

---

1. Kroeker, "Ironic Cage of Positivism," 95. Further references will be cited parenthetically in the text.

Kroeker is not sentimental but takes seriously spiritual experience and theological anthropology—aspects often considered too personal to be academic matters. Public and private, political and personal, are not binaries in Kroeker's philosophical theology. Unfortunately, this can lead to misunderstanding. In this instance, for example, Wiebe registers Kroeker's argument as having a "severely *ad hominem* character" (68).[2] Wiebe retorts with his own personal claims: Kroeker is "enamoured with Nietzsche's intellectual anarchy" and "thinks he alone has the right to access" a rhetoric of high moral purpose (68n4); his "implicit criticism" of Wiebe's project is that it doesn't "hold his interest" without "the kind of existential thought Kroeker craves" (73); and, he is "frightened" by Wiebe's work (74). This last assertion is worth repeating, which Wiebe does two more times. Not only is it "obvious that Kroeker fears" Wiebe's conclusions, it's also a fear seen in Plato. Both show "intolerance" and "disdain for scholarship" (79), which makes Kroeker's argument "unseemly at best" (70n5). In short, Kroeker's writing "is hardly becoming of serious academic discussion" (68). As rhetorically and intellectually divergent as Wiebe claims to be, the lady doth protest too much, methinks. Calling Kroeker "frightened," "enamoured," and "unseemly"—is this what appropriate and serious academic discussion looks like without spot or wrinkle on Wiebe's own terms? What is Kroeker's offense?

Wiebe offers one clue with dramatic description in his text: he misquotes and paraphrases Kroeker's critique of modern writing habits as "'overemphasizing scholarship'—which is for [Kroeker] a despiritualizing of thought, "*whatever that means*" (72, emphasis added). Wiebe takes issue with being compared to Nietzsche's account of "the spiritless character of modern scholarship." Wiebe is called to account for his lack of spirit, by which Kroeker means a lack of character. "The Ironic Cage" has as its epigraph a phrase from Camus in French that translates as: "When you don't have character, you have to have method." The issue is not just that scientific method is a poor substitute for character but also indicative of social corrosion—the very thing Plato is at pains to show Socrates was warning Athenians about all along. In other words, under scrutiny is what it means to take spirit seriously.

I highlight this exchange to illustrate the way Kroeker's work is part of productively challenging dialogues with his current and former graduate students and colleagues. His writing bears a feisty character, sure, which

---

2. Wiebe, "Argument or Authority in the Academy?" Further references will be cited parenthetically in the text.

makes some people uncomfortable. But for those of us who are equally convinced that philosophy and theology matter, Kroeker's character is one of the things we love about him. That we find this character in his published work is both singular and the bearing out of a true vocation.

And so I chance one maudlin remark here when I say that Travis became a father figure to me through his mentorship, which was indeed first and foremost an education of the affections. I risk saying this because I know many of his students, friends, and family have shared stories that resonate with the same experiential significance. I'll stop here to avoid embarrassing Travis or myself any further; these stories are better told with a glass of rioja at the faculty club, a pint of IPA at the Phoenix, or a dram of Knob Creek in a congenial living room in Hamilton's Kirkendall South neighborhood.

But what more accurate way is there to describe Travis's work as an academic, supervisor, and colleague? He disabuses us of our secondary-scholarship conceits, insisting instead that we engage primary texts vulnerably and erotically. He's open to guiding engagement with almost any body of literature as a search for an existential issue. Has any other supervisor in a religious studies department worked with students on authors whose range includes Arendt, Augustine, Barth, Benjamin, Berry, Charles Curran, Dostoevsky, Eckhart, Frye, Gadamer, Michael Henry, Illich, Jung, Kierkegaard, Levinas, Marion, Nietzsche, O'Connor, Pannenberg . . . ? And that's just to get us to the letter "Q." His criticisms arise when interpretations don't reach any personal import, when what is presented misses how far down it needs to go for the author. Travis never claims to be objective and instead reads others in a way to invest himself, read himself, to expose or uncover what is true or good in the apocalyptic sense. Travis's scholarship is radically anti-commodified in this way. Training students and dialogically engaging colleagues are never transactional: supervision isn't job training, publishing isn't individualistic gain, and academic achievement isn't ladder climbing. His is truly vocational work—invoking the transcendent—which can only be done by throwing himself into it, taking it personally. Travis's work is constituted by being in relation.

I'll end by returning to something truly perceptive in Donald Wiebe's response to Travis, an insight that characterizes Travis's work as a whole. Wiebe is right to call Travis "Plato's philosophical and theological counterpart." He understands theology as relational, sees the beginning of philosophy as the soul's naked astonishment of nature, reckons with truth as something arrived at dialogically and not possessed, articulates knowledge as ideas produced through love, and is sincere about the centrality of piety—qualities of character and their obligations whose measure is the Good beyond Being—for healthy communities, social justice, and political stability. While Travis does write on and about Plato, his true contribution is himself doing what Plato did. He'll talk to you about whatever you're interested in and help you see that what really attracts you to the topic and author is the Good. He takes you seriously and won't let social niceties get in the way of arriving at the truth. It's not always a comfortable experience, but when is opening the soul free from hardship? The sun burns the eyes.

In a book inspired by Giambattista Vico, Robert Pogue Harrison writes, "Vico needs heirs more than commentators." What he means is that "sometimes the best way to retrieve a legacy is by freeing it from its original framework and reinscribing it in new ones."[3] P. Travis Kroeker is one such heir of Plato. His messianic imagination retrieves what he sees as Plato's legacy and reinscribes it in new ones—literature, politics, ethics, religious studies. What he calls critical philosophical theology is Plato's legacy, a vocation into which he invites his students, friends, and colleagues. This invitation is erotic, it's generative, and I for one can't help but find it compelling. It's intellectually attractive and existentially irresistible. The work in this volume, this celebration, constitutes expressions from those of us who have in various ways and degrees found a loving attunement and calling in Kroeker's invitation.

Critical Invitations (Maxwell Kennel)

Moving beyond derivative and secondary interpretation that merely receives and repeats what is given, toward the courage to take up thinking and action and make new ways forward is a critical invitation that Travis extends to his students. The way that he extends this and other critical invitations—in his published work, seminars, and elsewhere—involves a series of subtle judgments that pick difficult paths between and beyond simplistic distinctions. In some ways, only the mixture of ideas and anecdotes can communicate the richness and depth of these critical invitations. Upon arriving at McMaster University's Religious Studies Department in the fall of 2016 to begin PhD studies under Travis Kroeker's supervision,

---

3. Harrison, *Dominion of the Dead*, xi–xii.

I had the sensation that I had become part of a lineage—something that surely comes with all of the complex problems of privileged succession and patrilineal descent, but which also has emancipatory potential and is part of all human desire for belonging, meaning, and continuity. When I met others who had been supervised by Travis, I heard stories of his supportive guidance and approach to what Joseph R. Wiebe calls "soul formation," and soon my own experience resonated with these accounts. For me, the sense of becoming part of a tradition of education belonging to Travis's students (following after the co-editors of this volume) was a therapeutic and challenging counterpoint to both the neoliberal university and the anxieties of some ecclesial institutions.

I had come to McMaster searching for a way to study the most important existential questions in critical dialogue with several disciplines and traditions. What I found was a pluralistic environment where I could study those questions while engaging with theological, philosophical, political, historical, and social-scientific methodologies. In this context, it was disorienting, challenging, and rewarding to learn from Travis. Sitting in his seminars required a close attention to texts that I was unaccustomed to, having come from a world of broad and abstract categories in literary theory and continental philosophy. By contrast, Travis calls his students to engage in close reading and disinvest from all investments insofar as they entrap thinking and action in ossified and idolatrous containers. When I speak to others who have learned from his teaching, I notice the same look in their eyes, the same careful and deliberate approach to the openness and limits of their subject matter, and the same commitment to educating the heart and the mind by mediating meaningfully between abstractions and particularities. Indeed, that is part of what this festschrift celebrates.

In 2018, following the release of *Messianic Political Theology and Diaspora Ethics*, I organized a student symposium on the book in the Department of Religious Studies at McMaster, together with Zacharie Klassen and Gerald Ens. My response to the book was highly critical. At the time, I did not understand how Travis could advocate for an unpossessive, sacrificial, and vulnerable disposition toward those violent situations that I believed (and in some sense still believe) call for decisive and effective action. His response in the symposium was a clear "no" to my questions about the possibility of opposing injustice with decisive force. At the time, I did not understand how he could advocate for what I thought was passivity in the face of injustice. But in the intervening years I have learned more, from him and others, about how a lighter and humbler touch, an unpossessive approach, and a careful but deliberate way of thinking and making decisions need not compromise on matters of urgency, justice, and violence. There is a way to respond decisively and seriously to concrete social problems and abstract theoretical aporias without resorting to the kinds of self-defeating possessive desire that violently seek to capture and securitize the world. My chapter in this volume represents a second attempt at responding to his work that focuses on the specifics and hidden potentials of this critique of possessive desire.

Years later, I watched a quite different polemical exchange unfold in the symposium on *Messianic Political Theology and Diaspora Ethics* on the Syndicate platform. Malinda Berry's response to Travis had misunderstood his work as belonging to a category of "Yoderian messianism,"[4] and Travis's response clarified his position and her misreading of him without reproducing something like Donald Wiebe's reactivity (narrated in the section above). But Travis's response still expressed anger and frustration with being misrecognized, concluding with these sentences: "Well, as Patrick Friesen said somewhere, so many Mennonites write because they're not allowed to fight. I'm grateful to Malinda Berry for her words."[5] The relationship between these two sentences is essential for the kinds of work, writing, and engagement that Travis teaches—implicitly and explicitly—in both his seminars and publications. Seeming opposites, like fighting words and gratitude—how can they coexist in writing or pedagogy?

The figure of the angry and resentful male is rightly criticized in many public and academic spaces today, and many toxic options present themselves for those who take on masculine identities, from Jordan Peterson's obfuscating absolutions of patriarchy to the powerful political economy of *ressentiment* mobilized by the American far right.[6] Short of some subcultures in heavy music and among therapists who use the Internal Family Systems model,[7] I have encountered few models or exemplars for working through and finding healthy expressions of negative emotions from the male subject position—unstable and constructed as it is. But in observing how carefully and intentionally Travis engaged with the complex dynamics of affect and recognition he encountered, from

---

4. Berry, "Yoderian Messianism Isn't My Cup of Tea."
5. Kroeker, "Personally, I'm a Coffee Drinker."
6. See Vogl, *Capital and Ressentiment*.
7. See Schwartz, *Introduction to Internal Family Systems*.

the institutional level to the scholarly sphere, I learned much about how to avoid the poison of *ressentiment* while finding healthy ways to express myself by writing in resonance with the many interests, attentions, affections, and felt senses that animate human communities.

Learning to be grateful and appreciative for the care and grace that one is shown while staying angry enough about those injustices and violences that mar our world is difficult work (and here I am thinking of Dorothee Sölle's critical and anticipatory interpretation of the present: "this is not it"[8]). Critiquing all forms of violence—across intersections of racialization, social and economic class, gender and sexuality, nationalism and settler colonialism, and beyond—requires an education of the heart that feels through and works with memory and trauma rather than repeating cycles of reactivity or artificially containing what ought to be expressed carefully. But those difficult ways through the deadlocks and double binds of anger and gratitude cannot be prescribed in advance. Instead, they must be worked through contextually, in ways that will always remain unpossessable, unfixable, ungraspable, and forever mysterious, being revealed only in messianic moments and flickers of fire and light. I am grateful to Travis for pointing down those difficult paths, and to the contributors to this volume for extending them.

Erotics and Incarnation (Grant Poettcker)

> "Each of us, starting on the left, should recite the fairest praise of *eros* that he can, and Phaedrus should be the first to begin" . . . "No one," Socrates said, "will cast a vote against you Eryximachus. For I would surely not beg off, as I claim to have expert knowledge of nothing but erotics."[9]

When celebrating his own *Doktorvater*, Travis Kroeker once drew a likeness between Jesus cleansing the temple, "whip in hand," and James Gustafson holding court in a theological ethics seminar, "refusing to allow scholars to proceed in a 'business as usual' manner."[10] Those of us who have participated in the liturgy of a seminar discussion or conference roundtable with Travis know that this tradition has been well and truly upheld. A certain energy hovers in the air: the electricity of mimetic

---

8. Sölle, *Truth Is Concrete*, 40.
9. Plato, *Plato's "Symposium"* l.177d–e.
10. Kroeker, "Theocentric Ethics and Policy," 19.

desire, the hint of anxiety, even a certain dread that the effort may sputter—alongside bright hope that the encounter may yet bear a truth capable of transforming the participants. The possibility of encountering truth ought to be the premise for all academic gathering, but the fact that the truth may offend acts as a powerful disincentive for authentic, truth-seeking dialogue. As a result, academic discourse tends to cluster at the poles of obsequious flattery or mistrust-inducing eristic; the best one can typically hope for is respectful compromise or a certain wit.

It is evident, then, both that Augustine's scathing remarks in *Confessions* about his teachers and the "academic game" remain lamentably relevant and that Travis's conference and seminar rooms look different because he has taken them to heart. This is fitting, since sustained attention to our heart's longings or affections and "erotics"—that is, the art of shaping the affections—is a central focus of Travis's work. As he puts it, "moral meaning is best discovered and communicated not in generic abstractions or formal codes that avoid discussion of the particular spiritual and moral commitments of real human beings."[11] To spin this positively, Travis's seminar and conference rooms feature an unusual intensity because they are places where the actual spiritual and moral commitments of their inhabitants are taken seriously, interrogated, and reshaped. I feel profoundly grateful to have been initiated into this existential reflection upon my own eros in just this way.

Travis's attention to our erotic attunement to our activities (inquiry, work, leisure, etc.) yields the corollary that we all have our affections shaped by powerful authorities. Yet Foucault has said the same in his reflections on "the will to know."[12] What distinguishes Travis's teaching and scholarly work is that it consistently returns to the scandalous claim that Messiah Jesus bears a liberating authority, that is, an authority that unmasks the way the regnant authorities' ontology (materialism), aesthetics (subjectivism), morality (professional "responsibility," which reduces morality to law) and epistemology ("objectivity") enslave those who would be learners. As a result, if Travis may be said to "bear the whip," he does so with a wonderful generosity and an uncommon humility. He bears an invitation neither into Gustafson's own theological iconoclasm[13] nor

---

11. Kroeker, "Messianic Freedom and the Secular Academy," 50.
12. Foucault, *Lectures on the Will to Know*.
13. Kroeker, "Theocentric Ethics and Policy," 19. In the same essay, Kroeker judges Gustafson to have an insufficiently personal conception of divine agency (23).

into a hidebound orthodoxy closed off from secular voices, but into an existential relation with the Word that is both true and the Truth.

Accepting this invitation requires a good deal of unlearning of today's established verities and habits of mind, which easily worm their way into the affections of self-relating selves. This was certainly true of my experience, as I recall sitting in seminars, thesis meetings—even defenses—dizzied by what I could recognize as erudition while also unable to grasp the source of the line of questions streaming at me. Yet does dialectical education not *require* that learners pass through a certain strangely humanizing humiliation and embarrassment? I insist on calling it humanizing, though, because this was just my experience with Travis. Initiation into proper eros is risky for all parties. But with it comes the promise of a more fully human life, a life that sets aside what disincarnates and that picks up "the one thing that is needful." My hope is that the essays that compose this collection will honor the eros for incarnation that Travis has practiced in his scholarship and teaching, for which I am truly grateful.

Faithful Postures (Paul Doerksen)

I first encountered Travis Kroeker through reading and reviewing his book *Christian Ethics and Political Economy in North America: A Critical Analysis* for the *Journal of Mennonite Studies*. That book introduced me to the kind of constructive work I would encounter and learn to appreciate more fully over the years—philosophical theology that draws on traditions both Christian and secular to cast light on our current situations, always drawing the reader to join in these historical conversations in ways that seek to reveal important realities, including our own delusions and distortions of those realities.

It's not my purpose to summarize or categorize that constructive work under conventional categories such as political theology, ethics, and so on, even though Travis has contributed significantly to many such fields. Rather, I want to recall a conversation in which I was remarking (without much insight) about the "posturing" I thought I observed in academic life. To which Travis pointed out that much of our lives consist in learning and practicing just how and when to take varied right and faithful postures on the places and relationships in which we find ourselves, and that these non-identical postures are not hypocritical.

And whatever posture we take is not simply a matter of social or even religious convention; rather, we are confronted by the consideration of a messianic posture, one that is rooted in the renunciation of possessive and distorted desire even while it embraces "proper use and enjoyment: a secular life in which we 'make use of earthly goods like pilgrims, without grasping after them.'"[14] The resistance here is not an abstraction, some notion of autonomy or independence for its own sake, but a resistance to power grabbed for its own sake or for self-promotion and aggrandizement, lusting after wealth and influence, after mammon. We are called to resist grasping, instead sacrificially offering up to God our affection in action. Instead of exercising power in conventional ways, we are offered the possibility of embracing "weak messianic power," which entails an endlessly self-emptying dispossessiveness rather than acquisitiveness and accumulation.

This kind of dispossessive power opens the way, sets the direction not for worldly power, recognition, and reputation but for quotidian service to the least, lowly, and despised. It is precisely in this expression of kenotic love, as displayed in Christ's life, teachings, and death, that we can begin to experience real freedom, not by possessing rights "but precisely by using the world 'as if not,' in a dispossessive manner that assesses the value of each particular thing or relation with reference to the passage of God in the world."[15] This living "as if not," this dispossessive exilic love is a perpetual challenge, both in the living and recognition of it, since the markers that are used so often to assess a career are virtually incapable of describing such work; even if those conventional markers such as publications, promotions, and awards are present, something more can still be present, even if largely hidden. Therefore, I have learned from Travis, whether in observing, reading his work, or carrying on a treasured friendship, that whatever stance to which I'm called, whether that of spouse, teacher, parent, child, friend, and so on, I ought to seek to embrace a kenotic dispossession, offering each of those relations up to God in the embodiment of affection in action, which calls for lifelong discernment. For this learning, and for valued, ongoing friendship, I am grateful.

---

14. Kroeker, *Messianic Political Theology*, 7; quoting Augustine's *City of God*.

15. Kroeker, *Messianic Political Theology*, 32. I'm drawing more broadly here on several chapters of Kroeker's book, especially the introduction and first chapter.

Summary of Themes

It is fitting that a volume of essays, conversation, and poetry written in honor of Travis Kroeker is as diverse and wide-ranging as his own work. This makes the editors' task in organizing such a volume challenging, although it is one joyously undertaken.

The first of the three sections under which chapters have been grouped, titled "Engaging Messianic Politics," gathers the contributions that engage most directly with Kroeker's own contributions to messianic political theology. Some of these chapters highlight distinctive emphases within Kroeker's work, such as his concern for the problems that institutions and authority structures pose for the mediation of divine love (Gregory Wiebe and Joseph R. Wiebe's essay), or for the ways that possessive desire—and instrumental programs that attempt to manage possessive desire—create new forms of hell on earth (Maxwell Kennel's essay). Others explore the central tensions that arise from Kroeker's insistence on a messianic mode of political theology: Matthew Thiessen ponders the exilic "in-between" posture that apocalypticism requires, and Philip Ziegler considers why Kroeker's messianism avoids the abstraction and formalism characteristic of other messianisms. Similarly, Eric Gregory asks how, having properly avoided celebrating nationalism or valorizing the nation-state, one might understand the idea of particular nations, and Gerald McKenny interrogates the way this-worldly order (*nomos*) relates to the eschatological order of the reign of Christ.

The second section, "Extending Apocalyptic Theology," contains contributions that explore areas of theological and ethical questioning opened by Kroeker's work, or which elaborate upon the ideas of authors that are key to Kroeker's own thought. Nancy Bedford's essay extends Kroeker's critique of political Augustinianism to decolonize and thereby reclaim the concept of grace. Douglas Harink's and Justin Klassen's essays, inspired by Kroeker's critique of reductive and mechanical images of creation, respectively work toward a messianic theology of science and an ecotheology. Paul Doerksen elaborates a notion of urgent patience that is sensitive to the anti-incarnational tendencies in both modern haste and romanticized slowness. Rachel Matheson and Stephen Westerholm take up topics not directly engaged by Kroeker but which bear upon his interpretations of Simone Weil and the Apostle Paul, as Matheson addresses Weil's mystical theology of work and Westerholm extends the apocalyptic dimension of Paul's notions of justification and the righteousness of God.

The final section, titled "Exploring Literary Revelations" collects contributions that critically engage with literary sources in modes inspired by or consonant with Kroeker's own approach. Bruce Ward uses Augustine, Pierre Corneille, and Fyodor Dostoevsky to explore the finely balanced duel between historical power structures and the messianic community. Sarah Stewart-Kroeker compares Augustine's relationally oriented conception of sexuality with Foucault's subjectively focused one to open into a discussion of Casey Plett's fiction, literature that is also profitably explored by Grace Kehler later in this section. Grant Poettcker's essay contrasts the ways Elaine Scarry and Dostoevsky defend beauty and underlines the latter's insistence that beauty be understood apocalyptically. And Chris Huebner develops faith as a theological and epistemological virtue by way of Shakespeare's *Othello* and Hrotsvit of Gandersheim's *Sapientia*.

Whether taking up Kroeker's ideas, extending them in new directions, or taking on his approach to literature, these contributions represent only a few of the ways the provocation offered in Travis Kroeker's writing may be worked with, for, or against. Each essay expresses his influence by finding things to uncover, by tarrying with texts to see what a theological, ethical, or literary framework might reveal. The authors don't just use literary and philosophical texts as a lens to understand theological concepts, but rather approach these texts as if they are not distinct from theology. In this way each chapter offers to readers a unique demonstration of how to understand and explore what we're calling a messianic imagination.

As a whole, the volume is meant to delineate a messianic political and theological vision, test the relationship between theology and ethics, and integrate theology and literature. As a response to Kroeker's own messianic imagination, it manifests the vast horizon of his work. The editors' hope in putting that horizon on display for readers is not to achieve comprehensiveness but spark inspiration. If readers are so provoked, there's much more to find in the list of Kroeker's publications found at the back of the volume. More than that, however: if, friendly reader, you find a moment in these pages that calls to mind a fictional scene that brought real tears, a philosophical argument that sent you spiraling into a rage, or a theological insight that triggered an ecstatic realization, then you know the experience of sitting with texts that open the soul in search of its divine source. Kroeker's work is about how that search can be an academic pursuit, which needs no commentary but rather calls for tenacious and imaginative companions.

Bibliography

Berry, Malinda. "Yoderian Messianism Isn't My Cup of Tea." Response to Symposium on *Messianic Political Theology and Diaspora Ethics*, by P. Travis Kroeker. Syndicate, July 2019. https://syndicate.network/symposia/theology/messianic-political-theology-and-diaspora-ethics/.

Foucault, Michel. *Lectures on The Will to Know: Lectures at the Collège de France, 1970–1971 and Oedipal Knowledge*. Edited by Daniel Defert and translated by Graham Burchell. New York: Palgrave Macmillan, 2013.

Harrison, Robert Pogue. *The Dominion of the Dead*. Chicago: University of Chicago, 2003.

Kroeker, P. Travis. *Christian Ethics and Political Economy in North America: A Critical Analysis*. Montreal: McGill-Queen's University Press, 1995.

———. "The Ironic Cage of Positivism and the Nature of Philosophical Theology." *Studies in Religion/Sciences Religieuses* 22 (1993) 93–103.

———. "Messianic Freedom and the Secular Academy: Educating the Affections in a Technological Culture." *Consensus* 31 (2006) 41–57.

———. *Messianic Political Theology and Diaspora Ethics: Essays in Exile*. Eugene, OR: Cascade, 2017.

———. "Personally, I'm a Coffee Drinker." Reply to Malinda Berry, Response to Symposium on *Messianic Political Theology and Diaspora Ethics*, by P. Travis Kroeker. Syndicate, October 2019. https://syndicate.network/symposia/theology/messianic-political-theology-and-diaspora-ethics/.

———. "Theocentric Ethics and Policy." *Annual of the Society of Christian Ethics* 17 (1997) 19–27.

Plato. *Plato's "Symposium."* Translated by Seth Benardete. Chicago: University of Chicago Press, 2001.

Schwartz, Richard. *Introduction to Internal Family Systems*. 2nd ed. Boulder, CO: Sounds True, 2023.

Sölle, Dorothee. *The Truth Is Concrete*. Translated by Dinah Livingstone. London: Burns & Oates, 1969.

Vogl, Joseph. *Capital and Ressentiment: A Brief Theory of the Present*. Translated by Neil Solomon. London: Polity, 2022.

Wiebe, Donald. "Argument or Authority in the Academy? On Kroeker on *The Irony of Theology*." *Studies in Religion/Sciences Religieuses* 23 (1994) 67–79.

———. *The Irony of Theology and the Nature of Religious Thought*. Montreal: McGill-Queens University Press, 1990.

Poems

John Terpstra

Dedication

A personal note is called for here, since my appreciation is for the person rather than the teacher, academic, or writer. When I was at a particularly low spot in my life, so low that I was lying in the grass staring up at the night clouds, which were raining down, Travis came outside and lay in the grass beside me. Did we say much? I don't recall. I do recall that after a time he helped me up, led me indoors, and helped me into bed. It was very Jesus-like. The poems that I write come from a certain conviction about the world and our place in it. At our deepest level, Travis and I share this conviction. He is a friend, and a brother.

Ceremony

Some ceremony is involved
in hauling the bicycles up from the basement,
angling their awkwardnesses
under ductwork, around the stairwell landing,
and through the needle's eye of the side door,
as one wheel spins free, ticking.

The sun was singing down, loud and glorious,
as we wove our two thin tire-lines through town
and to the bay, then through and around surprising
numbers of walkers, strollers, roller-
bladers of varying degrees of proficiency, and other

cyclists, all of us twisting and braiding
our various momentums together
like a fat rope played out by the water's edge,

and the gravel swallowed our tires as we left the paveway
and headed toward the point, while volleyed
in and out of hearing on the wind we heard the beat
of some hydraulic jack driving posts into the earth,

or some jack's boom box, I said,

but came upon the backs of three white
T-shirts there instead, and the draped jet
hair and braids of two men and a woman
sitting facing the open blast
furnace of light on the water,
in the sky, and drumming
the sun down,
singing rhythmic undulations over
the chanted surface of the bay,

a song that went nowhere, musically,
and could have gone there forever—
        and the gravel
swallowed our tires again, as we quit
the landfill point to be home before dark,
and all I wanted to convey is the deep enjoyment
of our early summer evening ride, the unexpected
explosion of people at the new waterfront park
three generations after industry and E. coli
drove them all away, and the three first-peoples,
this late in the game, chanting and drumming
the sunset as an event
in which they were participant,
while we looked on.

Topographies of Easter

We are walking in the mild mid-winter
snow and thin ice, up Coldwater Creek,
its many tributaries, their steep ravines
tracing the blue and brown lines that wind
dizzily over the unfolded whiteness of our new
map, like staves for the crazy earth song we've been
sight-reading with our feet. We are singing the impossible
pitch of these slopes and cliffs, losing our place
in a landscape that lives to improvise, and the map
helps, but nothing written is in stone,
and it's always a revelation, stopping to
compare what's on paper with being there.

Because I did not for a moment doubt in childhood
the story of this rising, shall I, now
I am wiser? The world still has no
boundary. The lines still shiver and wave;
the impossible takes place; people are kind.
And these woods are still as real and magic
as when I first chased and followed any path
that found me, and just as fearful, and brown death
still haunts the green, discolouring all
in brilliant falls ground to sodden mulch,
from which, in deepest regions of the wood,
the bright stem still rises, witnessed by
those few who run like children home to tell us.

I'll say this: whom she supposed to be
the gardener sings and dances the contour lines
that are his body; this body that is broken
by time and season and violence too deep
for us to wonder at the source, broken
into beauty that lures our present rambling
and leads us to the edge of this escarpment,
where the waters fall, where all our many streams

cascade and plunge, in curtain and ribbon, over
terrace and washboard
                    (our terms for the living text:
earth's open veins)
                and where we meet her,
who has run and sung and danced these trails
since the day she first saw
the massive rock dislodged
from the cliff-face
                of any reasonable expectation.
And all these years removed from childhood
we still leap aboard, to feel if it shifts
or moves us, trusting and not trusting,
not willing and willing
                    the rock to roll on.

Conviction

The preacher stands in the middle of an island
holding the world in one hand.
Today the world is orange.
It grows on a tree that grows
on a small plot of ground that is on the island.
A disciple has climbed into the tree
and dropped the orange world
to a second disciple,
who offers it to the preacher,
who stands holding in her right hand
the world, and in the left a machete.

She stands her small plot of ground, the preacher.
The blade slips under the skin
and the orange world begins to spin
as she pares.
Our fascination grows
as the latitudes unravel and dangle
a loose spiral
that disconnects from the pole and falls to earth,
and the orange world turns pulp white.

To each of us she offers just such
a soft and unprotected world,
its two hemispheres clinging together
from the knife sliced not quite through
the equator,
which is where she lives.

To receive from her
we must accept the fruit,
the blade that she withdraws
from the world she places in our hands—
and goes to pare new worlds,
as the juice from this, her gift
and her conviction
springs fresh to our tongues.

Engaging Messianic Politics

1

Mediating Divine Love in the Messianic Imagination

GREGORY D. WIEBE AND JOSEPH R. WIEBE

> I offer these reflections not as an expert Mennonite theologian nor from an academic or ecclesial ivory tower, but rather as someone struggling to give an account of what it means to be answerable for what I have been given to be and to do.[1]

The Erotics of the Messianic

ONE OF THE PERENNIAL problems that Christians and their ecclesiastical institutions run into is the stifling of the very love of God they mean to mediate and make present in the world. This can occur most perniciously through a kind of fetishization: a misplaced fixation on—and, indeed, an attempt to fixate—the modes and media of love's manifestation as though those modes and media were ends in themselves rather than means of making divine love present. Of course, in Christian understandings of God's love, such means might include nearly anything, not least ethnicities, traditional cultural practices, various social structures, or ecclesiastical institutions of authority themselves. The possessive use of these means is something Marie-José Mondzain calls an

---

1. Kroeker, "Anabaptists and Existential Theology," 86.

"empire over emotions,"[2] as when penitence is used as a Machiavellian masquerade for the propping up of authority structures, or when reconciliation is merely a justification for scapegoating. It is within these broader Christian theological conversations on the role of Christians and their institutions to mediate divine love—and their frequent failure to do just that—that Travis Kroeker locates his work.

A key theme Kroeker uses in his engagement with these questions is that of eros.[3] Namely, this particular failure of churches to mediate divine love, even using their mechanisms of mediation perniciously for imperialistic or Machiavellian ends, is in some significant sense a failure or elimination of eros. Eros here refers to the ancient Greek notion (god, really), but Kroeker appeals to it particularly in terms of its use in the work of Plato. To Kroeker, the messianic is erotic in the specific sense in which Plato understood the structure of the soul as moving toward the highest human experiences through the pushes and pulls of attraction within human drama.[4] But he reads it equally in light of the Christian sense of incarnation, which maintains that divine love is embodied unpretentiously and with humility, and yet by this very posture resists reigning political and sacerdotal powers fallen from grace. These two senses are brought together in the imagination as a spiritual vision of reality revealed through risky relationships that engender non-idealistic, non-ideological insights of what is true, good, and beautiful in creation. A messianic imagination is an affectionate perception of the world that sees by and seeks to enact divine love in ways that oppose exploitative, unjust systems.

The ancient Greek notion of eros included the deluded, possessive desires that are at the heart of social problems. But for Kroeker, read in light of the Incarnation—that is, in light of the Messiah—erotic moments can enable us to change, turn away from self-love to love of others. These moments are messianic insofar as their vulnerable love incarnates divine sovereignty.[5] It's not just self-giving love, the hallmark of romance, but part of an anti-imperialist, anti-possessive political economy. That is, the messianic imagination is part of the messianic community, which is

2. Quoted in Kroeker, "Scandalous Displacements," 94.

3. See his 2013 J. J. Thiessen Lectures, *Empire Erotics and Messianic Economies of Desire*.

4. See his account of Socrates's description of erotic movement in Plato's *Phaedrus*, in Kroeker, "Sexuality and the Sacramental Imagination," 126–27.

5. Kroeker and Ward, *Remembering the End*, 169–70.

not defined institutionally in the abstract but relationally between actual humans. Thus for Kroeker, it may be a church community, but it very well may not, and it is such manifestations of the messianic community that aren't narrowly ecclesial that draw his particular interest. Here, non-institutionally mediated divine love is incarnated economically and politically in defiance of both modern culture's cult of individualism and state-sponsored exploitation.[6] Moments of conversion are instances of turning around through erotic memory as part of a messianic community threatened by disincarnation and anti-erotic forces.

This messianic imagination is a significant theme of Kroeker's writing. We see Kroeker not just writing *about* the messianic imagination, however, but writing through it and with it as well. His writing is something of a lesson in messianic erotics that constitutes a theological education of the affections in both its content and its style. Desire, in Kroeker's theological ethics, is the faculty leading the insurgency against Mondzain's ecclesial "empires over emotion." We will demonstrate this by identifying some of his key sources and modes of scholarly engagement—namely, Augustine and with Augustinians—and locating him as he reads these sources within his own ecclesial tradition. How Kroeker draws on Augustine and argues with Augustinians, how Kroeker engages with Mennonite writing and enters relationships with non-Mennonite neighbors both reveal and perform the erotics of a messianic imagination.

For Kroeker, Augustine opens up the question of mediation: how to manifest servant messianism beset by pitfalls. What is missed by the Augustinians with whom he engages (notably Charles Taylor and John Milbank) is that messianism involves everything—the existential, the familial, the civic, and the cosmic—and cannot be reduced to any one of these or systematized apart from the loves of actual humans. Kroeker's writing attempts to manifest his own messianic call of this nature by making the soul the key site of messianism. Yet the soul is not merely or reductively the individual alone, insofar as its erotic creative power is moved by spiritual causality. That is, the soul's affections reveal the divine connection between the existential, kinship, and civic communities.

Kroeker situates his work on the soul and mediation within the Mennonite tradition. While he admits he's not a "formal member of the

---

6. For example, see Kroeker's account of messianic mediation in Herman Melville's *Moby Dick*, where Pip, Fleece, and Queequeg's manifest pattern of suffering servanthood is contrasted with Ahab's "restlessly desiring, rights-bearing ego." Kroeker, "Saint Paul at Sea," 117.

Mennonite church," his work contributes to what he refers to as Anabaptist theology.[7] As a polygenetic conglomerate of sixteenth-century anticlerical movements without doctrinal, liturgical, or social cohesion, Anabaptism doesn't have a theology per se. Nevertheless, there is justification for treating the theologies of the living traditions that understand themselves to be connected significantly to the Radical Reformation—engaged dialogically if not ecclesially with one another—as Anabaptist theology, and that will be our approach in this essay. Kroeker comes from the *Kleine Gemeinde* community, the "little church" Mennonites, but engages with writers from the Mennonite Brethren,[8] Brethren in Christ,[9] Hutterite,[10] Amish[11] communities, and conference Mennonites.[12] He does so to delineate a particular image of existential theology.

Augustine and Augustinians

Part of what it means for Kroeker to be an Anabaptist theologian entails resistance to the constitutive dualisms of certain significant streams of Protestant theology. In a passage Kroeker quotes, the essayist Wendell Berry comments that he was never satisfied by the Protestantism he inherited "because of the dualism of soul and body, heaven and Earth, Creator and creation—a dualism so fierce at times that it counted hatred of this life and this world as a virtue. From very early that kind of piety was distasteful to me."[13] This dualism Berry names exists as a part of Protestantism's protest against the Roman church, but one that implicates Anabaptist churches as well. World denial has an ancient history in Roman Catholicism, and yet one can with very good justification see its sacramental theology as exactly a form of works that unite the soul and body, just as one can the traditional Anabaptist concern with good works. Therein, however, lies a different danger—not of dualism

---

7. Kroeker, "Anabaptists and Existential Theology," 83.
8. Kroeker, "Anabaptists and Existential Theology," 84.
9. Kroeker, "Rich Mennonites in an Age of Mammon," 212.
10. Kroeker, "Rich Mennonites in an Age of Mammon," 213.
11. Kroeker, "Rich Mennonites in an Age of Mammon," 216.
12. Kroeker, "Rich Mennonites in an Age of Mammon," 216. "Conference Mennonites" refers to denomination members within Mennonite General Assembly and General Conference Mennonite Church as well as to the church conference denominations that emerged after they amalgamated in 2002.
13. Quoted in Kroeker, "Sexuality and the Sacramental Imagination," 135n6.

but conflation—to which Kroeker tries to stay equally attuned. In some sense, Kroeker's notion of the messianic imagination can be understood in terms of an attempt to navigate between two pitfalls: resisting the degradation of the Spirit into formless naval-gazing, private romance, or ahistorical sentimentality on the one hand, while resisting the reduction of the Spirit to manifest institutions, on the other. In other words, if a kind of dualistic hatred of this life and this world is a problem, so too is an all-too-easy identification of the Spirit with the forms of this world, which, as Kroeker will remind us by quoting Saint Paul, are passing away. Navigating such waters, Kroeker looks to various authors for helpful orientation, including Berry, as above, but also Augustine of Hippo.

That Kroeker would look to Augustine is important, because in the hands of many other interpreters, Augustine represents exactly the kind of approach to theology Kroeker claims needs to be avoided. One can see this clearly in his article "Augustine's Messianic Political Theology: An Apocalyptic Critique of Political Augustinianism." The *political Augustinianism* of the title is a technical term in Augustinian studies for the blurring of the distinction between ecclesiastical and governmental authority.[14] Its logic can be seen by beginning with the notion, developed in *The City of God*, that there are two constitutive citizenships of humanity: that of Christ, destined for eternal life; and that of the devil, destined for eternal judgment. These citizenships are manifest in the church and all other earthly (especially imperial) citizenships, and while they will lead to utterly distinct destinies in the final resurrection at the eschaton, they nevertheless intermix in the present life. As such, good governance over any earthly city—that is, in those polities that involve governance over all humans born naturally in their realm, as opposed to churches that govern only those born also of the Spirit in Christ—will of necessity involve restraint of the wicked by force. A key component of all political Augustinianism adds to this the conviction that it is precisely the Christian culture of orienting to the true nature of things, manifest most clearly in the humble servant kingship of Christ, that constitutes the best quality of rulers, such that even *earthly* cities are best governed by *Christian* rulers.[15] This proper orientation of Christian rule for Augustine, however, involves rulers directing those they govern toward true worship as part of the responsible use of power given to them by none other than God.

14. See Kries, "Political Augustinianism," 657–58.
15. Cf., for example, Williams, "Politics and the Soul"; and Dodaro, "Augustine's Secular City."

Concomitantly, this will involve a ruler's use of means at their disposal to support the church and impose limitations against those who oppose the church as false idolaters.[16]

Kroeker begins his essay, however, with something Charles Taylor calls *hyper-Augustinianism*.[17] If political Augustinianism represents a certain orientation of ecclesiastical culture toward political responsibilities, hyper-Augustinianism seems to represent the zealous desire to systematize this conflation into a kind of straightforward theocracy. In Taylor's conception this paradigmatically Calvinist political theology (though it can also be found among Catholic thinkers) takes the Augustinian political trajectory sketched above and unites it with a juridical-penal understanding of atonement and all-too-neatly resolves constitutive Christian tensions between redemption and judgment, mercy and wrath, and love and anger into dichotomies, and then maps those dichotomies onto salvation and damnation, good and evil, and, ideally, ruler and ruled. Kroeker summarizes:

> This logic is tied to a pernicious interpretation of suffering and punishment as a part of a providentially governed "divine pedagogy," in a narrative of total human depravity and limited atonement. Politically this view entails the belief that the godly minority should exercise political control so as to restrain evil and promote civil order. Hyper-Augustinians emphasize divine punishment, foster a seamless and puritanical connection between piety and social order, and emphasize the transformation of the will in which virtue requires the disciplined, institutional imposition of the ordering of the good. But for hyper-Augustinians there are also real limits to such institutional, sociopolitical (re)ordering and reform due to the pervasive, incorrigible fact of human sinfulness, which must simply be coercively restrained in the earthly city.[18]

If the trajectory of political Augustinianism makes Kroeker uncomfortable, it is in no small part because it always risks becoming a caricature of itself in hyper-Augustinianism. In *The City of God*, the earthly

---

16. See, for example, Augustine's Letter 185.8, and the classic statements on Christian rule in the examples of Constantine and Theodosius I, the "mirror of princes," in *City of God* 5.25–26. See also Baynes, "Political Ideas of St. Augustine's De Civitate Dei," 300–302.

17. Taylor, *Secular Age*; see Kroeker, "Augustine's Messianic Political Theology," 46n1.

18. Kroeker, "Augustine's Messianic Political Theology," 46–47.

city promulgates false religious practices in imitation of the false gods its inhabitants worship, demons whose desire is only to deceive and possess; but it is difficult not to see this kind of hyper-Augustinianism, too, as an effort, in the name of Christ, to "bind men more tightly, as it were, in civil society, so that they might likewise possess them as subjects."[19]

Kroeker's essay is full of references to interpreters of Augustine who try in one way or another to navigate these waters while remaining faithful to Augustine's understanding of the Christian message. Taylor's own sense of how to resist this risk emphasizes divine compassion instead of penal pedagogy, and the community of neighbor love above an institutional church. In other words, he prescribes a kind of liberal Catholic political theology that commends a disenchanted Christian ethic stripped of manifest markers of Christian religious identity.[20] This seems to Kroeker insufficiently "theological" and "existential." He cites the work of John Milbank as a kind of alternative to Taylor's vision that seeks not a furthering of the modern project of disenchantment, but rather a *re-enchantment* of social structures in a recovery of Christendom that seeks precisely to reinvest the larger corporate body with such markers of Christian religious identity as Taylor seems to downplay.[21] This is much more straightforward political Augustinianism, and as such bears the risks described above. What is more, though, for Kroeker, is that Taylor and Milbank seem to represent two sides of the political Augustinian coin, which seeks an institutional-political solution to what is fundamentally a spiritual problem.

It may seem, then, that what Taylor and Milbank try to address at an institutional level is properly dealt with only at the level of the individual soul. Problems appear here too, however, to the extent that this might be understood as a kind of "disembodied inner selfhood." Another interpreter of Augustine makes a brief appearance, this time Robert Markus and his concept of the secular, which shifts all manifest—that is, apocalyptic—opposition between the two cities to the last judgment, containing it for the time being in the soul of the believer and not as a matter of public institutional embodiment.[22] In other words, the way Kroeker

---

19. Augustine, *City of God* 4.32.

20. Kroeker, "Augustine's Messianic Political Theology," 47.

21. Milbank, "Closer Walk on the Wild Side." See Kroeker, "Augustine's Messianic Political Theology," 47–48.

22. Markus, *Christianity and the Secular*. See Kroeker, "Augustine's Messianic Political Theology," 54, including n7.

positions himself in the conversation is not to say that spiritual matters are personal as opposed to institutional, much less vice versa, but exactly that they pervade all levels of the cosmic order. Thus, while the paradigmatic issue with various forms of political Augustinianism is that they reduce the spiritual problem of humanity to the level of political institutions, it is more broadly the case that any attempt to reduce the problem of human sinfulness to a single level of existence represents something less than the fullness of the theological vision Augustine offers.

In an effort to understand this vision more fully, Kroeker introduces the notion of *spiritual causality*.[23] This is his term for the nexus of things Augustine discusses in, among other places, book 5 of *The City of God* to account for God's foreknowledge of all things, and why it does not contradict free human will. All things that are and happen, Augustine says there, are the product of some will. But even those things caused by animals, humans, or angels, are so caused by the participation of those creatures in the power that the divine *spiritus vitae*, the Breath of Life, gives to them for that purpose. The key point of this for our purposes is that the divine Breath of Life, "the real cause which causes and is not caused,"[24] is thus itself the participable order and principle of all created things. With participation, Plato emerges for Augustine (and thus also for Kroeker) as an important figure of comparison. In the context of the polemics of *The City of God*, Plato is the only "natural philosopher" of the pagans worthy of the name. To Augustine, Plato recognizes that God transcends the soul as the immutable light of wisdom but bestows blessedness upon the soul through participation in that unchanging light. Because of this, among pagan philosophers "only Plato's theology is," in Kroeker's words, "truly theological."[25]

But as anyone who has read *Confessions* book 7 attentively will know, as high as Augustine's praise for Plato is, he maintains Plato is missing something (literally) crucial. *That* the light of wisdom is participable is indubitable; *how* is the question, and the Platonic philosophy of grasping the truth only by a purified mind is insufficient. What is missing is penitence, humility, the form of a servant, the cross—in short, the Incarnation. The model of participation that Christ gives is not one of philosophical, dialectical purification of the intellect. "The key to spiritual causality is now to

23. See Kroeker, "Augustine's Messianic Political Theology," 51–53.

24. Augustine, *City of God* 5.11; quoted in Kroeker, "Augustine's Messianic Political Theology," 52.

25. Kroeker, "Augustine's Messianic Political Theology," 57.

be found in an embodied model that nevertheless is claimed to be the very spiritual principle underlying all created reality, and this embodied model takes the form of a lowly servant, not an exalted ruler."[26]

The whole question, in other words, is one of mediation, how participation in the Holy Spirit is made manifest in the world, the proper modes of embodying the human relation to eternity.[27] But the messianism in Jesus of Nazareth reveals that this manifestation has not just any character but that of humility, service, and penitence. What is more, this mediation will inevitably evoke opposition and rivalry from the world that serves and thus mediates not the divine Breath but demonic spirits, and which is thus never far from turning those participating in the true order of the cosmos into martyrs, that is, witnesses to that very true messianic order. The opposition between the flesh and the spirit, named by Paul and explored by Augustine, cannot be reduced to the opposition of institutional authorities, like church and state, nor to the opposition of private versus public, or vice versa. Rather, they

> belong to very different orientations of life that extend from the inner conscience of each human being . . . to household relations, to cities and peoples, to the cosmic ordering of all things in keeping with the spiritual causality of divine causality apocalypsed in Christ—an apocalyptic sovereignty that may not be institutionalized in any authoritative human cultural form but that lives by faith, oriented toward the invisible Sovereign It worships not only in its ritual forms but in all acts of loving service in the world.[28]

For Kroeker, the messianism of Jesus of Nazareth, as understood by Augustine of Hippo, is both fully personal and fully public. But his caution about political Augustinianism and concomitant resistance to reducing messianism to any one form or level of mediation raises questions exactly to the extent that it resists easy solutions, whether individual, political, or ecclesiastical. It is clear that Kroeker perpetually refuses to nail down messianic mediation and is critical of others where he thinks they do, in order to encourage his readers never to forget that they must always do the existential work of figuring out how to manifest

---

26. Kroeker, "Augustine's Messianic Political Theology," 57.
27. See Kroeker, "Augustine's Messianic Political Theology," 48, 58.
28. Kroeker, "Augustine's Messianic Political Theology," 49; see also 60.

this relation to the eternal in their own lives. Kroeker's is a messianism always in search of modes of manifestation.

Mennonite-Situated, Relational Theology

Kroeker's reflections on what Anabaptist existential theology entails are investigations into the sacramental particularity of Mennonite servanthood, that is, into the mode of its messianic embodiment. Existential work in general consists in the soul's movement toward its source by way of penitential tears and humble, loving servitude. Kroeker's reflections on the specifics of Anabaptist existential theology are pertinent to Mennonite identity insofar as they address two isolationist temptations that resemble the Augustinian pitfalls named above. First, Mennonites from the imperial Russia migrations in the late nineteenth and early twentieth centuries—of which Kroeker and the brothers Wiebe are descendants—often use their biological genealogy to establish particularity, reifying bloodline into an ethnic identity. Mennonite ethnicity is considered religious insofar as its heritage is part of a communal ecclesiology, and yet it is detachable from theological commitments. A person with a family name that traces back to Mennonite villages in Ukraine can be recognized as Mennonite and claimed as part of the tradition. Knowing a few verses of "This world is not my home," some *Plautdietsch* phrases, and how to make *zwieback* is a bonus; these are examples of embodied practices that both signify Mennonite tradition yet have little theological import. Mennonite as an ethno-religious identity retains a particularity that mediates nothing divine. Second, Mennonites who are more theologically convicted are less concerned about how that faith is embodied. Aspects that were once hallmarks of Mennonite practices—sharing common meals, pacifism, adult baptism, anti-clerical leadership—have become commonplace Protestant characteristics.[29] In their attempt to connect with others in both evangelical and interdenominational contexts, Mennonites have downplayed or elided their particularity. Mennonite theology that focuses on doctrine or institutional structures is generically, not particularly, embodied.

Whether Mennonites have isolated their bodies from theology or their convictions from embodiment, Kroeker demonstrates that Mennonite reliance on ethnicity for particularity is insufficiently messianic.

---

29. Kroeker, "Anabaptists and Existential Theology," 90.

In both cases but in different ways, Mennonites use their family name to connect current practices and beliefs with traditional community life relegated to the past. For Kroeker, the particularity of Mennonite servanthood is in its relationality, its kinship; however, understood existentially and sacramentally rather than abstract and possessive. Mennonite relationality as kinship, rather than ethnicity, is the theological model for messianic community. It is the movement of embodied souls toward the transcendent source through attraction and affection, seeking community. It serves rather than possesses.

Kroeker's vision for the form of Mennonite humility comes from Mennonite gulag experiences. In these memoirs, both fictional and not, one sees how "true human identity is not one rooted in ethnicity or in the achievements of a people, but rather one rooted in the self-emptying humility of Christ."[30] Aspects of identity that are human-derived cannot withstand the gulag's denigration. What's left after the loss of everything through hardship is the *imago Dei*, the image of the suffering servant. Waldemar Wolff, a character in a fictional Mennonite memoir, says to his beloved in a Siberian camp: "When our existence here—after the loss of our former prosperity and social status—has torn the last shred of self-respect out of us . . . we won't even want to admit that we are Mennonites, or claim any status or identity for ourselves at all." What is the meaning of pain in a Siberian forest camp on the Mezen River? "Nothing."[31] Yet Wolff's reflections on this "nothing" show its message of love. In the camp, the real threat is not what causes suffering but the temptation to become indifferent because of it: "The most insidious enemy in camp life is the kind of spreading indifference which begins as callousness towards fellow sufferers and ends as a general apathy."[32] The enemy is a relational disease. The narrator claims that in exile, all "share a common identity now which transcends ethnic and cultural identities. In exile there are no strangers."[33] Against the anti-erotic force of indifference, the faith that survives is a witness to divine self-sacrificing love, which is the only thing that gives meaning to these lives—not suffering, ethnicity, or tradition. A vision of cruciform relationality emerges in Siberia's forest camp.

Such negation is necessary for Mennonites who, wittingly or not, worship mammon and are in need of the humility that

30. Kroeker and Ward, "Gulag Ethics," 185.
31. Quoted in Kroeker and Ward, "Gulag Ethics," 195–96.
32. Quoted in Kroeker and Ward, "Gulag Ethics," 194.
33. Quoted in Kroeker and Ward, "Gulag Ethics," 194.

imitates—embodies—this relationality. Here we see how Mennonites are witness to divine love rather than only victims of political persecution: when cultural, social, vocational, and ethnic identities are stripped away to nothing and what's left is not indifference but an experience of the truth and mystery of divine love. In another memoir, the main culprit of Mennonite ingratitude to divine love is possessiveness, which is seen acutely in property acquisition. Mennonites had developed a strong desire to acquire land: "Some had one, two, even three farms, others had no land. . . . By 1905 nonresistant Mennonites had become landlords."[34] These Mennonites who cry "land, land" need conversion through penitence.[35] Possessiveness, like indifference, is anti-Christ because anti-erotic and therefore requires conversion through penitence.

Kroeker's writing performs an erotic dialogue that demonstrates a penitential conversion. In some essays, he chastises Mennonite theologians for largely ignoring contemporary Anabaptist communities as a funding current for theology. For example, he advocates for dialogue with communities like the Amish, not for "protecting ethno-religious identity" but rather for seeking out a model of theology that is "a nonviolent resistance of globalizing capitalism."[36] But it is Kroeker's conversation with Red River Métis scholar Carole Leclair that embodies his own Augustinian-Platonic—Anabaptist existential—theology.

In the essay's introduction, written together, Leclair and Kroeker summon ethicists to begin with stories rather than theoretical frameworks or an eye toward solutions. The essay offers a new path, one that begins awkwardly with personal stories moving vulnerably with hope and uncertainty toward a relationship. Or as they put it, a journey toward respect by attending to divided worlds of experience.[37] Kroeker begins with his personal experience and positionality: born in a rural Mennonite community, whose family was ignorant yet privileged, and who experienced a spiritual wound after the culture shock of moving to Winnipeg. He shares his experience reading *Black Elk Speaks*, which models a dramatic openness that Kroeker sees as constituting a path for identity and connection with others beyond ideologies. This path is "opening one's heart to pain," which Kroeker follows by listing his own pain over what Mennonites have caused and felt because of

---

34. Quoted in Kroeker and Ward, "Gulag Ethics," 196.
35. Quoted in Kroeker and Ward, "Gulag Ethics," 197.
36. Kroeker, "Rich Mennonites in an Age of Mammon," 217.
37. Kroeker and Leclair, "Mennonite and Métis," 200.

colonialism.[38] The movement along this path is away from "prideful possession" and toward relationality; he transitions to the story about how he met Carole Leclair.[39] Drawing on figures and arguments endemic to his writing, he outlines a case for spiritual disciplines that obviate colonial tendencies. A "messianic ethic . . . is rooted in a self-emptying movement of dispossession . . . to get beyond possessive identities and aspirations altogether via the gift of a healing rooted in penitence—for Mennonites, a penitence for participating in the destructive domination and appropriation of peoples and lands."[40]

Leclair replies generously yet critically to Kroeker. This movement is no easy journey. She's cautiously nervous and with good reason, given how appropriation and tokenism are hallmarks of settler academia. But it turns out they grew up on the same land, merely fifty kilometers apart, and "the land connected us" even though they have very different relationships with that land.[41] Travis meets her with protocol, bringing tobacco as a gift for their conversation, which begins with pain. The Dominion of Canada gave Mennonites the land of her nation's territory; Mennonites were heavily involved in the Oklahoma Territory land grab. Kroeker responds with penitence, which Leclair hesitatingly accepts as part of their conversation, again for good reason. Is it personal or merely "Christian," that is, a habitual gesture without material substance? Leclair tells her own stories from her heritage, sharing not only who she is and her family's experience but how it exposes the colonial legacy in institutional Christianity. Here Leclair notes that her conversations with Kroeker "take a different turn."[42] Through Kroeker there is a change of direction, a turning around, a conversion. They don't leave convictions or identity behind—Kroeker never detaches himself from his heritage or tradition—but the conversation is a spiritual discipline: "These healing talks work against estrangement and indifference."[43] The dialogues themselves are not enough to achieve healing, reparations, sovereignty. But, as Leclair and Kroeker say in their introduction, it's a beginning and part of the work for change that outlines this work as necessarily messianic for Mennonites.

38. Kroeker and Leclair, "Mennonite and Métis," 202.
39. Kroeker and Leclair, "Mennonite and Métis," 203.
40. Kroeker and Leclair, "Mennonite and Métis," 205.
41. Kroeker and Leclair, "Mennonite and Métis," 206.
42. Kroeker and Leclair, "Mennonite and Métis," 210.
43. Kroeker and Leclair, "Mennonite and Métis," 210.

Conclusion

Understanding Kroeker's work as a lesson in messianic erotics that constitutes a theological education of the affections risks offense. Indeed, his work embodies this risk—what Annie Dillard calls the "scandal of particularity."[44] His critical attention to figures who mediate a desire for anti-imperial and anti-possessive moments is singular among theological ethicists because it is the attentiveness of a deviating imagination. His is an affectionate perception that sees into the deeper meaning of dramatic moments of love others find uncomfortable.

Take an illustrative example: during the time we were both in graduate school, a visiting scholar presented a paper on Wendell Berry to the department. In the conversation that followed, Kroeker referred to the pivotal moment in Berry's novel *Remembering* that marks the point when the protagonist, Andy, reaches the nadir of his journey. It's both an emotional and physical low point when Andy remembers a conversation he had as a child with his grandma about raising chickens. Gathering eggs, Andy tells his grandma, "You know, you can just order the chickens from a factory now and they send them to you through the mail." To which she responds, "But this is the best way, aint it?"[45] In our academic context, Kroeker spoke what he has elsewhere written: Andy's "turning is marked by a memory of sexual love embodied in his grandmother," whose husband has just died, "to help her and to provide her company."[46] Andy's sexual desire is shaped by a love of raising chickens he shares with his grandma. His problem is a series of bad relationships based on his refusal to be vulnerable; he wants to claim a strong position in the community and in his marriage based on what he can do and produce. His love is not properly attuned to the divine in the sense that he refuses to trust that what he can offer in his woundedness as a one-armed man will be accepted and part of the community's social life; that he's part of something bigger than himself that is mysterious because it cannot be seen or proven and also exists to restore things wounded and divided. Here we have a moment of love between Andy and his grandmother that is both part of a political economy deemed replaceable by dominant economics as well as an erotic memory that pulls his desires toward home. Kroeker describes it as a "memory of love and sexual begetting,"

44. Quoted in Kroeker, "Postsecular History or Figural Messianism?" 343.
45. Quoted in Kroeker, "Sexuality and the Sacramental Imagination," 129.
46. Kroeker, "Sexuality and the Sacramental Imagination," 129.

an "insemination that gives birth much later to his loving return."[47] Andy is reminded of the community that has claimed him, its relational form that constitutes a political economy, in an erotic memory with his grandmother. Andy's small, rural town in Kentucky—not San Francisco or even the church of Peter and Paul—is the messianic community. A child's shared affection for raising chickens with his grandma—not a man's intimate connection with his wife—is an erotic relation with wholeness, with the divine presence in all creation.

As one might guess, the visiting scholar found this reading to be offensive. And why shouldn't he? The direct connection of the development of sexual desire with one's grandmother risks calling to mind, shall we say, a certain confusion of roles. But this is hardly more risky than the Christian tradition's own overlapping symbolism of Mary as both the queen at the right hand of the messianic king, and, herself an image of the church, also as the bride of Christ. That is not supposed to encourage calling forth lewd thoughts either. Rather, it is an instruction about how the Spirit that is intended to unite and vivify the marital relationship is the same one God gives to unite different generations of a family, whole communities and cities, and the entire cosmos. One ought to relate to one's grandma differently than to one's spouse, but what Kroeker seems to see is that within these different relations dwells the same eternal Spirit these relations help make manifest in very real ways in our lives. Thus, the themes of erotics and messianism are here intended to help convey the sense in which divine eros seems to be the driving force behind everything Kroeker does, as a scholar, as a speaker, as a teacher.

With this comes no small measure of risk: of offending, of uncomfortable confrontation, of being misunderstood, of misunderstanding. And it is not our purpose here to contend that Kroeker gets every reading or relation "right." Rather, it is to account for the palpable sense of importance in his every engagement, as though any moment might sacramentally bear forth a revelation of eternal significance. In light of this, his assumption of such risks is intelligible: this is someone struggling "to give an account of what it means to be answerable for what I have been given to be and to do." It is not enough to seek establishment of the right ecclesiastical or sociopolitical configurations, to be known by a certain familiar clan name, or to possess the correct arguments. It is to push hard to look through these things as modes of messianic

---

47. Kroeker, "Sexuality and the Sacramental Imagination," 130.

manifestation meant to convey the aspect of what is eternal within, to which one can relate through experience. For Kroeker's students, this is not just a training for a profession (though it is certainly that) but the cultivation of a counterinsurgency through the exploration of scholarship aimed at mediating divine love. Kroeker's tutelage is defined by caring enough—about the material, about the books and their characters and their nuances, about theological teachings and their coherence, about interlocutors and their arguments, and about students themselves—to speak about and argue over things like they matter. It is a form of scholarship difficult and personal, and something of a rarity. "But," we might agree with Andy's grandma, "this is the best way, aint it?"

Bibliography

Augustine. *The City of God Against the Pagans*. Translated by R. W. Dyson. Cambridge: Cambridge University Press, 1998.

Augustine. *Letters 156–210*. Translated by Roland Teske. Hyde Park, NY: New City, 2004.

Baynes, Norman H. "The Political Ideas of St. Augustine's De Civitate Dei." In *Byzantine Studies and Other Essays*, 288–306. London: Athlone, 1955.

Dodaro, Robert. "Augustine's Secular City." In *Augustine and His Critics: Essays in Honour of Gerald Bonner*, edited by Robert Dodaro and George Lawless, 231–59. London: Routledge, 2000.

Kries, Douglas. "Political Augustinianism." In *Augustine Through the Ages: An Encyclopedia*, edited by Allan D. Fitzgerald, 657–58. Grand Rapids: Eerdmans, 1999.

Kroeker, P. Travis. "Anabaptists and Existential Theology." In *Messianic Political Theology and Diaspora Ethics: Essays in Exile*, 83–96. Eugene, OR: Cascade, 2017.

———. "Augustine's Messianic Political Theology: An Apocalyptic Critique of Political Augustinianism." In *Messianic Political Theology and Diaspora Ethics: Essays in Exile*, 46–63. Eugene, OR: Cascade, 2017.

———. *Empire Erotics and Messianic Economies of Desire*. Winnipeg: Canadian Mennonite University Press, 2016.

———. "Postsecular History or Figural Messianism?" *Political Theology* 24 (2023) 342–46.

———. "Rich Mennonites in an Age of Mammon: Is a Messianic Political Economy Possible?" In *Messianic Political Theology and Diaspora Ethics: Essays in Exile*, 211–20. Eugene, OR: Cascade, 2017.

———. "Saint Paul at Sea: A Mystical-Political Reading of *Moby Dick* via Stanislaus Breton." *Pro Ecclesia* 26 (2017) 111–18.

———. "Scandalous Displacements: 'Word' and 'Silent Light' in *Irma Voth*." *Journal of Mennonite Studies* 36 (2018) 89–100.

———. "Sexuality and the Sacramental Imagination: It All Turns on Affection." In *Wendell Berry: Life and Work*, edited by Jason Peters, 119–37. Lexington: University of Kentucky Press, 2007.

Kroeker, P. Travis, and Carole Leclair. "Mennonite and Métis: Adjacent Histories, Adjacent Truths?" In *Messianic Political Theology and Diaspora Ethics: Essays in Exile*, 199–210. Eugene, OR: Cascade, 2017.

Kroeker, P. Travis, and Bruce Ward. "Gulag Ethics: Russian and Mennonite Prison Memoirs from Siberia." In *Messianic Political Theology and Diaspora Ethics: Essays in Exile*, 185–98. Eugene, OR: Cascade, 2017.

———. *Remembering the End: Dostoevsky as Prophet to Modernity*. Boulder, CO: Westview, 2001.

Markus, Robert A. *Christianity and the Secular*. Notre Dame, IN: University of Notre Dame Press, 2006.

Milbank, John A. "A Closer Walk on the Wild Side." In *Varieties of Secularism in a Secular Age*, edited by Michael Warner et al., 54–82. Cambridge, MA: Harvard University Press, 2010.

Taylor, Charles. *A Secular Age*. London: Belknap, 2018.

Williams, Rowan. "Politics and the Soul: Reading the *City of God*." In *On Augustine*, 107–29. London: Bloomsbury, 2016.

2

Wrestling with Apocalyptic Eschatology and the Task of Political Theology

MATTHEW THIESSEN

ERNST KÄSEMANN FAMOUSLY CLAIMED that "apocalyptic was the mother of all Christian theology."[1] Käsemann here acknowledges that both Jesus and the Jewish sect that arose in his wake were indebted to ancient Jewish apocalyptic hopes and expectations. New Testament scholars and theologians alike have sought to grapple with the apocalyptic origins of Christianity, striving to make these origins sensible in very different contexts. Most difficult for this theological task is the awkward fact that both Jesus and Paul believed that the eschaton was imminent. And both Jesus and Paul were wrong. Stating it so baldly often raises the hackles of many a biblical scholar or theologian, let alone layperson. And understandably so. No Christian *wants* Jesus to be wrong. (Paul, on the other hand . . .) I am not entirely convinced that apocalyptic was the mother of all Christian theology,[2] but I am convinced that the unfulfilled apocalyptic hopes

---

1. Käsemann, *New Testament Questions of Today*, 102.

2. As Cyril O'Regan puts it, "the history of theology seems largely to be the history of the marginalization of apocalyptic." O'Regan, *Theology and the Spaces of Apocalyptic*, 15. And long before O'Regan, Albert Schweitzer claimed that "the whole history of 'Christianity' down to the present day, that is to say, the real inner history of it, is based on the delay of the Parousia, the non-occurrence of the Parousia, the abandonment of eschatology, the progress and completion of 'de-eschatologising' of religion which has been connected therewith." Schweitzer, *Quest of the Historical Jesus*, 328.

of Jesus and Paul (and others in the early Jesus movement) ought to be the mother of all Christian political theology.

Unfulfilled Apocalyptic Hopes

The 1892 publication of Johannes Weiss's book *Die Predigt Jesu von Reiche Gottes* necessitated a full-scale reconsideration of Jesus's proclamation of the kingdom of God.[3] Rather than understanding this kingdom to be a reference to the church or to some sort of interior disposition, as was a common theological interpretation in his day, Weiss argued that the kingdom Jesus preached was rooted in Jewish apocalyptic hopes about a very real and manifest overhaul of the current state of the cosmos. Weiss argued that Jesus initially thought that this would happen during his lifetime. But when this kingdom failed to materialize, Jesus modified his eschatological calendar, becoming convinced that the kingdom would come shortly after his own death. This death, Jesus believed, would serve as an eschatological catalyst in bringing about the kingdom. When Weiss speaks about the apocalyptic thinking of Jesus, then, it is clear that he means *specifically* a belief in the imminent and obvious transformation of the cosmos.[4]

Each of the Synoptic Gospels transmits a saying of Jesus that appears to point in this direction. In Mark 9, Jesus tells his disciples, "Truly I say to you, there are some standing here who will not taste death until they see that the kingdom of God has come in power" (Mark 9:1).[5] Matthew modifies this saying slightly: "Truly I say to you, there are some standing here who will not taste death until they see the Son of Man coming in his kingdom" (Matt 16:28), while Luke follows Mark quite closely: "Truly I say to you, there are some standing here who will not taste death until they see the kingdom of God" (Luke 9:27). On a straightforward reading of the various forms of this statement, it looks as if Jesus expected the apocalyptic eschaton to break in imminently and powerfully in the lifetimes of at least some of his own disciples. The messianic Son of Man would rule.[6] Most historical Jesus scholars think this saying goes back

3. For the English translation of this short but powerful work, see Weiss, *Jesus' Proclamation of the Kingdom*.

4. Käsemann too thinks that the early Jesus movement held to an "imminent expectation of the *parousia*." Käsemann, *New Testament Questions of Today*, 109n1.

5. All quotations from Scripture are my own translation.

6. On ancient Jewish messianism, see Novenson, *Grammar of Messianism*.

to Jesus and that Mark (and Matthew and Luke, following Mark's lead) sought to minimize the scandal of this incorrect eschatological proclamation by redefining what Jesus meant through placing it immediately before the story of Jesus's transfiguration. But if Jesus meant to refer to his transfiguration, then the kingdom has come and it has gone, and those who follow this Jesus are two thousand years down the historical road with little to show for it. Additionally, the Gospel of Mark contains a lengthy apocalyptic speech of Jesus that ends with him telling his disciples, "Truly I say to you that this generation will not pass away until all this happens" (Mark 13:30). And the Gospel of Matthew contains an even more explicit hope of an imminent eschaton. There Jesus tells his disciples, "Truly I say to you that you will not have finished going through all the towns of Israel before the Son of Man comes" (Matt 10:23). This messianic coming, to put it bluntly, did not happen.

While the Gospel of John does not contain these particular claims, it ends with another piece of evidence that Jesus's words were initially understood to imply an imminent coming of God's kingdom. There, the resurrected Jesus eats with Peter and asks him, "If I want him [i.e., the beloved disciple] to remain until I come, what does that have to do with you? Follow me!" (John 21:22). In an authorial aside, John informs his readers that this statement was the reason that Jesus's early followers believed that the beloved disciple would not die before Jesus returned, but then makes the grammatical observation that Jesus's words were not a statement of fact but a conditional statement: "*If* I want . . ." Apparently, according to John, Jesus did not want him to remain until his coming! To be sure, the Jesus of the Gospels acknowledges that he does not know when the kingdom of God will actually come (Mark 13:32; Matt 24:36), but other statements suggest the belief that, whatever the precise moment, it was going to happen very soon.[7]

Turning to the apostle Paul, the evidence of his belief in the imminent end is even more compelling.[8] In what most scholars believe to be his earliest letter, Paul tells the Thessalonians that when the resurrected Jesus returns, "We who are alive, who are left, will be caught up in the clouds together with them to meet the Lord in the air; and so we will be with the Lord forever" (1 Thess 4:17). Christian readers naturally read themselves into the "we" of this verse, but this occasional letter intends to refer to Paul

---

7. Schweitzer argued for the "thoroughgoing eschatology" of Jesus in *Quest of the Historical Jesus*, an interpretation reinvigorated by Allison, *Jesus of Nazareth*.

8. See Kensky, "Paul and the Apocalypse of the Gospel."

and first-century residents of Thessalonika, not to us. In other words, Paul anticipated that some (perhaps most?) of his first readers would be alive when Jesus returned.[9] This expectation was so powerful that a second letter, whether penned by Paul or one of his followers, was needed to assuage the anxieties of those who thought that perhaps the end had already come and that they had missed it (2 Thess 2:2).

Such thinking fits with Paul's claims that "the time has grown short" (1 Cor 7:29), that the "structure of this cosmos is passing away" (7:31), and that "the ends of the ages have come" (1 Cor 10:11). While these passages from 1 Corinthians do not explicitly address the absolute imminence of the eschaton, Paul's words about the resurrection of the body do: "We will not all die, but we will all be instantly transformed, in the twinkling of an eye, at the last trumpet. For the trumpet will sound, and the dead will be raised imperishable, and we will be transformed" (1 Cor 15:51–52). As in 1 Thessalonians, Paul refers here to both himself and his intended readers, first-century residents of the city of Corinth. And to those in Rome, Paul claims that now is the time to wake up, because "salvation is nearer to us . . . the night has advanced and the day is near" (Rom 13:11–12). Such statements led Albert Schweitzer to conclude over a century ago that "from his first letter to his last Paul's thought is always uniformly dominated by the expectation of the immediate return of Jesus."[10]

Such textual evidence from the earliest years of the Jesus movement shows that the movement was dominated by an imminent apocalyptic expectation that the resurrected Jesus would return in glory and transform both humanity and the entire cosmos. It is not surprising, therefore, to see early discomfort with and responses to what biblical scholars refer to as the delayed parousia.[11] For instance, the author of 2 Peter claims that some people are mocking God, asking, "Where is the promise of his coming [parousia]? For ever since our fathers died, all things continue as they were from the beginning of creation!" (3:4). To this question, quite understandable if one has been led to believe that Jesus would return imminently, the author responds by quoting Ps 90—"with the Lord one day is like a thousand years, and a thousand years are like one day" (2 Pet 3:8; cf. Ps 90:4)—before appearing to quote Paul's imminently apocalyptic

9. Luckensmeyer, *Eschatology of First Thessalonians*.

10. Schweitzer, *Mysticism of Paul the Apostle*. See now the updated treatment of Fredriksen, "*Al Tirah* ('Fear Not!')."

11. See Grässer, *Das Problem der Parusieverzögerung*.

words from 1 Thess 5:2 about the Day of the Lord coming like a thief (2 Pet 3:10). The theo-logic of the use of this Psalm is that the parousia has not, in fact, been delayed, since what seems like a thousand years to humans is only a day to God.[12] Even if they are fifty, one hundred, or nine hundred years from Jesus's resurrection, they are still only one day removed. It is still the Day of the Lord.

Theological efforts to minimize the scandal of a delayed parousia have trickled down through time,[13] resulting in biblical theologians, perhaps most famously N. T. Wright, claiming that Jesus's and Paul's apocalyptic language should not be taken literally, but figuratively or metaphorically.[14] For Wright, "if Jesus expected the end of the world, then he was mistaken," a possibility that he clearly finds too unpalatable for his theological stomach.[15] This strategy of metaphorization serves as a convenient way to admit that Jesus and Paul are apocalyptic thinkers, while entirely redefining what apocalyptic expectations actually were in order to align with contemporary Christian concerns.

Political Theology

At the age of twenty, I desperately wanted to be a theologian. I soon realized that whatever intellectual gifts I may have, they do not extend to the realm of deep, constructive theological work. So instead I settled for the role of a pedantic Bible scholar. But it has repeatedly struck me that this issue of the delayed parousia in the first century intersects with central themes that run through the work of Travis Kroeker. The theme of apocalyptic especially weaves its way through his *Messianic Political Theology and Diaspora Ethics: Essays in Exile*. These diverse essays range through thoughtful discussions of Plato and Isaiah, Martin Luther and Thomas Müntzer, Oliver O'Donovan and John Howard Yoder, and a whole host

---

12. See especially Bauckham, "Delay of the *Parousia*."

13. In fact, such concerns continued into the second and third centuries CE, as Siker, "Parousia of Jesus," has shown.

14. On Jesus, see Wright, *Jesus and the Victory of God*, 339–68. In his earlier volume, *New Testament and the People of God*, 280–338, Wright argues that this eschatological thought was shared by their Jewish contemporaries. See here the trenchant criticisms of Allison, "Jesus and the Victory of Apocalyptic"; and more broadly, Allison, "Problem of Apocalyptic." But well before Wright, Ladd had already sought to defuse the theologically troublesome apocalyptic message via metaphorization. See Ladd, *Presence of the Future*; and more recently, Witherington, *Jesus Quest*, 96.

15. Wright, *Jesus and the Victory of God*, 95.

of other interlocutors along the way. What has struck me repeatedly as I have worked through these essays is the theme of apocalyptic.

The pedantic biblical scholar in me is tempted to point out that Travis uses the term *apocalyptic* in a way that differs from how it is generally understood in early Jewish and Christian scholarship,[16] but I nonetheless believe that there is a fruitful intersection of these two different meanings that surfaces within the context of an ancient attempt to defuse the tension of a delayed parousia. After seeking to minimize the problem of Jesus's long-delayed return, the author of 2 Peter shows that he still subscribes to apocalyptic thought himself. Jesus will return like a thief (cf. Matt 24:43; 1 Thess 5:2). It could happen at any moment and in an unexpected and unannounced way. It did not come when we thought it would come. But it will come when we do not think it will come. The author calls his readers to live their lives in the midst of this dual uncertainty: "Since all these things are to be dissolved in this way, what sort of persons ought you to be in leading lives of holiness and godliness, waiting for and hastening the coming of the Day of God" (2 Pet 3:11–12).

The embarrassment or scandal of the delayed parousia or eschaton is a scandal in different ways for different people. For Christians with a high Christology, the scandal is the question of, as Dale Allison puts it, "How could God incarnate be mistaken in his eschatological expectations?"[17] For Christians who view Jesus primarily or predominantly in terms of a moral exemplar or teacher of timeless moral values, what are they to do with his embarrassingly fervent apocalypticism?[18] For both, who wants Jesus to share anything in common with modern doomsday thinkers? For all Christians, the question persists: What do Jesus's teachings, what does Jesus's life mean here and now? The absurdity or difficulty or impossibility of answering that question is only heightened when one grapples with the fact that Jesus did not appear to envisage *our* here and now. If the eschaton had been approaching in the first century CE, was Jesus just teaching an "interim ethic," as Schweitzer argued?[19] Or do those moral teachings apply now, and if so, how?

It seems to me that the task of both theological ethics (more broadly) and political theology (more narrowly) is one of wrestling with the fact that the kingdom is both here and not here. The ends of the ages

---

16. The pedantic in me just did point it out.
17. Allison, "Problem of Apocalyptic," 107.
18. See Miller, *Apocalyptic Jesus*.
19. Schweitzer, *Mystery of the Kingdom of God*, 55.

have come and not come. We are not supposed to be here and yet here we are. As Daniel Colucciello Barber puts it, "Christians are those who identify with a messianic hope that seems to have failed, but that cannot have failed."[20] Our lives are lives in tension, stuck between two worlds: the world that is and the world that is to come. Consequently, all theological ethics and all political theologies are but mere "essays in exile," whether their authors remember this fact or not. All Christian theology and ethics are written without a clear roadmap for what we are to do and how we are to live in this awkward and rather extended moment of the *ends of the ages* (1 Cor 10:11). One can glimpse a bit of the resulting variety, although I am tempted to call it chaos, of Christian political theology in Joan Lockwood O'Donovan and Oliver O'Donovan's *From Irenaeus to Grotius: A Sourcebook in Christian Political Thought*.

One sees further glimpses of the possibilities of political theology in Travis's writings, which discuss many of the same sources found in O'Donovan and O'Donovan but also bring to the fore political theologies in various Anabaptist registers.[21] Kroeker's patient work comes through in his careful, sensitive readings of theologians such as Augustine and Luther, who are often vilified or ignored by Mennonite and Anabaptist theologians. He rightly acknowledges that "the use that is made of apocalyptic language can take many different theological, ethical, and political forms."[22] Nonetheless, his work cautions against dominant domestications of the apocalyptic thinking of Paul and Jesus and the early Jesus movement. On the one hand, the kingdom of God "cannot be simply a 'doctrinal' or 'religious' or 'otherworldly' teaching, nor indeed is it a category that only applies pietistically to the inner movements of individual hearts; it has ethical and political dimensions and implications."[23] That sort of eschatology is spiritualized, internalized, and made otherworldly. And on the other hand, Kroeker denounces the material and this-worldly eschatology of the "Constantinian Christian empire" because it is "rooted in a falsely realized eschatology,"[24] noting that as the Christian church gains power and becomes more visible, its Christ-like character conversely becomes more invisible. Such a criticism seems especially pertinent at a time when more and more Christians, most notably in the

20. Barber, "Immanent Refusal of Conversion."
21. See also Klaassen, *Living at the End of the Ages*.
22. Kroeker, *Messianic Political Theology*, 208.
23. Kroeker, "Overcoming Historicism."
24. Kroeker, *Messianic Political Theology*, 118.

United States but also around the world, are subscribing to various forms of brash and unapologetic Christian nationalism.[25]

Conclusion

In response to Schweitzer's reading of Jesus and Paul as thoroughgoing apocalyptic thinkers whose ethics were interim ethics, the American Unitarian minister and Harvard University theology professor Francis Greenwood Peabody claimed that if Schweitzer were right, "the ethics of the Gospels would give us a teaching, not designed for this world, but preparatory for another."[26] Peabody rejects this possibility, but, ironically, his claim approaches the truth. In fact, it is not merely the Gospels but the entire New Testament that provides its readers with an ethics preparatory for another world. That other world was just on the horizon for the New Testament writers. That is not a situation dissimilar to our own. We remain in diaspora, we remain in exile, but it is a diaspora or exile that is markedly temporal in nature. The end has come and it has not come.[27] We remain in the now/not-yet of the two ages, wrestling with how to live in this world even as we constantly look for and anticipate another world where "all created reality will be drawn up through death into eschatological completion, the 'all in all' of divine love."[28]

The apocalypse both reveals and conceals. And much remains hidden. Travis's extensive writings seek to bring to the surface some of what is hidden, to shine light on those fissures in the fabric of our world where the apocalypse breaks through. Apocalyptic thinking must live inside the tension that the end should have come and yet has not come. It is both here and not here. When I read through Travis's wide-ranging and probing writings, I see him wrestling to find those moments of "here-ness"—the apocalypse is near you, on your lips and in your heart. At the same time, one can see Travis's wrestling with the non-here-ness in his repeated recalling of the apostle Paul's words: "Let even those who have wives be as those who do not, and those who mourn as those not mourning, and those who rejoice as those not rejoicing, and those who

---

25. On this phenomenon, see Goldberg, *Kingdom Coming*; Whitehead and Perry, *Taking America Back for God*; and Martin, *Gospel of J. Edgar Hoover*.

26. Peabody, "New Testament Eschatology and New Testament Ethics," 308.

27. On one recent theological creative effort to grapple with the nature of Christian time, see Jervis, *Paul and Time*.

28. Kroeker, *Messianic Political Theology*, 143.

buy as those not having, and those who deal with the cosmos as those not dealing with it" (1 Cor 7:29–31).

Paul himself explored ways to continue on in this world in ways that made sense of the apocalyptic inbreaking of the Messiah that did not live up to the apocalyptic expectations he and others cherished. This advice to the Corinthians of living in the world as if not (*hōs mē*), a phrase repeated five times in this passage from Paul, suggests, as Travis puts it "a using that is not proprietary, not related to human sovereignty or juridical ownership."[29] Although Travis does not use the term *Gelassenheit*, I wonder whether this life lived in the tension of "as if not" connects to or makes sense of the Mennonite principle of yieldedness, or letting go of one's attachments to the things of this world.[30] *Gelassenheit* is an apocalyptic posture: what one has now, sweet and precious as it may be, is but temporary and pales when compared to the apocalyptic hopes that have animated Jesus, Paul, and all those who belong to that small apocalyptic Jewish sect turned Christianity.

Inhabiting the in-between, where the church points back to the Lamb that was slain and forward to the kingdom of God, living between the crushed hopes of those who cry out, "But we had hoped that he was the one who was about to redeem Israel" (Luke 24:21) and the exuberant celebration of those who wait for "God to be all in all" (1 Cor 15:28): this is the task of political theology, something that earlier theologians such as Käsemann sought to retrieve for Christian theology.[31] Travis's writings, too, repeatedly invite us into the awkwardness and discomfort of this in-between-ness, right where we belong.

Bibliography

Allison, Dale C. "Jesus and the Victory of Apocalyptic." In *Jesus and the Restoration of Israel: A Critical Assessment of N. T. Wright's Jesus and the Victory of God*, edited by Carey C. Newman, 126–41. Downers Grove, IL: InterVarsity, 1999.

———. *Jesus of Nazareth: Millenarian Prophet*. Minneapolis: Augsburg Fortress, 1998.

———. "The Problem of Apocalyptic: From Polemic to Apologetics." In *Apocalypticism, Anti-Semitism and the Historical Jesus: Subtexts in Criticism*, edited by John S.

---

29. Kroeker, *Messianic Political Theology*, 78.

30. See, for example, Klaassen, "'Gelassenheit' and Creation"; and Snyder, "*Gelassenheit* and Power."

31. See the appreciative treatment of Siggelkow, "Ernst Käsemann and the Specter of Apocalyptic."

Kloppenborg and John W. Marshall, 98–110. *Journal for the Study of the New Testament* Supplement Series 275. London: T. & T. Clark, 2005.

Barber, Daniel Colucciello. "The Immanent Refusal of Conversion." *Journal for Cultural and Religious Theory* 13 (2014) 142–50.

Bauckham, Richard J. "The Delay of the *Parousia*." *Tyndale Bulletin* 31 (1980) 3–36.

Fredriksen, Paula. "*Al Tirah* ('Fear Not!'): Jewish Apocalyptic Eschatology, from Schweitzer to Allison, and After." In *"To Recover What Has Been Lost": Essays on Eschatology, Intertextuality, and Reception History in Honor of Dale C. Allison Jr.*, edited by Tucker Ferda et al., 15–38. Novum Testament Supplements 183. Leiden: Brill, 2021.

Goldberg, Michelle. *Kingdom Coming: The Rise of Christian Nationalism*. New York: Norton, 2007.

Grässer, Erich. *Das Problem der Parusieverzögerung in den synoptischen Evangelien und in der Apostelgeschichte*. Beihefte zur Zeitschrift für die neutestamentliche Wissenschaft 22. Berlin: de Gruyter, 1957.

Jervis, L. Ann. *Paul and Time: Life in the Temporality of Christ*. Grand Rapids: Baker Academic, 2023.

Käsemann, Ernst. *New Testament Questions of Today*. Translated by W. J. Montague. London: SCM, 1969.

Kensky, Meira Z. "Paul and the Apocalypse of the Gospel." *Interpretation* 76 (2022) 328–38.

Klaassen, Walter. "'Gelassenheit' and Creation." *Conrad Grebel Review* 9 (1991) 23–35.

———. *Living at the End of the Ages: Apocalyptic Expectation in the Radical Reformation*. Waterloo, ON: Institute for Anabaptist and Mennonite Studies, 1992.

Kroeker, P. Travis. *Messianic Political Theology and Diaspora Ethics: Essays in Exile*. Eugene: OR: Cascade, 2017.

———. "Overcoming Historicism: Weak Messianic Apocalypticism." Syndicate, June 16, 2014. https://syndicate.network/symposia/theology/the-heterodox-yoder/.

Ladd, George Eldon. *The Presence of the Future: The Eschatology of Biblical Realism*. Grand Rapids: Eerdmans, 1974.

Luckensmeyer, David. *The Eschatology of First Thessalonians*. Novum Testamentum et Orbis Antiquus 71. Göttingen: Vandenhoeck & Ruprecht, 2009.

Martin, Lerone A. *The Gospel of J. Edgar Hoover: How the FBI Aided and Abetted the Rise of White Christian Nationalism*. Princeton, NJ: Princeton University Press, 2023.

Miller, Robert J., ed. *The Apocalyptic Jesus: A Debate*. Santa Rosa, CA: Polebridge, 2001.

Novenson, Matthew V. *The Grammar of Messianism: An Ancient Jewish Political Idiom and Its Users*. New York: Oxford University Press, 2017.

O'Donovan, Joan Lockwood, and Oliver O'Donovan. *From Irenaeus to Grotius: A Sourcebook in Christian Political Thought*. Grand Rapids: Eerdmans, 1999.

O'Regan, Cyril. *Theology and the Spaces of Apocalyptic*. Milwaukee: Marquette, 2009.

Peabody, Francis Greenwood. "New Testament Eschatology and New Testament Ethics." In *Transactions of the Third International Congress for the History of Religions*, edited by Percy Stafford Allen and John de Monins Johnson, 2:305–12. Oxford: Clarendon, 1908.

Schweitzer, Albert. *The Mystery of the Kingdom of God: The Secret of Jesus' Messiahship and Passion*. Translated by Walter Lowrie. New York: MacMillan, 1957.

———. *The Mysticism of Paul the Apostle*. Translated by William Montgomery. Baltimore: Johns Hopkins University Press, 1998.

———. *The Quest of the Historical Jesus: A Critical Study of Its Progress from Reimarus to Wrede*. Translated by W. Montgomery. London: A&C Black, 1910.

Siggelkow, Ry O. "Ernst Käsemann and the Specter of Apocalyptic." *Theology Today* 75 (2018) 37–50.

Siker, Jeffrey. "The Parousia of Jesus in Second and Third Century Christianity." In *The Return of Jesus in Early Christianity*, edited by John T. Carroll, 147–67. Peabody, MA: Hendrickson, 2000.

Snyder, C. Arnold. "*Gelassenheit* and Power: Some Historical Reflections." *Vision* 5 (2004) 6–13.

Weiss, Johannes. *Jesus' Proclamation of the Kingdom of God*. Translated by Richard Hyde Hiers and David Larrimore Holland. Philadelphia: Fortress, 1971.

Whitehead, Andrew L., and Samuel L. Perry. *Taking America Back for God: Christian Nationalism in the United States*. Updated ed. New York: Oxford University Press, 2022.

Witherington, Ben. *The Jesus Quest: The Third Search for the Jew of Nazareth*. Downers Grove, IL: InterVarsity, 1995.

Wright, N. T. *Jesus and the Victory of God*. Minneapolis: Fortress, 1996.

———. *The New Testament and the People of God*. Minneapolis: Fortress, 1992.

3

The Price of Christian Messianism

Philip G. Ziegler

I

GERSHOM SCHOLEM FUNDAMENTALLY CHALLENGED our understanding of the history of Judaism by his pioneering studies of its enduring mystical and messianic aspects. By demonstrating the dynamic importance of both these currents in the development of Judaism up and into the modern era, Scholem called into question the received historiography of the *Wissenschaft des Judentums* in which he himself had been trained, securing a new and fundamental appreciation for the internal diversity of Jewish life and thought. As regards messianism, his massive study of the seventeenth-century Sabbatian movement—*Sabbatai Sevi: The Mystical Messiah 1626–1676*—underwrote several smaller studies,[1] including the programmatic essay whose argument most concerns us here: "Toward an Understanding of the Messianic Idea in Judaism."[2]

As its title suggests, Scholem's essay addresses the recurrent logic of the messianic as it has unfolded "under the conditions of exile as a primary reality of Jewish life" and within the interplay of the "conservative,

---

1. Scholem, *Sabbatai Sevi*, represents a revision and augmentation of the original Hebrew edition first published in 1957.

2. Scholem, "Toward an Understanding." The German original is collected in Scholem, *Judaica*, 1:7–74.

restorative, and utopian" forces shaping rabbinical Judaism.³ He suggests that the messianic arises in the interplay of the restorative and utopian impulses, that is, from the interchange of forces pursuing the recovery of a lost and idealized past, with those driving toward a state of affairs that has never yet been. Seemingly contradictory, these impulses are in fact entangled in a "dialectically linked tension," for the past to be restored is always ideal and not actual, and the utopian vision is always furnished by imagined transformations of the old. Crucially, Scholem observes, forged in this way, the messianic idea "always occurs in the closest connection with apocalypticism;" indeed, apocalypticism "appears as the form necessarily created by acute Messianism."⁴ The apocalyptic transformation of the deliverances of the law and the prophets associates the messianic idea with "the catastrophic and destructive nature of the redemption on the one hand and the utopianism of the content of realized Messianism on the other," ensuring that, as Scholem explains, "Jewish Messianism is in its origins and by its nature . . . a theory of catastrophe" that emphasizes "the revolutionary, cataclysmic element in the transition from every historical present to the Messianic future."⁵ This element of catastrophe—itself the expression of the radical contradiction of what is by what will be—obtains finally because everything in *this* redemption is ascribed to God and achieved by God. This theological truth sometimes funds mystical quietism, but it also regularly provokes "messianic activism" expressed in diverse political and chiliastic programs.⁶

As regards the latter activism, Scholem observes that whenever Christians have grown dissatisfied with their own "chemically pure inwardness," they have reached back to the Jewish messianic vision of a public historical redemption, and he cites the early Anabaptists as a representative case.⁷ Within the history of Judaism itself, such explosive messianic energy has largely been checked and channeled either by the ordered world of *halakhah*, that is, of personal and communal Torah

---

3. Scholem, "Toward an Understanding," 2–3.
4. Scholem, "Toward an Understanding," 4.
5. Scholem, "Toward an Understanding," 7.
6. Scholem, "Toward an Understanding," 14, 15. Among such mystical activists in modern times one thinks of figures like the "militant mystic" Abraham Heschel, the "mystic rebel" Dorothee Sölle, and Johann Baptist Metz and his "mysticism of open eyes" keyed to human suffering. See Heschel, *Thunder in the Soul*; Sölle, *Silent Cry*; Wind, *Dorothee Soelle*; as well as Metz, *Passion for God*.
7. Scholem, "Toward an Understanding," 17, 16. In this way, he observes, "Judaism has again and again furnished Christianity with political chiliastic Messianism."

observance, or else by rationalist ethical prudence of the sort championed by Maimonides, Moses Mendelsohn, and Hermann Cohen. Configured in this way, messianism (re-)appears within Judaism as a kind of anarchic disturbance: Scholem tellingly invokes the apostle Paul's talk of the "freedom of the children of God" in this regard.[8]

Scholem's essay culminates with a provocative observation concerning *der Preis des Messianismus,* "the price demanded by Messianism, the price which the Jewish people has had to pay out of its own substance for this idea which it handed over to the world."[9] Precisely because "every attempt to realize it tears open the abysses which lead each of its manifestations *ad absurdum,*" the messianic idea and its apocalyptic expression have generally been structurally contained, emerging within *halakhic* life only as a source of hope inspired by "the blazing landscape of redemption," yet never realized. Scholem contends that the effect of this has been to render the quality of actual Jewish existence ever "preliminary," "provisional," even perhaps "profoundly unreal": the messianic idea, he concludes, "has compelled a *life lived in deferment,* in which nothing can be done definitively, nothing can be irrevocably accomplished." Jewish existence has thus been incapable of "irrevocable action in the concrete realm," the quality of any and all of its historical action depleted and called into question by the absolute redeeming action expected of the Messiah.[10] In this way, the historic outworking of the messianic idea has, despite its marginal standing, played a decisive role in shaping Jewish existence in the world.

Jacob Taubes—Scholem's erstwhile student at the Hebrew University from 1949 to 1952—famously took issue with his teacher's particular "psycho-economic calculation of the price of messianism in Jewish history."[11] Taubes's critical assessment is written in an analytic-historical mode, yet his interest in the normative aspects of the messianic is evident throughout. Scholem's thinking distinguished sharply between the

---

8. Scholem, "Toward an Understanding," 21.

9. Scholem, *Judaica,* 1:73; Scholem, "Toward an Understanding," 35.

10. Scholem, "Toward an Understanding," 35 (emphasis original). For a searching reconsideration of these themes and their logic, see Beilek-Robson, *Another Finitude.*

11. Taubes, "Price of Messianism," the text of a paper delivered to the World Jewish Congress in 1979. Taubes offered a somewhat expanded version of the same in "Scholem's Theses on Messianism Reconsidered." On Taubes's intellectual debts and relation to Scholem, see Styfalls, "Deconstructing Orthodoxy." For an exhaustive account of Taubes's fascinating, complex, and morally ambivalent life, see Muller, *Professor of Apocalypse.*

public, communal, and historical redemption conceived by Jewish messianism and the private, personal, and inward redemption advanced by Christian messianism. For Taubes, the spiritual reconfiguration of the messianic idea is not something uniquely Christian but in fact a move intrinsic to messianic experience as such, a move that "belongs essentially to the career of that 'idea' if such an idea should have a career at all in an unredeemed world." As he explains, "Interiorization is not a dividing line between 'Judaism' and 'Christianity'; it signifies a crisis within Jewish eschatology itself—in Pauline Christianity as well as in the Sabbatian movement of the seventeenth century."[12] In both these instances, interiorization is not an abdication of the messianic—as Scholem held—but an outworking of the "inner logic of the messianic idea" and a crucial one at that, since forceful efforts to "actualize the messianic idea" on the level of world-historical existence lead "straight into the abyss."[13] In the case of Paul, all this is expressed specifically in the "abrogation of the law," which "follows strictly from his 'immanent logic' after acceptance of a Messiah justly crucified in consequence of the law" and the valorization of "conscience" as the organ of faith's fraught confrontation and negotiations with the world.[14]

As for the question of the *price* of messianism, Taubes seems to make two claims. First, inasmuch as a full world-historical prosecution of the messianic idea would prove catastrophic—and on this he agrees with Scholem—Taubes suggests the price of the interiorization of messianic redemption within subjective faith and hope is a price well worth paying. In this sense, "price" names all that is involved in managing the messianic idea so as to avoid the self-destruction of the community: for Scholem this price is the lamentable "deferred life," for Taubes the "interiorization" he thinks integral to messianism itself. In these reflections, neither thinker exploits the wider economic semantics of *oikonomia* that have become important and enrich more recent work in political theology.[15]

Yet second, and at the same time, Taubes also argues that withdrawal from history and "deferred life" are not in fact, as Scholem claims, the

---

12. Taubes, "Price of Messianism," 4.

13. Taubes, "Price of Messianism," 8–9.

14. Taubes, "Price of Messianism," 5. As Styfalls clearly discerns, Taubes's reading of Paul is and continues to be indebted to Scholem's analysis of messianism generally, and of Sabbatianism in particular. Styfalls, "Deconstructing Orthodoxy," 191–92.

15. See especially Agamben, *Kingdom and the Glory*; and for related discussion, di Somma, "Mystery of Economy."

price of messianism at all, for while the interiorization of the messianic idea does indeed refuse a certain "jump into history," by refusing one way of historical realization in the world it actually makes possible and ventures another. So, for example, he says the Pauline conscience "exists in constant tension with the world, forcing us to construct casuistries to bridge the gap between it and the realm of the world."[16] In an infamous correspondence with Carl Schmitt from the same year as his essay, Taubes appears to integrate these same two points when he asserts that while "the boundary between spiritual and worldly may be controversial and is always to be drawn anew," without this distinction "we are exposed to the thrones and powers that in a 'monistic' cosmos no longer know any Beyond."[17] In other words, it remains crucial to seat the messianic in the spiritual and not the worldly as such, yet precisely in so doing its unsettling significance for the world is secured and exercised. Taubes seems to suggest that what is at stake at the boundary between the "interiorized messianic idea" and the sociopolitical world is the effective exposure of the world to transcendence, even if the life of faith consists merely in ever so many humble experiments in "constructing casuistries" to forge the connection. So, not only the messianic idea but also therefore messianic life as well as messianic politics—the question of its shape and substance and promise and peril—are involved in any weighing up of the price of messianism.

II

We can go further. For in Taubes's judgment, the interiorization of the messianic idea is not its privatization; neither does it leave the historical world untouched. Rather, it entails a specific modulation of the manner of public life: its personal and communal outworking rightly exerts anarchic pressure on the *katechonic* forms of the world, in hope—and in indirect pursuit—of that redemptive catastrophe that just is the Messiah. The upshot is a specific sort of divestment from, disturbance of, and also finally uprising against the world as it is. Taubes sometimes speaks of this as a particular "nihilism," that is, the peculiar politics of that "weak

---

16. Taubes, "Price of Messianism," 5.

17. Taubes, *Political Theology of Paul*, 112, 102–3 citing from letter to Schmitt of September 18, 1979. This is also now available alongside other related material in Taubes, *To Carl Schmitt*; the specific remark cited is reproduced at 29–30.

messianic power" of which Walter Benjamin also famously wrote.[18] Taubes takes the theological aspect of Benjamin's thought with great seriousness, suggesting that his thinking "begins with the Messiah" and is "substantial" in this regard, rather than being hypothetical or merely aesthetic.[19] As he remarks, "Benjamin has a hardness similar to that of Karl Barth. There's nothing there having to do with immanence. From that one gets nowhere. . . . Something has to happen from the other side."[20] Taubes shares Benjamin's concern for the effective reality of transcendence and its messianic interruption of the immanent status quo.

The normative importance of this comes through most sharply in Taubes's exchanges with Schmitt. There Taubes speaks of himself as an "apocalypticist from below," or "of the revolution" whose worldview involves "no spiritual investment in the world as it is."[21] As such, he repudiates the politics of the *katechon* (2 Thess 2:6), a politics in which enforced order aims merely to restrain "the antichrist" and so also to hold off the eschaton.[22] This is the politics for which Schmitt qua jurist advocates, in keeping with the traditions of Christendom. Both figures work within a sharply dialectical understanding of the matter.[23] Taubes considers such politics and their preservation of the way things are as a legacy of how "Christian experience of the End of the World was domesticated and came to an arrangement with the world and its powers."[24] Yet when in

18. Taubes, *Political Theology of Paul*, 72. Cf. Benjamin, "Theses on the Philosophy of History," 197.

19. Taubes, *Political Theology of Paul*, 74–75. Taubes contrasts this with the status of the messianic in the famous "Finale" of Adorno, *Minima Moralia*, 247: "But beside the demand thus placed on thought, the question of the reality or unreality of redemption itself hardly matters." Cf. Stimilli, "Jacob Taubes."

20. Taubes, *Political Theology of Paul*, 75–76.

21. Taubes, *Political Theology of Paul*, 103. In reflecting upon Schmitt's position as the *katechon* for whom the apocalypse is "the adversary" and "who does everything to keep it subjugated and suppressed," Taubes comments: "That isn't my worldview, that isn't my experience. I can imagine as an apocalyptic: let it go down. I have no spiritual investment in the world as it is." Taubes contributed to the wide-ranging reconsideration of Gnosticism in postwar German theory and *belles lettres*, and this posture also reflects something of that. See Styfhals, *No Spiritual Investment in the World*.

22. For concise discussion of the exegesis of the text itself, see Ziegler, "How It Ends."

23. The inevitability and adequacy of this dialectical configuration is questioned in the recent work of Cacciari, *Withholding Power*.

24. Taubes, *To Carl Schmitt*, 13. He offers a related critique of Augustinian Christianity (following Erik Peterson) as a "domestication" of apocalyptic messianism; see Taubes, *Occidental Eschatology*, 79–80, 86. Kroeker's longstanding work on Augustine's

light of the messianic we accede to the truth that "immanence gets one nowhere" in matters of redemption, then ways of being in the world that aim to preserve the received immanent order of things—or perhaps to rearrange its elements while keeping the order as such intact—at best fail to express redemption's significance and at worst belie it. Importantly, the quality of the revolution in view is for Taubes always apocalyptic, that is, an opposition to the world in its schematic totality rather than a project to replace the current order with newer, better one.[25]

Said differently, it is not the apocalypse of eschatological redemption but rather the continuation of "this world" that is the catastrophe against which messianic life and politics protests. Glossing the sixth of Benjamin's "Theses on the Philosophy of History"—that "the Messiah comes not only as the redeemer, he comes as the subduer of antichrist"—Taubes stresses how the Messiah comes "as the subduer of 'what is,'" since "'what is,' is the antichrist."[26] In venturing this interpretation—that the messianic contradicts "the world that is" as "antichrist"—Taubes must have in mind Benjamin's other well-known aphorism: "That things 'just go on' *is* the catastrophe. It is not that which is approaching but that which is. . . . Redemption looks to the small fissure in the ongoing catastrophe."[27] On such a view, when the messianic makes its way through the cracks in the carapace of *this* world, "the mechanisms that stabilise this history by keeping the human locked within the confines of the given" suffer anarchic interruption.[28]

Variations on this theme continue to echo importantly in the work of other thinkers. One thinks, for example, of Jacques Derrida's assertion of the crucial political necessity of acknowledging the "undeconstructible" reality of "a certain experience of the emancipatory promise . . . perhaps even the formality of a structural messianism, a messianism without religion, even a messianic without messianism."[29] Even more recently, something uncannily similar appears in the work of the philosopher

---

political theology represents, in part, an effort to refute just such a reading.

25. Taubes, *Occidental Eschatology*, 9. This fact makes it difficult to know quite how to understand the force of "from below" and "of the revolution" in the remarks cited at the opening of this paragraph, with their evident associations with the idiom of class struggle.

26. Taubes, "Seminar Notes," 200.

27. Benjamin, "Central Park," 50.

28. Vandeputte, "Continuity as Catastrophe," 79.

29. Derrida, *Specters of Marx*, 74.

Byung-Chul Han. Central to his essay on *The Agony of Eros* is the claim that in our present moment we find ourselves locked within "the inferno of the same," as he styles it, such that "the arrival of the atopic Other"—the possibility of true transcendence—can and must "assume apocalyptic form." As he summarizes in language redolent of messianism: "Today, only an apocalypse can liberate—indeed, redeem—us from the inferno of the same, and lead us toward the Other."³⁰ In such lines of reflection we are reminded forcefully of the continued currency of the messianic idea and its apocalyptic form bequeathed to European thought.

To speak of "form" here is to observe how schematic and formal invocations of the logic of messianism can become. Our recourse to the abstract idiom of "the messianic" is already telling in this regard. This tendency toward abstraction affords theology a certain ecumenicity, allowing us to discern and express interesting ad hoc overlaps with other neighboring discourses and forms of thought. Yet it arises not only from the desire to make our second-order concepts available and intelligible to others; it also reflects a particular aspect of the historic unfolding of messianism itself.

In an extensive review essay and engagement with Scholem's study of Sabbatai Sevi, the New Testament scholar W. D. Davies draws particular attention to the fact that the messianic Sabbatarian movement "flourished apparently without much active interest among the masses of believers in the history and character of Sabbatai. What matters was *that* the Messiah has appeared, not *who* had appeared as Messiah."³¹ As he explains more fully:

> The end was at hand; deliverance was at the door. The results of this conviction were staggering. The one decisive factor was *that* the Messiah had appeared. Who he was, or what he was like, was for many unimportant. Interest in the personal character and conduct of Sabbatai was at best secondary and probably, among the majority of believers, non-existent. What made him significant was his role as the Messiah, proclaimed and authenticated by Nathan [of Gaza].³²

---

30. Han, *Agony of Eros*, 3.
31. Davies, "From Schweitzer to Scholem," 537.
32. Davies, "From Schweitzer to Scholem," 542–43.

There is, in other words, a kind of formalism native to this historically significant early modern messianic movement: abstraction from the who and what of the person of the Messiah is ingredient in it.

Now, Davies is interested in exploring the analogy between this and the earliest Christian movement, itself understood as an event of Jewish messianism illumined by Scholem's study. While he notes some possible parallels of this particular dynamic—for instance, a certain disinterest on the part of Paul as regards the details of Jesus's ministry—Davies ultimately finds here a notable difference. Scholem himself had sharply contrasted the characters of Christ and Sabbatai.[33] But Davies is interested in the differing *importance* of their characters to the respective messianic movements. His conclusion is this:

> As the very emergence of the gospels indicates, the character of Jesus at least, if not the inner recesses of his personality and minute biographical details of his life, in various degrees and dimensions remained central for early Christianity. That *he* was the Messiah was significant for early Christianity, in a way that Sabbatai Svi as a person was not for Sabbatianism. . . . The life of Jesus of Nazareth, as understood by his followers, was . . . an expression of *agape*. It could, therefore, always provide a corrective to any antinomian messianic licence that might emerge.[34]

Espied here is the material importance of the "what and who" of the figure of Jesus to determine the orientation and form of messianic life and politics of the first Christians. In short, early Christian messianism was apocalyptic, "but it was such under the constraint of the *agape* (to risk distortion through brevity) of Christ."[35] Davies himself gave maximal expression to this constraint when he famously claimed that "Jesus became the Torah of Christians."[36] But however expressed, Christian messianism is marked from the first by a quite *determinate* dynamism, its messianic form and redemptive protest against the world "as it is" being specifically shaped, we might say, by the politics of Jesus.

---

33. Scholem, "Crisis of Tradition," 62: "One cannot overlook the abyss which yawns between the figure of the Messiah who died for his cause upon the Cross and this figure [Sabbatai Svi] who became an apostate and played this role in disguise."

34. Davies, "From Schweitzer to Scholem," 554–55.

35. Davies, "From Schweitzer to Scholem," 556–57.

36. Davies, "From Schweitzer to Scholem," 555; citing the formulation from his own influential and earlier study, Davies, *Paul and Rabbinic Judaism*, 147.

III

The insight at which we have arrived by way of these terse engagements with Scholem, Taubes, and Davies is one Travis Kroeker has long advocated and elaborated programmatically with erudition, creativity, and patience. Perhaps particularly sharply in his extensive engagements with recent philosophical interest in Paul, Kroeker has pushed back against the abstract formalism of the messianic idea that is a recurrent feature of such work. As he writes, "The identity of the 'Christian' born by the messianic community, in other words, is not a new universalism that somehow transcends or escapes particularity and difference. . . . It is rather an identity 'in Messiah' that seeks the perfection of love not in the domination or possession of any part, but in the apocalyptic transformation of all partial things to their completion in divine love."[37] Likewise, to receive this new identity "in Christ"—to suffer and heed the calling of this One—does not mean "abandoning the world for an 'elsewhere'" but rather "dwelling within it in dispossession" so as to contest and confound it "from within" while "allowing the power of God to transform it."[38] Moving on this basis, Kroeker is able with especial acuity to state the price of Christian messianism. To the kenotic divine *agape* manifest in the suffering servant Messiah on the cross, there corresponds a human life of dispossession and self-giving service, an ethos of self-humbling love that pitches itself against the world "as it is" for the sake of others.

Christians, on Kroeker's account, quite properly ought to have no real "spiritual investment in this world as it is," since "messianic sovereignty dispossesses the faithful, as is indicated in the *hos me* logic of 1 Corinthians 7:29–31" and commits them to living in a manner which faithfully expresses their freedom vis-à-vis the world that is "passing away."[39] This messianic way of being in the world is aptly characterized as exilic, diasporic, and "jeremian" in its quality, as it is forever being made strange to the reigning commonplaces of the age. In all this, the decisive factor in setting the price of Christian messianism is the price paid by the Messiah himself: his own kenosis and *agape* fund and fashion the practices of dispossession, suffering love, nonviolence, and so on by which the Christian life takes issue with the world.

---

37. Kroeker, "Is a Messianic Political Ethic Possible?" 167–68.

38. Kroeker, "Living 'As If Not,'" 31.

39. Kroeker, "Is a Messianic Political Ethic Possible?" 167. Cf. Kroeker, "Living 'As If Not,'" 29, for a dense summary statement of all this.

Kroeker's theological vision invites us to consider that the price of messianism is a price well worth paying. This is not because its price is a prudent strategic investment in the work of the *katechon* to stabilize historical and sociopolitical existence, or a well-calculated tactical wager on the world-historical effectiveness of contrarian lives. Rather, it is well worth paying only because it is the price of concrete evangelical freedom, the price of inhabiting the world that is passing away in light of its redemption at the hands of a loving God, the price of fidelity to the crucified and risen Christ, and so the price of being properly unsettled by the strange "otherwise" movement and power of his Spirit. The outworking of "the messianic idea" in the Christian life is not a move within the politics of the world as it is, but rather faith's venture of another politics, namely, the politics of the reign of God.

Hence the price of messianism—Christianly understood—just is the cost of discipleship. From the perspective of messianic faith itself, such a cost is no cost at all. For as Massimo Cacciari has sharply reminded us, the gospel enjoins a quite specific "rendering unto Caesar" (Mark 12:17 and parallels).[40] The gospel story of Jesus and Caesar's coin serves as a parable of the *hos me* logic of the life of faith. Working this trope, we find that to return the coinage of the world to its issuing authority is not in fact a transaction in tribute to the *katechon*, not an investment of any kind in the world as it is. It is rather a liberation, a disposing of a burden and ridding oneself of an impediment. To dispossess oneself of earthly coinage, as it were, is to depose the authority invested in the circulation and operations of that coinage. As such, it is an "unpolitical" gesture in Cacciari's sense, that is, a radical critique of the political seated in a reversal of value that opens up another politics, a "grand" politics, whose grandeur lies not in its scale but in the freedom of its messianic calling.[41]

Bibliography

Adorno, Theodore. *Minima Moralia: Reflections from Damaged Life*. Translated by E. F. N. Jephcott. London: Verso, 1978.

Agamben, Giorgio. *The Kingdom and the Glory: For a Theological Genealogy of Economy and Government*. Translated by Lorenzo Chiesa and Matteo Mandarini. Stanford, CA: Stanford University Press, 2011.

Beilek-Robson, Agata. *Another Finitude: Messianic Vitalism and Philosophy*. London: Bloomsbury, 2019.

---

40. Cacciari, *Withholding Power*, 43–47.
41. Cacciari, "Nietzsche and the Unpolitical," 95.

Benjamin, Walter. "Central Park." Translated by Lloyd Spencer and Mark Harrington. *New German Critique* 34 (1985) 32–58.

———. "Theses on the Philosophy of History." In *Illuminations*, translated by Harry Zohn, 196–209. Boston: Houghton Mifflin, 2019.

Cacciari, Massimo. "Nietzsche and the Unpolitical." In *The Unpolitical: On the Radical Critique of Political Reason*, 92–103. New York: Fordham University Press, 2009.

———. *The Withholding Power: An Essay on Political Theology*. Translated by Edi Pucci. London: Bloomsbury, 2018.

Davies, W. D. "From Schweitzer to Scholem: Reflections on Sabbatai Svi." *Journal of Biblical Literature* 95 (1976) 529–58.

———. *Paul and Rabbinic Judaism*. 2nd ed. London: SPCK, 1958.

Derrida, Jacques. *Specters of Marx*. Translated by Peggy Kamuf. London: Routledge, 1994.

Di Somma, Emilio. "The Mystery of Economy: Exploring the Threshold Between Theology and Economics." *Review and Expositor* 116 (2019) 83–92.

Han, Byung-Chul. *The Agony of Eros*. Translated by Erik Butler. Cambridge, MA: MIT Press, 2017.

Heschel, Abraham. *Thunder in the Soul: To Be Known by God*. Edited by Robert Erlewine. Walden, NY: Plough, 2021.

Kroeker, P. Travis. "Is a Messianic Political Ethic Possible?" In *Messianic Political Theology and Diaspora Ethics: Essays in Exile*, 144–70. Eugene, OR: Cascade, 2017.

———. "Living 'As If Not': Messianic Becoming or the Practice of Nihilism." In *Messianic Political Theology and Diaspora Ethics: Ethics in Exile*, 15–33. Eugene, OR: Cascade, 2017.

Metz, Johann Baptist. *A Passion for God: The Mystical-Political Dimension of Christianity*. Translated by J. Matthew Ashley. New York: Paulist, 1998.

Muller, Jerry Z. *Professor of Apocalypse: The Many Lives of Jacob Taubes*. Princeton, NJ: Princeton University Press, 2021.

Scholem, Gershom, "The Crisis of Tradition in Jewish Messianism." In *The Messianic Idea in Judaism and Other Essays on Jewish Spirituality*, 49–77. New York: Schocken, 1971.

———. *Judaica*. Volume 1. Frankfurt: Suhrkamp, 1981.

———. *Sabbatai Sevi: The Mystical Messiah, 1626–1676*. London: Routledge & Kegan Paul, 1973.

———. "Toward an Understanding of the Messianic Idea in Judaism." In *The Messianic Idea in Judaism and Other Essays on Jewish Spirituality*, 1–36. New York: Schocken, 1971.

Sölle, Dorothee. *The Silent Cry: Mysticism and Resistance*. Translated by Barbara and H. Martin Rumscheidt. Minneapolis: Fortress, 2001.

Stimilli, Elettra. "Jacob Taubes: Messianism and Political Theology After the *Shoah*." In *Depeche Mode: Jacob Taubes between Politics, Philosophy, and Religion*, edited by Herbert Kopp-Oberstebrink and Harmut von Sass, 68–81. Leiden: Brill, 2022.

Styfalls, Willem. "Deconstructing Orthodoxy: A Failed Dialogue Between Gershom Scholem and Jacob Taubes." *New German Critique* 45 (2018) 181–205.

———. *No Spiritual Investment in the World: Gnosticism and Postwar German Philosophy*. Ithaca, NY: Cornell University Press, 2019.

Taubes, Jacob, *Occidental Eschatology*. Translated by David Ratmoko. Stanford, CA: Stanford University Press, 2009.

———. *The Political Theology of Paul*. Translated by Dana Hollander. Stanford, CA: Stanford University Press, 2004.

———. "The Price of Messianism." In *From Cult to Culture: Fragments Toward a Critique of Historical Reason*, edited by Charlotte Elisheva Fonrobert and Amir Engel, 3–9. Stanford, CA: Stanford University Press, 2010.

———. "Scholem's Theses on Messianism Reconsidered." *Social Science Information* 21 (1982) 665–75.

———. "Seminar Notes on Walter Benjamin's 'Theses on the Philosophy of History.'" In *Walter Benjamin and Theology*, edited by C. Dickinson and S. Symons, 179–214. New York: Fordham University Press, 2016.

———. *To Carl Schmitt: Letters and Reflections*. Translated by Keith Tribe. New York: Columbia University Press, 2013.

Vandeputte, Tom. "Continuity as Catastrophe: Origins of a Thesis in Walter Benjamin." *New German Critique* 50 (2023) 59–82.

Wind, Renate. *Dorothee Soelle—Mystic and Rebel: The Biography*. Translated by Nancy Lukens and Martin H. Rumscheidt. Minneapolis: Fortress, 2012.

Ziegler, Philip G. "How It Ends: Brief Remarks on Reading 2 Thessalonians 2:1–12." *Pro Ecclesia* 31 (2022) 41–48.

4

Do Nations Have Souls?
An Augustinian Inquiry with a Canadian

Eric Gregory

TRAVIS KROEKER IS A soulful political theologian, attuned to the desires of the heart and the rule of the slain Lamb. Perhaps there should be no other kind. More than most, his Anabaptist writings trouble me in the ways good theology should. Part of this trouble emerges from a shared Protestant admiration for—and critical fascination with—Augustine's story of two cities unfolding from Babylon to Jerusalem. Augustine is a key interlocutor for Kroeker's sustained project of recovering a messianic political theology and diaspora ethics.[1] Kroeker agrees with my own efforts to move beyond narrow and constrained liberal readings of *City of God* in order to render a more christological approach to political Augustinianism that takes, among other things, his dynamic account of nonpossessive neighbor love seriously. But he finds them insufficiently apocalyptic, exilic, and agonistic.[2] Too much Rawls and Niebuhr, not enough Paul and Isaiah. Too much priestly Calvinism, not enough prophetic Radical Reformation. My Augustinian civic liberalism has yet to learn the power of "parabolic reversal" (32). It is a criticism that keeps me up at night, though I have sought in my own way to recover a more

---

1. Kroeker, *Messianic Political Theology and Diaspora Ethics*. Further references will be cited parenthetically in the text.

2. Kroeker, "Secular—The Political."

biblical, and so more apocalyptic, reconstruction of Augustine precisely in terms of a messianic understanding of history and politics.[3] I suspect that effort remains insufficient. But it is part of ongoing dialogue with my fellow low-church, high-Christology Augustinian, one I hope this strange, unsystematic inquiry advances.

The strangeness allows several senses. It is odd to honor someone attracted to sacramental ecclesiocentrism with a provocation about nations, especially at a time when the rebellious nations are angry. Perhaps nations, for an Augustinian, are simply fallen sites of moral injury. Nations, it would seem, are not theologically interesting other than as characteristic sponsors of our disordered loves. The internationalism Augustine knew was the Roman Empire, which prided itself on allowing many nations to flourish provided they paid minimal homage to the *imperium*, a pride he was keen to unmask. *City of God* reads as Augustine's version of the 1619 Project, a retelling of foundings to demythologize whitewashed histories. Nations are simply a part of the violent trauma and imperial domination in our sin-soaked drama of postlapsarian history. Kroeker's gentile ancestors, like ancient Israel, were victims of the nations and their injustices.[4]

On one interpretation, to the extent Augustine desacralized politics, so too he strips the nations of their spiritual pretensions. The less said about them, the better. Nations have enough defenders. Long before postcolonial theory, these strange creatures of spirit rather than flesh proclaimed the nations belong to the old age. Nations are historical, not eternal. The heavenly *patria* is what really matters, even on earth, as Augustine tells Nectarius in Letter 91. The time of nations is literally running out. The people of God are a "kinship of promise" (165), adopted into a new *ekklesia*, a new holy nation (1 Pet 2:9).

There are nations and there are souls, but their combination is imagined and consequential. Nations do not have souls in any meaningful metaphysically realist sense. As Simone Weil argues, "a nation as such cannot be the object of supernatural love. It has no soul. It is a Great Beast."[5] There is a patristic discussion of the angels of nations, but I could not find meditations on the soul of nations in Augustine's corpus. My goal, however, is to think with a different imagination, given Augustine's

3. See Gregory, "Remythologizing Augustine."

4. Note, however, Kroeker's recognition of the complicity of apocalyptic Mennonites in the neoliberal project of Canadian statehood (*Messianic Political Theology*, 215).

5. Weil, *Gravity and Grace*, 169.

and Kroeker's active imagination for a corporate spiritual world beneath the surface of apparent reality.

Kroeker's soulfulness is not limited to a restless struggling with the fifth-century African bishop who famously longed to know only God and the soul. The drama and the poetry of Kroeker's distinctive political theology is shaped by existentially vulnerable encounters with others, both real and imagined. Intellectually, these include an eclectic mix of thinkers who disturb conventional streams of political theology: Plato, Fyodor Dostoevsky, Henri de Lubac, Jacob Taubes, Giorgio Agamben, Walter Benjamin, Ivan Illich, Eric Voegelin, George Grant, John Howard Yoder, and Stanley Hauerwas. Kroeker is both a charitable interpreter in these encounters and a critical conversation partner. Plato, Voegelin, and Grant are at the front of my mind, alongside his Jewish interlocutors.

Augustine's critique of earthly republics is tethered to his identification with a messianic body on pilgrimage in this age, a *corpus mysticum*. This identification with the *totus Christus* funds a standing vigilance against idolatry and "subverts any merely human claim to sovereignty and political authority" (17). So too for Kroeker. His work reads Augustine alongside a range of modernity critics that expose the spiritual crisis of both post-Hobbesian political theory and the lived reality of mass society this side of capitalism and technological globalization. But, like Augustine, he also recognizes that diverse "identities as mode of worldly belonging—national, cultural-linguistic, ethnic and ecclesial—seem unavoidable" (2). In the remarkable close of book 2 of *City of God*, for example, Augustine calls upon the *Roman* character (could we say soul?) to seize the heavenly country. Much depends, then, on how followers of Christ as members of his body relate to these identities. Kroeker, following Paul, admonishes living *hos me*, "as if not" possessing them (1 Cor 7). He calls for a dwelling in dispossession, "a monasticism in the world" (8). Yet this messianic consciousness of dispossession extends beyond the individual to "household relations, to cities and peoples, to the cosmic ordering of all things" (49). This extension taps into the persistent interest in the relation between wholes to parts spread across Augustine's theology. Kroeker cares about the "embodied Mennonite soul" (88). What might it mean to care about a Canadian one?

The "Christendom" debate between Oliver O'Donovan and Stanley Hauerwas has mainly been framed in terms of the spiritual authority of the church and the "sword-bearing authority of the state" (9). But Kroeker's critical insights take us well beyond abstract formulations of church and state or church and world, or even what he calls the "politically correct Canadian version" of multiculturalism (76). With both O'Donovan and Hauerwas, he accents particular communities and a sense of place in the face of a sterile cosmopolitanism and the "technological paradigm of statist sovereignty" (75). He claims the Bible "celebrates plurality and diversity as the gift of creation" (75). Against gnostic pretense, the messianic community is "not a new universalism that somehow transcends or escapes particularity and difference" (167). Clearly there is no room for a state church in Kroeker's pilgrim politics. Surprisingly, however, the nation as embodied site of cultural difference plays an elusive role in Kroeker's publications. It is partially surprising because his earliest work bemoans the "often ignored Canadian approaches in the discussion of North American religious ethics and public life."[6] In this essay, however, I am not simply asking the extent to which Kroeker's political theology is a Canadian one. I suspect the answer to that question is as complicated as his relationship to the Mennonite tradition. The primary question is more existential and theological: What, to Kroeker, is Canada? How, if at all, might he describe Canadian nationhood (or peoplehood) given his interest in a political theology where "real people and communities dwell" (87)? Where might the peculiar people of Canada figure in his call for "an eschatological vision of the relation between the visible and invisible rule of God" (129).[7]

In his first book, Kroeker argues that political theology seeks to "discern the meaning of particular concrete political realities in relation to the larger purposes of the created order."[8] Nations, whether imagined or not, are concrete political realities. They loom large in the Bible, especially in the Hebrew prophets, Paul, and Revelation. They also play an important role in books 15–18 of *City of God*, which Kroeker also highlights (6). Kroeker tells us that "political philosophy or theology, therefore, is a matter of the proper symbolization of human nature and society in relation to the divine order of reality in creation" (44). The political symbolism of "Israel and the nations" is as pronounced in Augustine and his Bible as Kroeker's preferred notion of "exile-exodus-diaspora" (2). All these texts figure throughout Kroeker's writing. But

6. Kroeker, *Christian Ethics and Political Economy*, xiv. This book, for example, highlights the distinctiveness of Canadian socialism (38).

7. The text here comes from a revealing passage where Kroeker criticizes both Yoder and O'Donovan for their account of political and ecclesial authority.

8. Kroeker, *Christian Ethics and Political Economy*, 127.

there seems to be only passing reference to the idea of the *nation*, which I here distinguish from both *nationalism* and the modern (secular) *nation-state*. These references typically involve the notion of the church's "prophetic witness of Jesus to the nations."[9] Or, following Yoder, the way in which the body of Christ is a social body that "represents the rule of God for the nations" (116), with Paul as a "Jeremian prophet to the nations" (164). Intriguingly, nations also appear in his late meditation on First Nations and "traditional indigenous knowledges and practices" (200). Where do (gentile) nations fit in his repeated claim that "types of community or political order, as Plato recognized long ago, are types of (shared) soul"?[10] Does Canada have a soul?

I doubt I need to motivate practical concern for debates about the idea of a nation, especially those negotiating tensions between liberal democracy, international legal order, and the need for national belonging. Such tensions are readily apparent in debates over immigration, public education, racism, religious liberty, national symbols, collective memory, and foreign policy. Think of the populist upheavals named Trump, Modi, and Brexit, widely seen as responsive to the neglect of local attachments by a technocratic, cosmopolitan elite wedded to economic globalization, financial deregulation, and supranational political integration. They are similar phenomena that once inspired Kroeker's fellow Canadian Christian to write one of the most important works of Canadian political thought: *Lament for a Nation: The Defeat of Canadian Nationalism*.[11] Kroeker is influenced by Grant's account of the ways in which market capitalism colludes with American liberalism to dissolve traditions of virtue. But the references are to Grant's *Technology and Empire* and *English-Speaking Justice* (64–65 and 173–74). For Grant, Canadian nationalism was meant to be a bulwark against homogenizing American imperialism. Grant holds that "one distinction between Canada and the United States has been the belief that Canada was predicated on the rights of nations as well as on the rights of individuals."[12] Lament implies attachment and a political sociology of

---

9. See, for example, Kroeker and Ward, *Remembering the End*, 111.

10. Kroeker and Ward, *Remembering the End*, 225.

11. Grant, *Lament for a Nation*. Interestingly, Grant's call for a religious equanimity in the face of loss ends where Augustine's *City of God* begins, with a reference to Virgil's *Aeneid*: *Tendebantque manus ripae ulterioris amore* ("they were holding their arms outstretched in love toward the further shore," 347).

12. Grant, *Lament for a Nation*, 292.

nationhood. In part, this essay is an effort to imagine how Kroeker might respond to the character of Grant's lament.

While often framed in terms of a cosmopolitan left against a nationalist right, there is a growing archive of so-called liberal nationalism in the United States. Consider Jill Lepore's *This America: The Case for the Nation* and Stephen Smith's *Reclaiming Patriotism in an Age of Extremes*. They recall a Tocquevillian conception of America that is primarily creedal and aspirational, but relies on feelings of inclusion and mutual recognition. Others, like sociologist Philip Gorski, have also called for a new vital center, a rededication the tradition of Robert Bellah's civil religion, complete with civic holidays, character education, and national service.[13] Augustinians are supposed critics of civil religion. Given the alternatives in our non-ideal world, I am cheering for these efforts to foster a liberal patriotism that might respond to the polarization and fragmentation that afflicts our society. But I am dissatisfied with a too-easy contrast between benign patriotism and xenophobic nationalism. Both tend to collapse the history of nations into the history of nationalisms.

A nation may be dedicated to a proposition, as Michael Lind wrote in his jeremiad against democratic universalism, but "it cannot be a proposition."[14] Like many scholars, I am attracted to so-called civic nationalism, a constitutional patriotism of ideas consistent with liberal values that are rationally chosen by free and equal individuals. But I have come to reconsider claims that any political community rests upon dense ethnocultural and extrapolitical features and habits. Nations are typically rooted in language, history, and territorial continuity, though there are many stateless nations. They allow us to recognize a political community as more than *simply* a collection of individuals. It is the "we" of "we the people," a group that supervenes on the separate, autonomous individuals. This is not to emphasize some crude, fixed notion of shared descent (let alone racial purity) or to deny the value of individuality. But as medieval historian Walter Pohl has argued in relation to biblical imagery of *ethnos* or *gens*, they point to evolving characteristics that distinguish peoples in ways that provide "orientation in a complex social world" and reproduce "the ties that hold a group together."[15] Nations, on this view, might be fictions rather than essences with a natural kind, a *demos* rather than an

---

13. Gorski, *American Covenant*.
14. Lind, *Next American Nation*, 5.
15. Pohl, "Disputed Identification," 17.

ethnos. They need not be considered part of a created order with an eschatological destiny. In another sense, however, they incarnate contingent expressions of human flourishing that are worthy of attachment and gratitude. We might even consider them individual perfections of universal human goods that in a sense create another wider self, a plural person under divine providence. The idea of the American people, for example, is a central feature of American democratic thought.

America's Catholic, Augustine-quoting president, Joseph Biden, frequently speaks about "the battle for the soul of the nation." In 2017, for example, he invoked the phrase after white supremacists marched on Charlottesville, Virginia. It was the signature theme of his 2020 campaign and his speech to the nation just before 2022 midterm elections.[16] When Biden talks about the soul of the nation, it is neither the Platonic soul, aching to get beyond the material world, or the Augustinian soul turning to a God within and beyond. I suspect it is also not the metaphysics of group agency or a reference to German Romantics or New England Puritans, who also invoked the phrase. It is a figure of speech, a metaphor, an analogy, a projection of imagination, a piece of presidential rhetoric in the furniture of American civil religion. Politics reflects the character of a people, what Biden in his 2021 inaugural address associated with Augustine's "common objects of love."[17] Soul language, to borrow from Melvin Rogers's recent survey of African American political thought, "conveys those ethical characteristics that define who we are . . . as when we speak of fighting for the 'soul of the nation.'"[18] Nations have character.

Asking whether such nations have souls as well as character is a somewhat playful exercise, one route into this fraught terrain. A Catholic theology of nationality by a Welsh Jesuit begins by stating that in some circles, "to suggest that nationality might have a spiritual value would appear as respectable as asserting that dragons exist."[19] We tend to feel safer with the concept of the nation-state than with nationhood, especially when attached to spooky metaphysics that travel with toxic politics. There is a massive literature on nation and nationalism, divided between those who hold the nation to be an artificial creature of Western modernity after the Reformation, empowered by technology, states, and mass democracy, the "modernists"; and those who believe

16. Biden, "Remarks . . . on the Continued Battle for the Soul of the Nation."
17. Biden, "Inaugural Address."
18. Rogers, *Darkened Light of Faith*, 18.
19. Llwelyn, *Toward a Catholic Theology of Nationality*.

nationhood to be much older and more global, the "primordialists."[20] Nationhood is a prolonged problem in Christian theology, displayed in the recent turn to the national anthems in Christian liturgies around the globe that should scandalize not just Anabaptists and students of Hauerwas. Sociologists point to a major restructuring in American religion, emerging from empirical investigation of a nativist, anti-democratic, and authoritarian "ethnocultural" phenomenon that merges Christian and American identity, calling the government to promote Christianity in special ways.[21] It is a significant factor in the "great abdicating," the precipitous decline in church affiliation among young adults in the United States. Religious nationalism deserves a prophetic no, and most theologians since Barth agree.

African, Roman, and Christian, Augustine was something of a cosmopolitan, at least by late antique standards, and certainly relative to a biblical world that more tightly bound cult, ancestors, and ethnic deities. He tells us that he wanted to be friends with angels, our fellow citizens and creaturely neighbors of an expansive universe. Augustine dreamed of a world of complete intimacy, a time when the "thoughts of each of us will then also then be made manifest to all."[22] It is telling that a book, a child, and conversations with his mother are central to his conversion to a God who also is a community of persons who act corporately, one being in three persons. Hannah Arendt, who admired Augustine's emphasis on natality, named this aspect of Augustine's otherworldly thought his most anti-political: democratic politics privileges respect, not loving intimacy. Politics is about statecraft, not soulcraft. Abandoning mythic talk, like that of souls, is thought to be the best path toward a deliberative and rational politics.

Augustine unmasked the myths of Rome as imperial ideology and posited universal norms that rise above the horizon of the nation. But he was neither a liberal nor a rationalist of this kind. John Locke, in fact, grounds his influential theory of democratic representation in a striking rejection of Augustine's corporatist doctrine of original sin. It was too collective. Living in a world mediated by nations frustrates an Augustinian desire for intimacy in the widest possible set of relations, divine and human. We should not, Augustine counsels, be mesmerized

---

20. Smith, *Ethnic Origins of Nations*.
21. See Gorski and Perry, *Flag and the Cross*.
22. Augustine, *City of God* 22.29.

by the "splendid names of things when hear of 'peoples', 'kingdoms', and 'provinces.'"[23] Like the Stoics, however, Augustine imagined the social world as a series of concentric circles. Each circle marks off a degree of social distance between the self and various others. One's family, friends, and neighbors are, in Augustine's ancient context, normally nearby. A person has special obligations to each, depending on one's roles in relation to them. Beyond these circles of proximate obligation, there are strangers, who are normally both physically and socially distant. Strangers who happen to become proximate, such as the resident alien, have the obligations and rights of visitors—the same ones I would have if I were in their land or neighborhood. It is a recurring impulse and a familiar metaphor that contemporary cosmopolitans, including Martha Nussbaum and Peter Singer, find inspiring in their efforts to ground a universal ethics for a universal community of equal standing.

The God Augustine confesses, however, is different from Stoic (or Platonic or Kantian) divinity that neither has preferential loves nor providential plans for peoples and persons. His God, it seems, also saves peoples, not just individuals. Determining and affirming these identities is a complicated historical task, one that Augustine attempts in long (mostly unread) sections of *City of God*, detailing the eschatological mystery of Israel and gentile nations, who in historical time still have their limited task in their "diversity of customs, laws, and traditions."[24] A lost created unity of blood gives way to the election of Israel and the historical plurality of nations. They are best governed, Augustine hopes, in multiethnic federated republics, giving rise to what Peter Brown has aptly described as "micro-Christendoms," where particular identities are seen as diverse incarnations of the church universal rather than a uniform *populus Christianus*.[25] The long durée of Christian political thought reveals many efforts to make sense of the *gentes* of the post-Roman West, fitting their new worlds into the biblical drama of Israel and the nations. Acts 17, for example, seems to charge nations with a providential role in history: "from one man he made all the nations, that they should inhabit the whole earth, and he marked out their appointed times in history and the boundaries of their lands." It was a favorite verse of lost-cause segregation theologians in the American South, the pro-apartheid Dutch Reformed Church, and frequently cited by Pastor

23. Augustine, *City of God* 4.3.
24. Augustine, *City of God* 19.17.
25. Brown, *Rise of Western Christendom*.

Robert Jeffress, whose 2017 Inauguration Day sermon compared Donald Trump to Nehemiah, rebuilding the walls of the nation, restoring a godly nation with a divine mission.

Augustine's God is also the same God in whose name Paul of Tarsus prophesied the apocalyptic erasure of master and slave, male and female, Greek and Jew. Galatians 3:28 is a frequent verse in Kroeker, but also the preferred verse that liberal Protestants in United States and liberal Orthodox theologians in Russia invoke against their new Christian nationalism. For Paul, "this world in its present form is passing away" (1 Cor 7:31).[26] Followers of the Christ should look to the "Jerusalem above," destabilizing Roman conceptions of national and ethnic distinctions, perhaps inventing a new semantic field of individualized *ethne*: Christ-fearing pagans, the *goy*, turning nations into spiritualized gentiles who join Israel without becoming Jews, and challenging all political communities.[27] The book of life only has personal names, an Augustinian theme that Søren Kierkegaard trumpets in his more existentialist defense of distinctive individuality as a divine gift.

Augustine's God is, of course, also Isaiah's and Amos's God. The prophets portray the nations as a mere drop in the bucket, a little dust on the scales of divine judgment. The defeated nations count for nothing, Isaiah says, from the perspective of eternity. Israel is a nation that has escaped the nations, survived their injustices. But when God gathers "all flesh" before the divine presence, it is as nations that they assemble and as members of nations that they come forward as witnesses to God's reign (Isa 42, Jer 1, Ps 47, Amos 9). Zechariah even imagines nations will be "like a clan in Judah" (Zech 9:7). John of Patmos sees these nations bringing their glory before the throne of God, prophesying the leaves of the tree of life will be "for the healing of the nations" (Rev 22:2). The nations are not denied, even if, strangely, they have returned after being destroyed by the rider on the white horse and deceived by the dragon.

Augustine is a biblicist, and there is a lot of nation-talk in the Bible. In the Hebrew Bible, we find prophetic visions of God bringing justice to the nations. Israel is a light to the nations. By emphasizing the Jewishness of Jesus and the New Testament, recent literature challenges any simple thesis that Christianity is universal and Judaism is particular. Denise Kimber Buell, for example, has argued that the notion of a Christian

---

26. All quotations from Scripture are from the NIV.
27. Ophir and Rosen-Zvi, *Goy: Israel's Multiple Others*.

erasure of nationality is not tenable historically or scripturally.[28] According to Buell, well-meaning universalism faces an ethical paradox by valorizing non-ethnic, universal Christianity against ethnic, particular Judaism, sustaining both anti-Judaism and anti-racism at the same time. Early messianic Christians, to be sure, wrestled with the charge they had disturbed the way of classifying people. They created the category of gentile, and then made gentiles unintelligible by preaching that equality in Christ shatters all other communities for those who have another city to love, a new covenant that gathers all peoples.

Soul-talk about nations has an ancient resonance with the Platonic tradition, given Socrates's famous analogy of the city and the soul. It is a central theme of the *Republic*. The analogy is a heuristic that tests the meaning of justice in both the city and the soul. Both are always at risk of civil war. The just person harmonizes the parts of her soul, just as the city seeks a harmony of its parts, rendering Plato's varied psychological descriptions of the timocratic, oligarchic, democratic, and tyrannical. Social struggles are manifestations of struggles within each soul, and vice versa. Augustine, like Kroeker, shares with Plato an insistence on the priority of the goods of the soul over material goods. It is a priority that invites liberal concerns about their political visions. Famously, Karl Popper argued that the city-soul analogy promotes an organic theory of the state that sacrifices the welfare of individuals.[29] Much of Plato and Augustine scholarship rejects this metaphysical picture and its totalitarian implications, debating how best to relate the interests of the whole to its individual members.

Augustine does not confront in detail the problem of the individuation of souls and diachronic personal identity as discussed by later Scholastics and contemporary philosophers. But he does seem to pick up the Platonic tradition, likely meditated by Cicero, when, again in *City of God* book 4, just before the famous description of kingdoms without justice, he contrasts a principle of tranquility between two men and two families, two cities, and two kingdoms. It is consistent with his claim in book 1.15 that "the happiness of a city and of a man do not, after all, arise from different sources; for a city is nothing other than concordant multitude of men." The virtue by which a city is made happy is the same as that which makes for the blessedness of a virtuous soul. God's rule over the heavenly city is

---

28. Buell, "Challenges and Strategies for Speaking About Ethnicity."
29. Popper, *Open Society and Its Enemies*.

analogous to the soul's rule over the body. And yet, Augustine does not deny to the Romans, the Greeks, the Egyptians, and ironically, even the Babylonians, "the property of a people," famously defined as "an assembled multitude of rational creatures bound together by common agreement as to the objects of their loves."[30] My aim here is not to adjudicate competing interpretations of this passage other than to say we should distinguish Augustine from social contract liberalism and theocracy alike.[31] It is to draw attention to the notion of common objects of love for thinking about distinct political communities, even nations.

Augustine's loves offer a contrast with a true founder of modern liberalism who plays an important role in Kroeker's political theology: the Arminian and Pelagian Thomas Hobbes. Hobbes too stands in the afterlife of Plato's city-soul analogy, though more proximate to what had become known as the "body politic" tradition that dominated medieval and early modern political thought.[32] In the context of civil strife, Hobbes turns to that tradition in order to contrast something like Augustinian concord with a more extreme union: the artifice of many wills that create a civil person, a Leviathan. Interestingly, Hobbesian sovereignty is cast as "an Artificial Soul, as giving life and motion to the whole body."[33] This is the Hobbes that Kroeker charges with eviscerating the human soul (111) and presenting a false power to worship (72). It is a mechanistic science that rightly troubles any Augustinian. "In effect," Kroeker finds, "Hobbes's Christian political theology purges Christianity of any spiritual meaning" (73). Does Kroeker's messianic political theology purge the politics of nations of any spiritual meaning?

Hobbes's appeal suggests the language of the soul is one of those myths that endures even in the most avowedly secular politics. I suspect that I have taken the "soul of the nation" too seriously, and too literally for Kroeker. The provocation of this inquiry walks a narrow path that tries to keep many readings of Augustine and his Jewish scriptures in mind by distinguishing the nation from the modern state. Concern for a national soul is no doubt a dangerous myth. But I wonder if it is a useful one, even for those of us who want to sustain cosmopolitan hopes as

---

30. Augustine, *City of God* 19.24.

31. For the best recent discussions, see Lamb, *Commonwealth of Hope*; and Ogle, *Politics and the Earthly City*.

32. See Smith, "Democracy and the Body Politic." It would be interesting to compare this "body politic" tradition with John Howard Yoder's notion of "body politics."

33. Hobbes, *Leviathan*, 9.

big as Augustine's metaphysical universe that would put human politics in its relativized place. The outward form of the nation is passing away. Grant's lament admittedly was not a call for a new Canadian nationalism. It was a diagnosis of the necessity of its death in the modern age. But God gives life to the dead. Might Kroeker allow for a transfigured Canadian identity?

Bibliography

Augustine. *City of God Against the Pagans*. Edited and translated by R. W. Dyson. Cambridge: Cambridge University Press, 1998.

Biden, Joseph. "Inaugural Address." White House Briefing Room, January 20, 2021. https://www.whitehouse.gov/briefing-room/speeches-remarks/2021/01/20/inaugural-address-by-president-joseph-r-biden-jr/.

———. "Remarks by President Biden on the Continued Battle for the Soul of the Nation." White House Briefing Room, September 1, 2022. https://www.whitehouse.gov/briefing-room/speeches-remarks/2022/09/01/remarks-by-president-bidenon-the-continued-battle-for-the-soul-of-the-nation/.

Brown, Peter. *The Rise of Western Christendom: Triumph and Diversity, A.D. 200–1000*. Oxford: Wiley-Blackwell, 2013.

Buell, Denise Kimber. "Challenges and Strategies for Speaking About Ethnicity in the New Testament and New Testament Studies." *Svensk Exegetisk Arsbok* 49 (2014) 33–51.

Gorski, Philip. *American Covenant: A History of Civil Religion from the Puritans to the Present*. Princeton, NJ: Princeton University Press, 2017.

Gorski, Philip, and Samuel L. Perry. *The Flag and the Cross: White Christian Nationalism and the Threat to Democracy*. Oxford: Oxford University Press, 2022.

Grant, George. *Lament for a Nation: The Defeat of Canadian Nationalism*. In *Collected Works of George Grant*, edited by Arthur Davis and Henry Roper, 271–367. Toronto: University of Toronto Press, 2005.

Gregory, Eric. "Remythologizing Augustine: History and Politics at the Edge of Time." *Augustinian Studies* 55 (2024) 3–24.

Hobbes, Thomas. *Leviathan*. Edited by Richard Tuck. Cambridge: Cambridge University Press, 1991.

Kroeker, P. Travis. *Christian Ethics and Political Economy in North America: A Critical Analysis*. Montreal: McGill-Queen's University Press, 1995.

———. *Messianic Political Theology and Diaspora Ethics: Essays in Exile*. Eugene, OR: Cascade, 2017.

———. "The Secular—The Political: Augustine and Political Augustinianism in Twentieth-Century Political Theology." In *The Edinburgh Critical History of Twentieth-Century Christian Theology*, edited by Philip Ziegler, 237–61. Edinburgh: Edinburgh University Press, 2022.

Kroeker, P. Travis, and Bruce K. Ward. *Remembering the End: Dostoevsky as Prophet to Modernity*. Boulder, CO: Westview, 2001.

Lamb, Michael. *A Commonwealth of Hope: Augustine's Political Thought*. Princeton, NJ: Princeton University Press, 2022.

Lepore, Jill. *This America: The Case for the Nation*. New York: Liveright, 2019.

Lind, Michael. *The Next American Nation: The New Nationalism and the Fourth American Revolution*. New York: Free Press, 1996.

Llwelyn, Dorian. *Toward a Catholic Theology of Nationality*. New York: Lexington, 2010.

Ogle, Veronica Roberts. *Politics and the Earthly City in Augustine's "City of God."* Cambridge: Cambridge University Press, 2022.

Ophir, Adi, and Ishay Rosen-Zvi. *Goy: Israel's Multiple Others and the Birth of the Gentile*. Oxford: Oxford University Press, 2018.

Pohl, Walter. "Disputed Identification: Jews and the Use of Biblical Models in the Barbarian Kingdoms." In *Barbarians and Jews: Jews and Judaism in the Early Medieval West*, edited by Yitzhak Hen and Thomas F. X. Noble, 11–28. Turnhout: Brepols, 2018.

Popper, Karl. *The Open Society and Its Enemies*. Princeton, NJ: Princeton University Press, 2020.

Rogers, Melvin L. *The Darkened Light of Faith: Race, Democracy, and Freedom in African American Political Thought*. Princeton, NJ: Princeton University Press, 2023.

Smith, Anthony D. *The Ethnic Origins of Nations*. Oxford: Wiley-Blackwell, 1991.

Smith, Sophie. "Democracy and the Body Politic from Aristotle to Hobbes." *Political Theory* 46 (2018) 167–96.

Smith, Stephen. *Reclaiming Patriotism in an Age of Extremes*. New Haven, CT: Yale University Press, 2021.

Weil, Simone. *Gravity and Grace*. Repr. New York: Routledge, 1999.

5

Regnum Christi, Apocalyptic, and the Everyday
Engaging the Work of Travis Kroeker

GERALD MCKENNY

WHAT DO CHRIST'S INCARNATION, crucifixion, and resurrection mean for the forms of life in society, ranging from the household to the *polis*, within which human beings live their everyday lives? Christian eschatology typically locates the quotidian—the ordinary, or the everyday, as this essay names it—in the overlap of the new age that dawned with Christ's resurrection and the old age that continues until the final consummation of redemption. This overlapping of the ages raises the question of how to understand the rule of Christ in the present, when the world of the everyday proceeds along its ordinary course with little evidence of his rule. One historically prominent answer to this question is that until its final consummation, Christ's rule is visible in the church but not outside it, so that two different principles, or *nomoi*, govern human affairs: one that directly manifests Christ's rule and pertains to the church; and one that may serve Christ's rule but does not manifest it, and pertains to the world outside the church.[1] Despite the claim that this second nomos can serve Christ's rule even if it does not manifest

---

1. Kroeker questions whether Augustine's *City of God* 19 supports this position, but Aquinas clearly does. See his "On Kingship," book 2, 3 (1.14), 337–40.

it, Travis Kroeker argues that to authorize it is to sanction institutions and practices that operate according to principles that are antithetical to Christ's rule.[2] His alternative is an apocalyptic political theology for which the mystery of Christ's rule becomes visible in the world of the everyday even as it remains hidden in it.[3]

With their insistence on a present unveiling of Christ's rule, apocalyptic political theologies became popular in recent decades, when they could claim to speak for those who wanted to retain the expectation of an imminent break with unjust conditions without placing hope in enduring institutions and arrangements that would inevitably betray it. Kroeker's political theology emerged during this moment, but his answer to the question of Christ's rule in the world of the everyday transcends its origin. That answer rests on three claims. First, Christ's rule is kenotic. It is visible in the acts in which Christ emptied himself, took the form of a servant, and became obedient to death (Phil 2:2–11), so that his rule, and the hidden meaning of history, is the rule of the slain Lamb (Rev 5:1–14).[4] Christ's kenotic rule continues to be visible in the kenotic self-dispossession of other human beings who imitate Christ by "living as if not" (1 Cor 7:29–31); that is, by their non-possessive use of things that frees them for employment in service to others.[5] A kenotic Christology and a kenotic ethic thus constitute the nomos of Christ's rule. Second, Christ's kenotic rule becomes visible in the world of the everyday, not only in the church. Kroeker does not authorize one nomos for the church and a different one for the world. He eschews every form of "two roles" or "two nomoi" ethics in favor of one kenotic pattern of the rule of Christ that becomes visible in the church and, at least partially, in the everyday, from the household to the *polis*.[6] Third, Christ's kenotic rule is plainly not manifest in the

2. Kroeker, *Messianic Political Theology*, 4, 116–17, 124, 232.

3. On the simultaneity of the hidden and the visible and the cross and cruciform life in the world as making visible what is hidden, see Kroeker, *Messianic Political Theology*, 4, 6–7, 25–26, 53, 78–79, 86, 92, 126, 128–29, 135, 142, 148, 245.

4. Kroeker, *Messianic Political Theology*, 95, 134, 135, 151, 246. John H. Yoder also emphasized these two texts (see Yoder, *Politics of Jesus* 132–33), though Kroeker attributes his own emphasis on them to Augustine.

5. See Kroeker, *Messianic Political Theology*, 22, 29–31, 77–78, 167, 184, 204. Here Kroeker draws on Giorgio Agamben, Alain Badiou, Jacob Taubes, and other recent conveyors of a Pauline messianic political theology, though Augustine again is also a source.

6. See Kroeker, *Messianic Political Theology*, 1–2, 4–5, 5–6, 8, 53, 60, 62, 93–94, 95, 105, 106, 117, 121–22, 124, 126, 128–29, 135, 137, 146, 147, 148, 151, 234; Kroeker, *Empire Erotics*, 14–15, 45, 79; and Kroeker, "Apocalyptic Political Theology," 316–17.

regular workings of the everyday but becomes visible only by interrupting its established course and exposing its non-messianic character. What is interrupted by Christ's death and resurrection and the human kenotic acts that imitate and participate in it is the world of immanent causality and its self-possessing, self-aggrandizing forces, and what is exposed is a world that is passing away yet is also opened to its "beyond" and is set in motion toward its ultimate redemption.[7]

Kroeker's insistence that Christ's rule is visible in the everyday and that the nomos of the everyday must manifest his rule seems right, but it poses two questions that his opposition to the "two nomoi" eschatology leaves open. First, does Christ's kenotic rule exclude all non-kenotic aspects? Second, could his rule be visible in certain ordinary workings of the everyday as well as in their interruption and exposure? It is unclear whether Kroeker would answer these questions affirmatively, and this essay ends with reasons why he might not. But the questions prompt consideration of whether his apocalyptic political theology could accommodate aspects that are not directly messianic.

These questions can be clarified by considering objections to Kroeker's first and third claims. Regarding the first claim, Kroeker's emphasis on the kenotic character of Christ's rule decisively defeats objections that the rule of Christ is an inherently triumphalist theme. The same emphasis, however, prompts objections that kenotic themes of dispossession and taking the form of a servant perpetuate structural evils that dispossess people and render them subservient to others. Kroeker would presumably reply that for him dispossession does not mean not having things but rather renouncing sovereign control over them, and that service to others is not subservience to them but using the things of the world to benefit them. In short, Kroeker successfully parries common objections to positions like his. But must he hold that kenosis is not only decisive for Christ's rule but also exhaustive of it? And must he preclude non-kenotic aspects of Christology from figuring in Christ's rule?

As Kroeker acknowledges, apocalyptic political theologies are often, and not without cause, criticized for their hostility to the everyday, lived in the ordinary course of events, which is interrupted and exposed by the unveiling of divine rule.[8] Kroeker's third claim seems vulnerable to this objection. Is not the interruption of immanent causality by the event of cross

---

7. Kroeker, *Messianic Political Theology*, 25–26, 26–27, 78–79, 143, 157.

8. See, for example, Keller, *God and Power*; and Lilla, *Stillborn God*.

and resurrection, which Kroeker calls "*ex nihilo*-ism," a forceful intrusion? Is not the exposure of the world's transitory character, which Kroeker describes as a "*mē*-ontology" in which God chooses the things "without being" to bring to nothing the things that are, the annihilation of the world?[9] Are not this interruption and this exposure acts of violence?

Kroeker can plausibly deny that they are. The world of the everyday is for him God's good creation that is capable of being opened to the Messiah, so that his entry into it is no violent intrusion, while the bringing to nothing of the things that are reveals their passing away to be their true nature, acknowledgment of which enables us to love them as they are, in their contingency, rather than clinging to them or investing them with a false permanence that ultimately destroys them. This interruption and exposure do rule out "conservative" affirmations of the everyday as it now is and cast doubt on "progressive" programs of transformative action aimed at making it better. But just because this ethic seeks neither to preserve the institutions and arrangements of the everyday in their current form nor to reshape them in accordance with moral ideals or political demands does not mean that it is inimical to the everyday as such. Far from a violent intrusion, the messianic interruption transfigures the ordinary by opening it to the rule of Christ that is otherwise hidden in it, but which becomes visible in acts of kenotic self-dispossessing love for what is passing away.[10] And far from annihilation, the exposure of the world's transitoriness lends urgency to ethical action as an exhortation to use "the time that remains" for building up what is passing away, thereby "strengthening what remains."[11] Kroeker's apocalyptic theology thus joins others that vociferously deny that apocalypticism threatens everyday life.[12] Far from threatening the ordinary, acts of interruption and exposure participate in its redemption by Christ, since it is, for Kroeker, "the kenotic movement toward the 'unsavable' [that] effects salvation."[13] But does it follow that interruption and exposure are the *only* ways in which Christ's rule becomes visible? Might it also be discerned in *some*

---

9. Kroeker, *Messianic Political Theology*, 21, 29.

10. Kroeker, *Messianic Political Theology*, 25–26, 26–27, 77, 79.

11. Kroeker, *Messianic Political Theology*, 7–8, 247.

12. See Metz, *Faith in History and Society*; Kerr, *Christ, History, and Apocalyptic*; and Ziegler, *Militant Grace*.

13. Kroeker, *Messianic Political Theology*, 33.

ordinary workings of the everyday without prejudice to its greater clarity in interruption and exposure?[14]

In short: granting that Christ's rule must be visible in the world of the everyday and that the nomos of the everyday must be the nomos of Christ's rule, may Christ's rule include a non-kenotic aspect, and may it be visible in the ordinary workings of the everyday as well as in their interruption and exposure? An affirmative answer will endorse two nomoi. But it need not endorse the sharp distinction between the nomos of Christ's rule and that of the everyday that is classically expressed in Luther's "Temporal Authority" and the Anabaptist Schleitheim Articles. Luther famously distinguishes two governments: that of Christ and the Spirit, which produces righteousness; and that of civil law and the sword, which restrains evil.[15] Genuine Christians, if there are such, are governed by Christ's rule: they do not resort to coercive force for protection or to litigation for the redress of wrongs.[16] However, the same Christians who submit to the government of Christ when their own good is at stake are in principle obligated to exercise the government of civil law and sword when the benefit of others is at stake.[17] For themselves, Christians, living according to the rule of Christ, who himself did not resist evil, will gladly suffer injury or loss of goods at the hands of others, but they will not allow their neighbor, whom they love, to suffer the same.[18] Luther thus exemplifies what Kroeker rejects, namely, the authorization of a nomos that is antithetical to the nomos of Christ's rule.

Like Luther, the Schleitheim Articles focus on civil law and coercive force—in their nomenclature, the oath and the sword—as the characteristic functions of the civil government. As with Luther, the civil government with these functions is ordained by God but falls "outside the perfection of Christ." The crucial difference, of course, is that Schleitheim prohibits members of the believing community from participating in

---

14. An answer to this question is found in Janna Hunter-Bowman's account of how acts of war-torn Colombian communities exhibited interruptive (messianic) and gradual (institutional) eschatologies at different stages of conflict transformation. See Hunter-Bowman, *Witnessing Peace*.

15. Luther, "Temporal Authority," 92.

16. Luther, "Temporal Authority," 89.

17. Luther, "Temporal Authority," 94, 95–96, 97–98, 101–2.

18. If recourse to the sword and the civil law place the Christian outside Christ's government, wouldn't having recourse to them for the neighbor's sake keep her from Christ's government? Conversely, if the sword and the civil law are goods that genuinely benefit the neighbor, wouldn't they genuinely benefit the Christian as well?

these functions.[19] At least for Christians, no antithetical nomos is authorized. But despite this disagreement, both parties agree that the rule of Christ governs the actions of Christians qua Christian, while outside Christ's rule stand the political and judicial orders that restrain evil by means that fall outside the perfection of Christ and operate by principles that do not derive from or conform to the nomos of his rule.[20] This stance problematically constricts Christ's rule by limiting it to domains in which there is explicit subjection to it and consigns the everyday to a nomos that in its content is antithetical to that of Christ's rule.

Kroeker agrees with Luther that Christians are called to service to others, while he agrees with Schleitheim that the acts of Christians must conform to the nomos of Christ's rule rather than to that of the political and judicial orders, which for him as for Luther and Schleitheim are antithetical to the nomos of Christ's rule. But could the nomos of Christ's rule itself authorize a nomos of the everyday that differs from it but is not antithetical to it? Dietrich Bonhoeffer and Joseph Ratzinger agree that it could, and they invoke themes of apocalyptic theology to show how it does. Bonhoeffer characterizes God's justifying grace to the sinner as the "ultimate" reality that radically breaks with everything "penultimate" and stands in judgment of it, yet also establishes its reality as that which precedes the ultimate, much as for Kroeker the cross and resurrection interrupt the world of immanent causality while also exposing its reality as that which is passing away. Likewise, for Bonhoeffer the ultimate determines the penultimate as that which prepares the way for it, much as the world for Kroeker is opened by Christ's kenosis to his entry into it. Moreover, for Bonhoeffer it is the ultimate itself that requires the preservation of the penultimate, much as for Kroeker it is the messianic that requires service to the world that is passing away.[21] Finally, Bonhoeffer's concept of the penultimate is broad and indistinct, taking in the entire domain of ordinary life in which the full range of human needs are felt and met, much as Kroeker's concept of the ordinary eschews distinctions between the household and city, encompassing all forms of human organization of the everyday under the same kenotic

---

19. Baylor, "Schleitheim Articles."

20. It is true that for Luther the Christian's use of the law and the sword for the benefit of the neighbor is a work of love, which would seem to reflect the government of Christ. However, what the Christian does as an expression of love does not itself conform to the nomos of the government of Christ.

21. Bonhoeffer, *Ethics*, 146–70.

nomos. In contrast to Kroeker, however, Bonhoeffer distinguishes the nomos of the penultimate, which is accessible to reason, from that of the ultimate, which is not.[22] Thus, while the penultimate with its nomos is established by the ultimate, its activities conform to principles that are not themselves derived from the ultimate. The penultimate prepares for Christ's rule but does not manifest it.

Ratzinger identifies the martyr as an apocalyptic figure whose willingness to suffer at the hands of the state rather than do what is evil reveals the boundary of the state. Within its boundary, the state enjoys God-given authority to ensure peace and uphold the rule of law. The readiness of the martyr to submit to the ruling authorities confirms the authority of the state, which legitimately demands obedience within its domain, and affirms the state's nomos, which is reason. At the same time, the martyr's refusal to do what is evil, even to the point of suffering and death, discloses the point at which the state, by commanding what is evil, exceeds what it is entitled to demand of its citizens and must not be obeyed. Here, the martyr points beyond the state to a law that is above the laws of states and a shalom that is more definitive than the peace they offer.[23] And in all this, of course, the martyr only imitates Christ, who also distinguished the things of Caesar and the things of God and suffered willingly at the hands of a state that transgressed its boundary. Notably, for Ratzinger the martyr's obedience confirms reason as the proper nomos of the state. It is at the point where something commanded by the state would violate this nomos that another nomos is revealed, namely, the higher law and more definitive peace that are beyond the state and what it secures. As with Kroeker, the nomos of Christ's rule is revealed in the suffering and death of Christ and of the martyr who imitates him; but in contrast to Kroeker (and in agreement with Bonhoeffer), the very different nomos of the state is confirmed by the nomos of Christ's rule.

In short, for Bonhoeffer and for Ratzinger the kenotic nomos of Christ's rule authorizes a nomos that differs from it yet is not antithetical to it or even independent of it. But they go further by ultimately identifying this second nomos with Christ. For Bonhoeffer, "the relationship between the ultimate and the penultimate is resolved only in Christ," that is, in his incarnation, crucifixion, and resurrection in which are disclosed, respectively, God's love toward creation, God's judgment on

---

22. Bonhoeffer, *Ethics*, 174.
23. Ratzinger, *Values in a Time of Upheaval*, 22–23.

all flesh, and God's purpose for a new world.[24] For Ratzinger, to say that the proper nomos of the state is reason (*logos*) is to say that this nomos participates in Christ as the eternal Logos by which God created and which is reflected in creation—the very same Logos who in Christ's incarnation, suffering, and death is revealed as love.[25] Of course, this does not mean that the nomos of the state is identical in content to the nomos of Christ's kenosis. They are two distinct nomoi, one finding expression in just laws and justly secured peace and the other in kenotic acts. Yet both nomoi are christological, and both therefore disclose something of Christ's rule. Because the Logos who became incarnate and underwent suffering and death is also the Logos reflected in creation, reason as the proper nomos of the political order reflects the rule of Christ, even as his rule is most directly visible and its character, which is love, is most clearly disclosed in his incarnation, suffering, and death, and in acts by others that imitate these kenotic acts.[26]

So, Bonhoeffer and (especially) Ratzinger show how the rule of Christ may be manifest in the everyday in a nomos that is not kenotic and that may be found in the ordinary workings of political and judicial orders. This nomos is not identical in content to the kenotic nomos, yet both are nomoi of Christ's rule. The kenotic character of Christ's rule is neither denied nor marginalized here but is affirmed in its connection to Christ's role in creation and to his trinitarian personhood. The kenotic manifestation of Christ's rule in his incarnation, suffering, and death remains the definitive disclosure, as it reveals the character of the Logos as love. But the reflection of the Logos in a political order characterized by just laws and justly secured peace is nevertheless a genuine manifestation, and one that does not take the form of interruption or exposure.

This position can be rendered more concretely by considering an issue of great importance to Kroeker, namely, the response to evil. Kroeker shows how the kenotic rule of Christ counters pretensions of sovereign human judgment that underwrite judicial systems and reveals forgiveness and reconciliation as the characteristic divine responses to evil, in contrast to retribution.[27] On these grounds, he sharply distinguishes formal judicial systems, which operate according to the principle of

24. Bonhoeffer, *Ethics*, 157–59.

25. Ratzinger, *Values in a Time of Upheaval*, 112–13.

26. These moves allow political theology to do justice to Gen 1 and John 1 as political texts, along with Phil 2 and Rev 5.

27. Kroeker, *Messianic Political Theology*, 60–62, 95.

retribution, which is antithetical to Christ's rule, from more spontaneous practices of restorative justice, which for him involves countering evil with forgiveness and reconciliation in the awareness of shared guilt, all in accordance with Christ's rule.[28] As Kroeker's messianic ethic is not confined to the church, countering evil with forgiveness and reconciliation rather than retributive justice presumably applies outside the church as well as within it.

A time-honored objection to this kind of position insists that responses to evil on this side of the eschaton should not try to instantiate the nomos of Christ's rule outside the church, where, it is said, his rule is not yet manifest, while in the meantime evil persists and must be restrained by means that exhibit an antithetical nomos. Luther vividly presses this argument in his remark that one who, presuming that the world is populated with Christians and therefore has no need of sword or court of law, attempts to rule it according to the government of Christ "would be loosing the ropes and chains of the savage wild beasts and letting them bite and mangle everyone, meanwhile insisting that they were harmless, tame, and gentle creatures."[29]

This objection, of course, expresses the non-apocalyptic eschatology described at the beginning of this essay. Against it, Kroeker rightly insists that political theology should not authorize responses to evil that are antithetical to the nomos of Christ's rule but only responses that reflect that nomos. But two questions remain open. First, is the kenotic nomos of forgiveness and reconciliation applicable to responses to evil outside the church? Second, if it is not applicable, does it follow that responses to evil outside the church are left to the nomos of retributive justice, or do they fall under a non-kenotic but still christological nomos? Apropos of the first question, Oliver O'Donovan mentions several reasons why practices like forgiveness and reconciliation are not applicable outside the church. Human judgments on wrongdoing, he points out, do not meet sin with patient suffering, do not give rise to humble and trusting obedience, do not pour out the Holy Spirit on those who trust and obey them, and do not assure regeneration and new life.[30] These deficits (especially the last two) suggest that what responses to evil outside the church lack is access to sacramental grace, which is the context within which meeting evil with forgiveness and reconciliation is intelligible and effectual. The problem is

---

28. Kroeker, *Messianic Political Theology*, 92, 147, 155, 227, 232, 246.
29. Luther, "Temporal Authority," 91.
30. O'Donovan, *Ways of Judgment*, 86–87.

not, as Luther feared, that the rule of Christ is incapable of restraining evil. It is rather that the world of the everyday lacks the conditions of efficacy and intelligibility that make acts of forgiveness and reconciliation—which are not only difficult to achieve but often seem inappropriate to demand of those who have been wronged—attainable and thinkable.

This is not to say that the presence of sacramental grace guarantees the success of restorative justice. As the notorious case of John Yoder, which Kroeker discusses, illustrates all too well, practices of restorative justice by churches can egregiously fail those who resort to them.[31] It is also not to deny that even in the church, forgiveness and reconciliation may become attainable and intelligible only after grace has restored the agency of a survivor of wrongdoing. Finally, it is not to resolve the question of whether or when, given these failures and limitations, Christians should respond to evil by resorting to courts of law rather than to practices Kroeker favors. These are all urgent and weighty matters. The present point is simply that it is one thing for the church to face up to failures and limitations of forgiveness and reconciliation as responses to evil that are proper to it; it is another thing for the world outside the church, which lacks O'Donovan's conditions, to take up forgiveness and reconciliation as its own characteristic responses to evil.

Turning to the second question, it does not follow that the nomos of Christ's rule is visible only in ecclesial practices of forgiveness and reconciliation and not outside the church as well, or that the judicial order is simply left to the nomos of retributive justice—in short, that Luther was right. For one thing, forgiveness and reconciliation may take place outside the church in the kind of spontaneous acts that Kroeker has in view, which characteristically occur outside formal judicial systems. Moreover, it is notable that forms of restorative justice that fall short of forgiveness yet aim at some degree of reconciliation have succeeded within the judicial system itself. These points suggest that grace is operative outside the church as well as in it, making Christ's rule at least dimly visible there. Moreover, Ratzinger's position implies that the nomos of the Logos as reflected in creation will be visible wherever responses to evil are governed by reason. According to an influential tradition of legal thought, this occurs when judicial judgments adhere to the principle of equity, which qualifies the strict application of statutes to account for circumstances, for factors that may mitigate guilt, and so on.

31. Kroeker, *Messianic Political Theology*, 8–9. For the definitive account, see Goossen, "'Defanging the Beast.'"

Closely related to equity is mercy, which moderates judicial judgments to reflect judges' awareness of the imperfectness of their judgments, of their own guilt, and of the need of all human beings for divine mercy.[32] In the moderation of judgment by mercy the judicial system itself rejects pretentions of sovereign human judgment and acknowledges shared guilt—two points that Kroeker, as noted above, identifies as central to his messianic response to evil. Here, the nomos of the incarnate Logos, who humbled himself and shared human guilt, becomes at least dimly visible in human judgments in the judicial order.

Once again, this is not to deny or underestimate the egregious injustices of the current judicial system, especially in the United States, with its appalling disparities in who receives equity and mercy and in who lands in the system in the first place. Nor is it to deny that the exercise of equity and mercy is compromised by myriad distortions. Finally, this position has not demonstrated that equity and mercy are incompatible with retribution generally or with any given form of punishment, including incarceration. Again, these are all urgent and weighty matters. The point here is simply that the rule of Christ in the forms of equity and mercy is proper to the judicial order, which is therefore not simply left to the nomos of retributive justice but may in principle manifest Christ's rule, however dimly, even apart from the practices of forgiveness and reconciliation in which his rule is most definitively visible. To demand that judicial systems meet the standards of equity and mercy in all cases is to hold them accountable to their proper task as well as, implicitly, to call them to honor Christ's rule.

An apocalyptic political theology is arguably one that insists on the visibility in the present of the hidden rule of Christ. Like Kroeker's work, to which it is indebted at every point, this essay is an exercise in apocalyptic political theology. It is unclear, however, that Kroeker would accept the position it sets out. He may suspect that its invocations of just laws, justly secured peace, and judicial equity conceal aspects of a so-called nomos of reason that are antithetical to the kenotic nomos. More fundamentally, he may suspect that its trinitarian Christology compromises his messianic Christology and that its claim that Christ's rule may be visible in the ordinary workings of political and judicial orders is insufficiently skeptical of institutional forms.[33] However, these

---

32. This account of equity and mercy roughly follows O'Donovan's account; see *Ways of Judgment*, 95, 97–98.

33. Cyril O'Regan's category of "metaxic" apocalyptic theology applies to Kroeker to

suspicions arise within shared convictions that in the overlap of the ages the rule of Christ is visible outside the church as well as inside, that Christian political theologies should therefore not endorse any nomos of the everyday that is antithetical in content to the nomos of Christ's rule, and that Christ's rule is most visible in his incarnation, death, and resurrection and in acts that imitate them. And no one articulates these convictions better than Travis Kroeker does.[34]

Bibliography

Aquinas, Thomas. "On Kingship." Translated by G. B. Phelan and I. T. Eschmann. In *From Irenaeus to Grotius: A Sourcebook in Christian Political Theology*, edited by Oliver O'Donovan and Joan Lockwood O'Donovan, 330–41. Grand Rapids: Eerdmans, 1999.

Baylor, Michael G., trans. "The Schleitheim Articles." In *From Irenaeus to Grotius: A Sourcebook in Christian Political Thought*, edited by Oliver O'Donovan and Joan Lockwood O'Donovan, 635–37. Grand Rapids: Eerdmans, 1999.

Bonhoeffer, Dietrich. *Ethics*. Edited by Clifford J. Green and translated by Reinhard Kraus et al. Dietrich Bonhoeffer Works 6. Minneapolis: Augsburg Fortress, 2005.

Goossen, Rachel Waltner. "'Defanging the Beast': Mennonite Responses to John Howard Yoder's Sexual Abuse." *Mennonite Quarterly Review* 89 (2015) 7–80.

Hunter-Bowman, Janna. *Witnessing Peace: Becoming Agents Under Duress in Colombia*. New York: Routledge, 2022.

Keller, Catherine. *God and Power: Counter-Apocalyptic Journeys*. Minneapolis: Fortress, 2005.

Kerr, Nathan. *Christ, History, and Apocalyptic: The Politics of Christian Mission*. Eugene, OR: Cascade, 2009.

Kroeker, P. Travis. "Apocalyptic Political Theology: Response to Philip Ziegler's *Militant Grace*." *International Journal of Systematic Theology* 22 (2020) 313–26.

———. *Empire Erotics and Messianic Economies of Desire*. Winnipeg: Canadian Mennonite University Press, 2016.

———. *Messianic Political Theology and Diaspora Ethics: Essays in Exile*. Eugene, OR: Cascade, 2017.

Lilla, Mark. *The Stillborn God: Religion, Politics, and the Modern West*. New York: Random House, 2007.

Luther, Martin. "Temporal Authority: To What Extent It Should Be Obeyed" Translated by J. J. Schindel and revised by Walther I. Brandt. In *The Christian in Society II*, edited by Walther I. Brandt, 81–129. Philadelphia: Muhlenberg, 1962.

---

the extent that he centers "the self-gift of the divine," "embraces the rhetoric of the radically new," and "demonstrates disinterest in or hostility towards institutional Christianity and towards doctrine." See O'Regan, *Theology and the Spaces of Apocalyptic*, 28–29.

34. I thank Janna Hunter-Bowman for her helpful and insightful comments on an earlier draft of this essay.

Metz, Johannes Baptist. *Faith in History and Society: Toward a Practical Fundamental Theology*. Translated by J. Matthew Ashley. 2nd ed. New York: Herder and Herder, 2007.

O'Donovan, Oliver. *The Ways of Judgment*. Grand Rapids: Eerdmans, 2005.

O'Regan, Cyril. *Theology and the Spaces of Apocalyptic*. Père Marquette Lecture in Theology. Milwaukee: Marquette University Press, 2009.

Ratzinger, Joseph, Cardinal (Pope Benedict XVI). *Values in a Time of Upheaval*. Translated by Brian McNeil. San Francisco: Ignatian, 2006.

Yoder, John Howard. *The Politics of Jesus*. Grand Rapids: Eerdmans, 1972.

Ziegler, Philip. *Militant Grace: The Apocalyptic Turn and the Future of Christian Theology*. Grand Rapids: Baker Academic, 2018.

6

Critique of Possessive Desire

MAXWELL KENNEL

This is the mind of the messiah [referring to the servant ethic of Mark 10:43–44], and it does not take the erotic form of desire. It takes the humiliating and often invisible, strange-making form of sacrifice, which relates to the form of this world as a "passing away." Such witness—and I daresay it is a witness equally paradoxical in the church and in the world—bears testimony to the power of the Spirit that brings about not new human achievements but discloses the strange and strange-making passage of God in the world. It cannot be possessed; it cannot be restricted to the church; it can only be prepared for by repentance.[1] —P. Travis Kroeker

Let this preface, then, be a "counter-provocation" to Jim's [A. James Reimer's] bi-directional provocations, in the service of what I want to call a messianic political theology that is neither Catholic nor Protestant, neither Mennonite nor secularist, neither orthodox nor heterodox—in keeping with a Pauline economy (*oikonomia*, sometimes translated as "commission"; 1 Cor 9:17) that inhabits the mysterious freedom of messianic slavery in order to build up (*oikodome*; 1

---

1. Kroeker, "Making Strange," 98.

Cor 8:1, 10:23) the common world that is nevertheless passing away (1 Cor 7:31).[2]—P. Travis Kroeker

There is no salvation to be found in institutional, human, political, or religious powers or in identitarian moral purity. Everything in the world is secular, fragile, vulnerable, and mortal, kept alive by divine love, the divine breath. This is why Augustine is so deeply ambivalent about all justice claims. Like all virtue language tied to the knowledge of good and evil, as if this could be a humanly controlled or instituted techne, love and justice may quickly become destructive fantasies: the endless erotic pursuits of "final solutions" to the problem of evil, as it is humanly understood and imposed, that always end yet again in violence and death—new kinds of hell on earth.[3]—P. Travis Kroeker

WHAT TO SAY ABOUT the work of P. Travis Kroeker? How to write about, and in some senses address, an erudite, charitable, critical, and influential figure in the conversation on political theology (who was also my *Doktorvater*, in the very best sense of the term)? Below I want to draw out just one feature of his thought that I find most challenging, most provocative, and most helpful: the *critique of possessive desire*, a term for what one might call a methodology or paradigm that centrally animates Kroeker's unique messianic political theology, but which he does not possess or use in the traditional ways that methodologies are often instrumentalized. As expressed in the leading quotations above and on the back cover of his book *Messianic Political Theology and Diaspora Ethics*, Kroeker's work seeks to further "a messianic posture rooted in the renunciation of possessive desire that pertains to all aspects of everyday human life in the household (*oikos*), the academy, and the *polis*."[4] But what does this mean? What makes for a critique of possessive desire, and how does it feature in his work and the works of others?

---

2. Kroeker, "Foreword," ix–x.
3. Kroeker, "Postsecular History or Figural Messianism?", 344.
4. Kroeker, *Messianic Political Theology*, back cover.

Below I will survey some of Kroeker's writings in order to draw out the threads of the critique of possessive desire, with the ultimate aim of demonstrating that it sits within the heart of his work in ways that cannot be fully articulated, lest it lead those who articulate it into possessive self-defeat. I will begin with an account of the constellation of ideas and paradoxical ways of thinking that characterize the critique of possessive desire, and then I will highlight its presence in a sampling of Kroeker's unique political theology, before concluding with an account of salient parallels between Kroeker's work and writings by Hartmut Rosa and Reiner Schürmann—two unlikely dialogue partners who illuminate how the critique of possessive desire transcends the often-possessive distinctions between religion and secularity.

The Critique of Possessive Desire

The critique of possessive desire is certainly not singular (for it is only ever "a" critique of possessive desire), but it nonetheless appears as a golden thread woven through the history of religious, theological, and political thought, from the ancients to the medieval mystics to the moderns and postmoderns. The critique draws from many sources but is reducible to none, and it persistently works against the forces of pride, hubris, and *libido dominandi* that drive people to ruin. This distinctive approach to the problems posed by power, control, and possession is, in some ways, *not* distinctive, because the critique of possessive desire belongs to no one (otherwise it would become self-defeating in being possessed), and yet it is found in many specific places and times. Kroeker's work addresses many of these sources, sometimes through apocalyptic and messianic readings of figures like Augustine or Simone Weil, and often through literary-political readings of the great works of Western religious and theological thought. Even within the social-scientific and interdisciplinary field of religious studies there are elements of unpossessive deferral when scholars allow the self-understanding of those whom they study to take precedence over the imposition of ideal types or classifications. Unrestricted by field, discipline, time, and space, the insights and wisdom of the critique of possessive desire are in some respects perennial and diverse, but in the interest of clarity (the possessive character of which must be refused), here are its main contours.

When we talk about what a thing *is* (ontologically) as if we know something *about it* (epistemologically), using names and terms and concepts to point toward it (linguistically and communicatively) that are jointly grounded in their instrumental uses and polemical abuses by various people (politically and socially), being both normative and descriptive, then we attempt—and it is only ever an attempt—to fix upon that thing enough to say something meaningful about it that others will understand and appreciate. But the moment that desire for fixity lapses into anxious or controlling exercises of power, force, violence, or coercion (often motivated by the very understandable but highly manipulable desires for safety, security, and certainty), then we have lost something valuable, even sacred, and fallen into possessive self-defeat.

For example, in desiring to lock down a definition of a key term or definitively solidify a religious doctrine, the project of securing it causes its sacred, ineffable, sublime, and spiritual character to disappear. Possessive desire, from the level of concepts and ideas (where thinkers deal in ideal types that cloak normative uses of terms in the appearance of mere description) to social and material situations (where people act in violent, controlling, and possessive ways toward themselves and others), offends against the nature of things: the fact that all things are subject to change, and that all things are passing away and will always pass away. In some senses, it is a bold metaphysical claim to say that the way things are is reflected in the idea that we cannot possess or fix in place how things are, but in another light it is simply a piece of worldly wisdom that everyone knows without much need for reflection: nothing lasts forever, all things must change, and as soon as you think you've captured something you desire, it has escaped your grasp.

Travis Kroeker's Political Theology

In both his seminar courses and published works, Kroeker approaches the ideas and texts of others in a distinctive way that flows both from and toward his messianic political theology and diasporic ethics. Now, Kroeker's work is not unique inasmuch as it exemplifies and sometimes articulates this critique of possessive desire. But his work is exemplary of this paradoxical approach in ways that can be put in more precise terms (mindful, of course, that too much precision defeats the purpose of clarifying a critique of possessive desire). From his master's thesis on Karl Rahner and dissertation on political economy to his co-authored book on Fyodor Dostoevsky and articles on Mennonite political theology, to his lectures on empire erotics, his 2017 essay collection on messianic political theology, and his work on Miriam Toews—and especially in the pedagogical relay between gentle correction and insistence on detailed close reading that characterizes his seminar teaching style—Kroeker's critique of possessive desire has left an indelible mark on his many students (and in some ways appears to be inspired by his own teachers[5]).

In the introduction to *Messianic Political Theology and Diaspora Ethics*, Kroeker gives one of the more succinct and programmatic summaries of his theopolitical project. His approach to political theology understands the term to refer to "a normative discourse rooted in the conviction that political crises—in the complex etymological sense of events, issues, judgments and decisions related to crucial 'turning points'—may be best accounted for with reference to theological terms."[6] Political theology is certainly normative, and it is certainly a response to crises, but *how* its normative orientation relates to the secularization of concepts is what counts, and for Kroeker, I suggest that the normativity of political theology is characterized by the struggle with possessive desire. Kroeker's work consistently returns to themes of scandal, controversy, and agonism, but without the *ressentiment*, moral panics, and anxieties that afflict conservative political theologians who seek a regressive return to a time when Christian theology reigned. Instead, Kroeker critiques "the presumptive grasping of power" that characterizes human sovereignty and seeks a form of political education that asks: "Who is leading us out (*e-ducere*) of bondage into a more liberating, peaceful and just form of communal life and vision?"[7] Exilic and diasporic approaches, informed by messianic and apocalyptic readings of Augustine, Walter Benjamin, and the great works of the Western tradition are the ways in which Kroeker resists possessive desire without taking refuge in the fantasy that

---

5. Kroeker concludes his appreciation of his PhD supervisor, James Gustafson, by stating, "The Christian faith at its center confesses that both the content and the human form of divine wisdom is revealed in Christ—whose example of humility and serving love is scandalous to both such strategies. The wisdom of God is foolishness to discursive human reason (whether doctrinal or scientific) that seeks to possess certain knowledge for itself; and the power of God is weakness to those human traditions (whether religious or secular) that seek to control and dominate the saeculum. What the alternative might be is known only to the eye of faith." Kroeker, "Doubting Theology," para. 4.

6. Kroeker, *Messianic Political Theology*, 1.

7. Kroeker, *Messianic Political Theology*, 2–3.

people can be purified of their need for repentance and reconciliation, and without the trappings of fatalism or hopelessness.

Elsewhere, Kroeker pitches suffering love against educative violence,[8] and calls for an existential form of Anabaptist radicalism that draws from literary and philosophical sources to provide provisional answers to the most important existential questions.[9] Like a golden thread, the critique of possessive desire is woven through Kroeker's work up to his most recent essays on the scandalous drama of the Trinity (on which he advocates for a "vernacular mysticism" that calls Anabaptists to "become more radical in committing to the figural drama of the biblical witness that goes beyond conventional doctrinal or traditional logics in the service of the scandalous divine love for a sinful, suffering world"[10]), and on the concept of the secular and the political (in which he argues that "to the extent to which any retributive judicial practices are devoted to the possessive and dominating 'order' of the security state that claims to mediate a non-penitential justice, such practices are rooted in sinful necessity and contribute to the 'lie' of a strictly human sovereignty."[11]).

The essays in *Messianic Political Theology and Diaspora Ethics* further exemplify the delicate but persistent wisdom that comes from critiquing possessive desire by treating their sources, concepts, narratives, and ideas in ways that allow them to be themselves (letting them be) but also make incisive interventions that transform them. Whether by learning to live "as if not" by acknowledging the partial character of all knowledge while nonetheless seeking the fulfillment and recapitulation of time, or arguing that the pursuit of the political and public good requires existential reckoning that cannot be forced or imposed, Kroeker's writing is careful and humble but also persistent and assertive.[12] Through simultaneous critiques of the liberal forgetting of religion and investment in technocratic individualism, and the conservative desire to conserve what cannot be conserved, Kroeker encourages ways of thinking and interpreting the world that build up the secular from below by theological means.[13] In his close readings, each major text he engages with—Augustine's *Confessions*, Friedrich Nietzsche's *Thus Spake*

8. Kroeker, "Educative Violence or Suffering Love?"
9. Kroeker, "Anabaptists and Existential Theology."
10. Kroeker, "Scandalous Drama of Trinitarian Theology," 153.
11. Kroeker, "Secular—The Political," 253.
12. Kroeker, *Messianic Political Theology*, 33, 44.
13. Kroeker, *Messianic Political Theology*, 64.

Zarathustra, Herman Melville's *Moby Dick*, Thomas Hobbes's *Leviathan*, Plato's *Republic*, and so on—is treated with similarly unpossessive hands. Kroeker draws lessons, truths, and insights from these texts without reducing them to moralizing discourses or didactic expressions of moral purity. Kroeker's ethics is diasporic, seeing the scattering of languages after Babel as a divine gift of difference and resisting the "colonizing vision and monolithic ontology" of technological empires.[14]

This upbuilding work involves both an apophatic suspicion of names and language and a willingness to name realities in plural and dispersed ways, alongside an existential theological orientation that seeks truths in ways that require "both a certain sort of person and a certain kind of *techne*, or method."[15] Kroeker's existential Anabaptism, for example, reflects his position as "someone struggling to give an account of what it means to be answerable for what I have been given to be and to do."[16] Rather than another overly cognitive and abstract theology, Kroeker advocates for an existential theology rooted in real people and communities, "in communion that keeps faith with one another, the land, and God—embracing and embodying, in disciplined skills of love and care, a life-giving vision of peaceable justice."[17]

Grounded as it is in existential matters, Kroeker's work nonetheless holds its ground with a gentleness and care that understands how possessive, controlling, reactive, and anxious desires can cause the movements of life to bind and catch, often leading into self-defeating cycles where we create precisely what we fear. Only humility, repentance, and unpossessive holding of ideas and things can prevent—for example—the poison of *ressentiment* or the perpetuation of colonial violence (dynamics touched upon in Travis's exchange with Carole Leclair in chapter 12 of *Messianic Political Theology and Diaspora Ethics*). Encounters across lines of difference are essential spiritual exercises for holding knowledge of the world with open hands, and this disciplined unpossessiveness should emphasize how the "critique of possessive desire" (that is perhaps idolatrously named and unpacked in this chapter) is not the possession of any single figure and is expressed by many. So, I turn in conclusion to two others who have found its path and articulated its wisdom, if only to illuminate

---

14. Kroeker, *Messianic Political Theology*, 75.
15. Kroeker, *Messianic Political Theology*, 75, 83.
16. Kroeker, *Messianic Political Theology*, 86.
17. Kroeker, *Messianic Political Theology*, 87.

how this critique is a possession of no one but available to all, in ways that resonate with Kroeker's corpus.

Critiques of Possessive Desire in Hartmut Rosa and Reiner Schürmann

Hartmut Rosa's book *The Uncontrollability of the World* describes the *Unverfügbarkeit* of all things in a clear and accessible way—so deceptively simple it risks being overlooked. Rosa focuses on the elusiveness of control and the positive possibility of resonating with the world in ways that engage with its unpredictable and resistant character by carefully yet decisively mediating between that which we can and cannot control (as the Serenity Prayer articulates in popular form). He opens with the claim that modernity is based on the idea that the world is controllable, while "it is only in encountering the *uncontrollable* that we really experience the world."[18] The visibility, accessibility, manageability, and usability that we attribute to the world when we desire to possess and control things in it—from concepts to people—are each fundamentally challenged, for Rosa, by the world's mysterious withdrawal.[19]

Against these desires, he prescribes modes of affection, efficacy, emotion, and adaptive transformation by which we can come into greater resonance with the world. By resonating with the tension that animates the line between what we can and cannot control, Rosa thinks that we are not confronted with a contradiction but are witness to the semi-controllable character of the world.[20] Against possession and mastery, Rosa asks that simple existential question that confronts us each day: "To take control or let things happen?"[21] His answer is to pursue the latter, and his examples are simple and beautiful, from falling snow that cannot be taken in hand and held to the paradox of trying to fall asleep, wherein the more one tries the less likely sleep will arrive.

Another thinker who expresses a version of the critique of possessive desire is Reiner Schürmann, who is best known for his work on Martin Heidegger and his magnum opus, *Broken Hegemonies*.[22] Early

---

18. Rosa, *Uncontrollability of the World*, 1.
19. Rosa, *Uncontrollability of the World*, 19.
20. Rosa, *Uncontrollability of the World*, 41.
21. Rosa, *Uncontrollability of the World*, 60.
22. Schürmann, *Broken Hegemonies*.

in his career, Schürmann trained to become a Dominican priest and wrote theological texts that have recently been edited and compiled in a volume called *Ways of Releasement*—where "releasement" stands in for the German *Gelassenheit* and the French *délaissement*.[23] In these early writings, before Schürmann sought to quietly erase his theological past, he articulates a series of insights—many derived from Meister Eckhart—that resonate with the critique of possessive desire. For the early Schürmann, living according to the gospel means to free oneself from the "complications of language" in ways that understand that "to seek words is necessary; to find them is impossible."[24] Via Schürmann's related concept of "peregrine identity"—at once influenced by Heidegger, Eckhart, and the Bhagavad-Gita—we can see another exemplary expression of the critique of possessive desire, especially in his description of "true ascesis" as "the apprenticeship of saying and falling silent," where revelation is at once "radically incomprehensible" and renewed through contemporary language.[25]

It is in his interpretation of Eckhart that Schürmann's critique of possessive desire becomes most clearly expressed—for example, in Eckhart's statement that those who wish to understand his teaching about detachment (*Gelassenheit*) must themselves become detached.[26] But this is not a total detachment that dissociates from present things in space and time, but rather it is a way of becoming more present, listening more closely, and letting things be in ways that still act and decide. For Schürmann, critiquing possessive desire and living in *Gelassenheit* means "preserving the mystery of his path," giving "answers with silence," "wandering far from the origin but being called back to it," and being invited and called to "the infinite resignation of detachment."[27] This itinerant wandering means "crossing the nothingness that separates us from the emergence in which all things are one" in ways that release hold on binaristic oppositions, while bearing and grounding nothing, and avoiding all security and capture.[28] Not unlike Kroeker's diasporic approach, Schürmann's releasement means

23. Schürmann, *Ways of Releasement*.
24. Schürmann, *Ways of Releasement*, 11, 97.
25. Schürmann, *Ways of Releasement*, 99.
26. Schürmann, *Ways of Releasement*, 102.
27. Schürmann, *Ways of Releasement*, 112.
28. Schürmann, *Ways of Releasement*, 151.

letting go, unclenching [*Lâcher prise*], ceasing to lay hold of. Of oneself, of others, of the images of the past and the projects of the future, of God finally. This has nothing to do with desperate abandonment. On the contrary. It is a matter of supreme interest in everything that is. But to see what is, it is necessary to pull back and keep our hands off. Away from the haze, we have a future in place of apprehensions, and a heart in place of a past. Letting be [*Laisser* être]: this opens a path. An initiation, perhaps, but not a threshold crossed once and for all. Dare dispossession, with animal patience. These words say it well: peregrination, peril, experience. Our essential peregrination, the experience of ourselves, remains perilous.[29]

Kroeker, Rosa, and Schürmann each articulate a version of the critique of possessive desire, the mystical center of which can never be expressed but the contours of which represent one of the most urgent and serious ethical problems we are faced with. Consider Rosa's question again: "To take control or let things happen?" It can never be so simple as to choose one option over the other in a decontextualized way. Instead, the question is really about how one mediates between letting things be and taking action, or discerns between the moment of releasement and the moment of decision. If Schürmann's approach is to be taken seriously, any simplistic division of our thinking in two is given over to possessive self-defeat—for example, the notion that one must either take control or let things happen.

Self-Critique and Self-Defeat of Possessive Desire

Lest theologians be tempted to read such insights possessively as a coded crypto-theological validation of preexisting doctrines, or philosophers to see these ideas as grounds to rail against religious contamination, we must recognize that the critique of possessive desire—as expressed by Kroeker, Rosa, Schürmann, and many others—must cultivate an essential self-reflexivity that calls into question any settling or sedimentation of normative categories (including traditional scholarly disciplines and institutions of all kinds). This includes the ever-present temptation to divide the world into the categories of "religious" and "secular," as if nothing crossed or stood between these bounds.[30] No. Better to call all

29. Schürmann, *Ways of Releasement*, 152.
30. See my *Postsecular History*.

things into question, disinvest in all categories, and let the question be and remain a question that, although it may be answered in contextual ways in specific times and places, maintains its questionable status, lest it fall into a violent ontology of displacement.[31]

I want to emphasize again that if it is to have integrity, the critique of possessive desire must not be restricted to either the realm of concepts or the domain of practices. It is existential, which means it is always mediating between theories and practices. The critique of possessive desire is as much about the problematic and tragic binds that we fall into when we grasp too tightly and anxiously the things in our everyday lives as it is about the act of critique and the careful combination of inward self-critique and outward ideology critique. Both the way that one thinks about ideas and categories (for example, how signifiers point toward but do not capture or exhaustively represent what they signify) and the way that one acts (for example, how one resists patriarchal, colonial, classist, and other violent ways of treating others) must be shaped by this form of critique. Although we are not a unified "we," it is nonetheless true that we cannot think possessively and expect to act unpossessively, and we cannot act possessively and expect to think unpossessively.

This critical chiasmus and its self-reflexivity are essential, and they resonate with Kroeker's messianic, apocalyptic, exilic, and diasporic approach—one that sees the Messiah as a sacrificial servant who does not bow to earthly power but resists it from below without being drawn into its oppositional character; one that reads apocalypse as a figure for the world "in which the mystical body of Christ is constantly being crucified (in the church no less than in the world)";[32] and one that sees exile and diaspora as terms for an existential, spiritual, and real struggle with worldly belonging. Becoming unpossessive—or "living as if not"[33]—requires intentional mediations between all of the dichotomous distinctions that Western metaphysics has monstrously gifted the world. When Kroeker emphasizes the partial character of all knowledge in the secular present, and when he refers to the "kenotic movement toward the 'unsavable' that effects salvation,"[34] and when he suggests that we make the most of our time while echoing Paul's admonition to love your neighbor as yourself, he is pointing—and only ever pointing without capture—toward a

---

31. See my *Ontologies of Violence*.
32. Kroeker, *Messianic Political Theology*, 1.
33. Kroeker, *Messianic Political Theology*, 33.
34. Kroeker, *Messianic Political Theology*, 33.

worldly and divine wisdom that is not his own, yet which he has explored and developed in most of his work.

Doubtless Kroeker will be horrified by the fact that I have attributed to him a critique of possessive desire that is anything but his own possession, and doubtless he will reject any inference that he possesses the messianic mystery. This is part of his integrity. For even the activity of trying to summarize and articulate the critique of possessive desire in the way I have above is always at risk of falling into possessive self-defeat. While this essay has attempted to delineate the main contours of this approach—which has surely gone by other names in many other places—the risk is always that the effort to express something becomes a form of capture. This is part of the necessary integrity of any critique of possessive desire worth its salt (Matt 5:1–20). Nonetheless, if above I risk clarifying too much how this way of thinking is essential to Kroeker's project, I only do so because he is the one who taught it to me, and because he was a messianic figure in my own life, who showed up when I needed a teacher most, and did not teach by pointing to himself but by building up others.

Bibliography

Kennel, Maxwell. *Ontologies of Violence: Deconstruction, Pacifism, and Displacement.* Leiden: De Gruyter Brill, 2023.

———. *Postsecular History: Political Theology and the Politics of Time.* Cham, Switzerland: Palgrave Macmillan/Springer Nature, 2022.

Kroeker, P. Travis. "Anabaptists and Existential Theology." *Conrad Grebel Review* 17 (1999) 69–88.

———. "Doubting Theology: Wisdom—Divine and Human." *Christian Century* (June 29, 2004). https://www.christiancentury.org/article/2004-06/doubting-theology-0.

———. "Educative Violence or Suffering Love? Radical Orthodoxy and Radical Reformation." *Conrad Grebel Review* 23 (2005) 19–24.

———. "Foreword." In *Toward an Anabaptist Political Theology: Law, Order, and Civil Society*, by A. James Reimer and edited by Paul G. Doerksen, ix–x. Eugene, OR: Cascade, 2014.

———. "Making Strange: Harry Huebner's Church–World Distinction." In *The Church Made Strange for the Nations: Essays in Ecclesiology and Political Theology*, edited by Paul G. Doerksen and Karl Koop, 92–99. Eugene, OR: Pickwick, 2011.

———. *Messianic Political Theology and Diaspora Ethics: Essays in Exile.* Eugene, OR: Cascade, 2017.

———. "Postsecular History or Figural Messianism?" *Political Theology* 24 (2023) 342–46.

———. "The Scandalous Drama of Trinitarian Theology for a Radical Church." *Conrad Grebel Review* 37 (2019) 146–53.

----------. "The Secular—The Political: Augustine and Political Augustinianism in Twentieth-Century Political Theology." In *The Edinburgh Critical History of Twentieth-Century Christian Theology*, edited by Philip G. Ziegler, 237–61. Edinburgh: Edinburgh University Press, 2022.

Rosa, Hartmut. *The Uncontrollability of the World*. Translated by James C. Wagner. London: Polity, 2020.

Schürmann, Reiner. *Broken Hegemonies*. Translated by Reginald Lilly. Bloomington: Indiana University Press, 2003.

----------. *Ways of Releasement: Writings on God, Eckhart, and Zen*. Edited and translated by Francesco Guercio and Ian Alexander Moore. Zurich: Diaphanes, 2024.

Extending Apocalyptic Theology

7

Decolonizing Grace

Nancy Elizabeth Bedford

This essay is a heuristic exercise, an exploration of whether grace is or could be good news in the sense of being decolonial and decolonizing.[1] Given the premise that the gospel of Jesus is good news for the poor, for prisoners, for the oppressed (as laid out paradigmatically in Luke 4), I would think so—yet I haven't often heard or read about an explicit link between liberation and grace, much less between decoloniality and grace. When I ask whether grace is decolonial or decolonizing, I'm not trying to imply that grace is not experienced personally, subjectively, existentially, individually. But I don't think the lens of individuality is enough in thinking of grace. It is a both-and: I expect grace to be liberating for us both as individual persons in community and in wider structural settings. Yet has the theological *concept* of grace, the way we've thought of grace theologically, worked in such ways?

Another set of questions in thinking about grace emerges from another direction, namely whether the concept or framework of decoloniality or of decolonial thought (at least as we encounter it here in the global North) is actually liberating (and as such, grace filled). In other words, I don't only want to think of grace in terms of decoloniality, but also of decoloniality in terms of grace. I'm not impressed with a

---

1. Portions of this essay were presented at the meeting of the American Theological Society on April 1, 2023.

decolonial performativity that is all about certain ways of expressing oneself but seems to be (a) quite ignorant of how religion in general and the Christian faith in particular actually functions in the lives of people, and (b) incapable of much traction in day-to-day life, in the vicissitudes of living and dying in these times. I don't often find the writings of those who consider themselves decolonial thinkers very grace filled, though I very much appreciate the critical questions they pose to theology and to the church.

There is no decolonial theology without the decolonizing of theology, and there is no decolonial liberation without the liberation of decoloniality. For any of these processes to be possible, we require openness to movement, change, and transformation, dynamics that theology links to the waves and the wind of the Spirit. Along these lines, one of the dimensions that I think may be lacking in our recent liberationist and decolonial conversations is that of conversion: how to repent and change directions, how to be changed by the Spirit of life. I'm not referring to conversion to a certain religiosity or ecclesiastical institutionality, but to conversion or *metanoia* as transformation and as a process of continual healing, which I'm linking here to grace.[2]

In sum, there is movement in two directions in this heuristic exercise: How does grace (as an experience and as a doctrine) stand up in the face of the need for decoloniality (or liberation)? And how does decoloniality (or liberation) look in the face of grace?

The essay is influenced directly or indirectly by P. Travis Kroeker's work at three levels, at least. First, I appreciate how he does not simply "give away" the Augustinian tradition but is capable of retrieving it from a standpoint marked by an Anabaptist sensibility. We can see this, for instance, in the way he emphasizes Augustine's messianic political theology in order to critique a particular brand of political Augustinianism that does not take into account biblical apocalypticism.[3] Second, in his work there is a quiet but persistent thread that makes reference to Simone Weil (who in turn engages her own retrieval of Augustine); this has helped nudge me toward a (re-)consideration of grace that explicitly avoids disincarnation. Third, though he expresses it in terms or categories (such as "political theology" or "messianic ethics") different from those I usually employ, I see in Kroeker's writings a push against

---

2. See Bedford, "Looking Back and Looking Forward."
3. See Kroeker, *Messianic Political Theology*, 46–63.

docetic and colonizing distortions of Christian theology and practice, an emphasis that I admire and seek to emulate.

Grace as Pneumatologically Christological and Christologically Pneumatological

The first thing that strikes me as I look over the etymology of χάρις is that it derives from χαίρω: that which delights, often linked to beauty. In the classical age, χάρις was widely used in reference to the favor of the gods. In later antiquity and Hellenism, it usually referred to a ruler's favor and/or to supernatural power that streams from the transcendent realm. I find that it is worth keeping in mind the dynamic dimension of beauty and delight, as it helps me to avoid reifying grace only as a Pauline concept narrowly referring to the salvation event. The Septuagint primarily uses it to translate the Hebrew חֵן (chen): God freely extends Godself in grace or favor to bless God's people. Clearly, the idea of God's grace is not limited only to instances of the word χάρις in the New Testament: God's loving care and generosity is depicted in many ways throughout Scripture. Jesus, in the Sermon on the Mount, for instance, describes the "Father in the heavens" as One who "gives good things" to those who ask (Matt 7:21).[4]

In thinking of the use of χάρις in the New Testament, perhaps the most helpful insight is simply to remember that grace is not exclusively a Pauline theme. There is a theology of grace in Luke-Acts, as well as significant insights to be found in John and 1 Peter (not to speak of Hebrews and James).[5] Reading across all these strands, I find that grace is characteristic of the work both of Christ and of the Holy Spirit: said otherwise, it is pneumatologically christological and/or christologically pneumatological. By this I mean that the work of Christ moves us toward the novelty and creativity of the Spirit, and that the work of the Spirit is always attuned to the way of Jesus and reminds us of him (see John 14:25–26, 16:12–15). Following this trinitarian logic, if we are speaking in terms of Christ we do so pneumatologically, and if we speak in terms of the Spirit we do so christologically. Said otherwise, grace is always grounded (christologically) in the incarnation and it always capable

---

4. Notably, Luke's account of this names the Spirit as the gift given by the Father to those who ask (Luke 11:13). All quotations from Scripture are my own translation.

5. For instance, Jas 4:6 ("God, who gives grace to the humble"); Heb 4:16 ("Let us therefore approach the throne of grace with boldness, so that we may receive mercy and find grace to help in time of need"); and Heb 10:29 ("the Spirit of grace").

(pneumatologically) of doing a new thing. Wherever grace is at work, the fruit of the work of the triune God in the world is evident in hope, peace, confidence, transformation, joy, beauty, and justice.

The Spirit Is Called Grace:[6] The Forgotten Pneumatology in Augustine's Theology of Grace

In an oft-quoted passage of the *Confessions* (10.29.40), Augustine prays, "Give what you command, and then command what you will."[7] The prayer arises in a discussion of continence, which Augustine believes serves to counter our tendencies to dispersion and helps put us back "together." As he sees it, continence is only achievable as a gift of God, and so he asks God for it as a gift. When the English monk Pelagius hears this phrase, he reacts negatively because he thinks that the theology behind it implies that God is fractious and unreasonable, demanding something of us beyond our power. Yet if we read Augustine's prayer in the light of the connection between grace and christological pneumatology or pneumatological Christology, it appears to be simply an expression of Augustine's confidence in God, who by grace provides us with all that is needed in Christ by the Spirit.

As Paul puts it, God works to give us both the desire and the capacity to live according to God's will (see Phil 2:13), and without Christ, we cannot do the things we know we should (Rom 7:15–18). Or in the words of John, without Christ we can do nothing (John 15:5). What Pelagius seems to have thoroughly misunderstood—probably because he was coming from a much different theological anthropology—is the way in which Augustine's theology of grace presupposes that God's Spirit is *always already* present and working in our lives, whether we recognize that fact or not. Even if we—like the prodigal son and like Augustine himself in his self-depiction—flee to the "region of dissimilarity" and risk falling into pieces, God is closer to us than we are to ourselves (*interior intimo meo*), holding us together and awaiting us with open arms and graceful hospitality. Even an admission of the tiny inkling that we might be welcomed by God is in itself already a gift of grace, which is why Augustine can say that "to desire the aid of grace is the beginning of grace."[8]

---

6. Augustine, Sermo 144.1.
7. Such is Boulding's translation in Augustine, *The Confessions*, 299.
8. Augustine, *De correptione et gratia* [On reprimand and grace] 1.2.

Augustine's christological and pneumatological insight about grace—characteristic of the *Confessions* but also visible throughout his work—is what I want to underline in his theology of grace. I realize that both Augustine himself and many of the Augustinianisms that arose in his wake have sometimes acted dis-gracefully. I'm not trying to defend his every decision or theological emphasis (especially not his turn to state-sponsored violence against the Donatists, his nastiness in the anti-Pelagian struggle, or for that matter his incapacity to see women as full equals to men, save eschatologically). Yet I don't want to miss the opportunity of discovering liberating threads in his theology, especially because it is so influential.

In *On Grace and Free Choice* 1.1, Augustine describes two common errors with regard to the interpretation of grace: on the one hand, to preach and defend free choice in such a way as to deny or get rid of the grace of God; and on the other hand, to defend the grace of God in such a way as to deny human free choice.[9] I find it significant that when he is giving pastoral advice, as here to Valentine and his monks, he reflects a more evenhanded and balanced understanding both of God's grace and of human agency in responding to that grace than in his polemics. Needless to say, I prefer this Augustine to the one we see in the angry, frustrated, or irritated passages from his arguments with Pelagius or Julian of Eclanum, or in the pervasive pessimism about the human condition (and the very limited number of God's elect) that many theologies seem to have inherited from him in a "long, unhappy postscript."[10]

My pneumatological reading of Augustine pulls out what seems to me a promising strand from his thought rather than trying to reflect the whole of his theology of grace across his life. My hermeneutic probably reflects the fact that the theological anthropology of my own Anabaptist faith is perhaps not as bleak as that of the inheritors of the Augustinian tradition within the Magisterial Reformation. Early Anabaptists tended to reject the bondage of the will (alongside double predestination) and to be quite confident that with the help of the Spirit it is possible to follow Jesus with one's life and to become a participant in the divine nature. Significantly, they linked the work of grace to divinization—and

---

9. See Augustine, *On the Free Choice of the Will*, 141.

10. Such is Duffy's the insightful phrase at the end of his chapter on Augustine in *The Dynamics of Grace*, 106. I think it is probably also fair to say that in practice Augustine often "underestimated the universal scope of the revelation in Jesus Christ," as Haight states in *The Future of Christology*, 70.

thus directly or indirectly to pneumatology.[11] In other words, they saw grace as the dynamic work of God, whereby God renews the divine image in humans through the Holy Spirit, making us into partakers of the divine nature (2 Pet 1:4).[12]

As Juan Luis Segundo points out, one of the problems we face in dealing with the legacy of Augustine is that he was very good at showing the weaknesses in the teaching of Pelagius but "was not so clear in picturing how the grace of God made it possible" for humans to find ourselves in harmony with God.[13] It seems to me (once again) that the key to resolving that quandary is pneumatology. We often see in Augustine the insight that the Holy Spirit, who has been given to us—who is a gift to us—comes to the aid of our weakness and pours out the love of God. As he puts it in Sermon 144.1: "Without a doubt, the grace of God is a divine gift; at the same time, the Holy Spirit himself is the maximum gift of God and that is why the Spirit is called grace."[14]

Augustine quotes Rom 5:5 often, and amplifies it, for instance at the conclusion of his treatise *Nature and Grace*: "For this love is the grace of God through Jesus Christ, our Lord, who with the Father and the Holy Spirit has eternity and goodness forever and ever. Amen."[15] Likewise, he underscores the role of the Spirit in *The Spirit and the Letter*: "This love is being poured out in our hearts neither by the sufficiency of our own will nor by the letter of the law, but by the Holy Spirit who has been given to us."[16] His discussions of grace as it relates to the Holy Spirit often connect grace to love: "When love itself is poured out in the hearts of those who believe, it is the law of faith and the Spirit who gives life to their lovers."[17] Alongside Rom 5:5, Augustine often cites 1 John 4:13 to identify the Spirit as the divine love that is from God and is God, working in our hearts: "This gift moves the Christian to appreciate and desire God above all else and to love self, neighbor, and all lower goods for the sake

---

11. See Beachy, *The Concept of Grace*, 187–88 and 227–28.

12. As Beachy puts it, their emphasis was more ontological than forensic; see Beachy, "The Grace of God."

13. Segundo, *Grace and the Human Condition*, 19.

14. My free translation of "Gratia quippe Dei, donum Dei est. Donum autem maximum ipse Spiritus Sanctus est; et ideo gratia dicitur." Augustine, Sermo 144.1.

15. Augustine, *De Natura et gratia* [On nature and grace] 70.84.

16. Augustine, *The Spirit and the Letter* 33.59, in *Selected Writings*, 284.

17. Augustine, *The Spirit and the Letter* 17.29, in *Selected Writings*, 254.

of God's goodness."[18] The Spirit "implants love which makes the heart restless with desire for good."[19] In Augustine, then, divinizing grace is tightly connected to the work of the Spirit, grace that makes us adoptive children of God and partakers of the divine nature.[20]

I also wonder whether it is worth revisiting the relevance of Augustine's insights about original sin for the structural dimensions of sin. I don't mean that we need to posit original sin in the precise way that he delineates it, but I do think he is signaling an important insight about human systems. One error of Pelagius is to privatize sin and trust too much in the capacity of individuals to make "moral" choices, a mistake in the direction of disincarnation that Augustine does not seem to make. His theology points to something important about the ways systemic or structural sin affects us, even beyond our individual desires or choices. On the other hand, his detours into an overly rigid dichotomy between nature and grace or the contortions he feels are required to explain why an infant would need baptism are not—for me—the compelling side of Augustine's reflections on grace.[21]

What draws me in is Augustine's confidence in God's engagement with us and his recognition that grace is first and foremost about the Triune God's concrete and material love for us.[22] As he puts it, we are justified by the gift of the Spirit of God; by the gift of the Spirit "there comes to be in us a delight in not sinning so that we have freedom."[23] I interpret such freedom not as privatized and spiritualized (though it is deeply personal), but experienced as communal, material, political, and structural, and deeply responsive to beauty.[24] I don't forget that for all his linguistic competence and rhetorical gifts in Latin, Augustine was a "Latin African," not a European—a man experiencing God's grace in a

18. Burns, "Grace," 393.

19. Burns, "Grace," 395.

20. Phan, *Grace and the Human Condition*, 271–72.

21. Eastern theologians—I think rightly—from the first considered this a *theologoumenon* relating to the practices of his North African church; see McGuckin, *The Westminster Handbook*, 40 et passim.

22. Burns points out that Augustine's thinking about grace was "radically historical"; as seen in the *City of God*, he "found the effects of divine operation evident not only in the individual but also in the creation and development of society." Burns, "Grace," 395–96.

23. Augustine, *The Spirit and the Letter* 16.28, in *Selected Writings*, 252.

24. Augustine's *Confessions* 10.27.38 comes to mind, of course: "Late have I loved you, Beauty so ancient and so new."

colonized body and expressing it in a colonial tongue (and sometimes also distorting that grace in colonizing ways). With all Augustine's limitations, it seems to me that at its best, his notion of grace has a pneumatological dimension with deep implications for human life and liberation from the bonds of all that is penultimate. Therein lies for me the force (or the potential force) of his theology of grace.

Decolonizing Grace

As is the case with other key Christian theological categories (such as sin, redemption, conversion, mission), the notion of grace has been reduced or constrained in ways that colonize the concept and empty out much of its transformative and liberative potential. As a theologian, I seek to decolonize the theology I do, since I hope to allow (my) theology to "give more of itself" than it would if it were hybridized and cultivated only in particular fields that are convenient for the powers and the principalities. At the same time, as someone who believes the gospel of Jesus is truly good news for the poor, the prisoners, and the oppressed, I trust also that grace as it is actualized by the Spirit of God is in itself a decolonizing, a transformative, a liberating force, beyond the effectiveness—or lack thereof—of any theological maneuvers of mine.

Primarily, when I think about decolonizing theology, I mean developing concepts and practices that are in tune with the glorious freedom of the children of God and the thriving of creation (Rom 8:21). The process sometimes requires disarticulating hegemonic common sense about the "obvious" semantic parameters of a concept. It can also mean "provincializing" certain interpretations, in order to give traction to theological understandings that emerge from different places and spaces than those that gave birth to our dominant understandings of theological doctrines or concepts—in this case, grace.[25]

Admittedly, the idea of decolonizing is fraught. I could have said "liberating grace" to indicate something quite similar, following the lead of Leonardo Boff.[26] I still love the terms "liberating" and "liberation,"

25. I'm borrowing the metaphor from Chakrabarty, *Provincializing Europe*. To "provincialize" is not to erase or deny but to understand that thought (here, theology) is not "from nowhere," and that any theology, as emerging "from somewhere," is by definition limited, "provincial."

26. See Boff's 1976 book *A graça libertadora*, rendered in English as *Liberating Grace*.

given their proximity to "salvation" and their rich theological history in Latin America. However, for this essay I chose "decolonizing" because I want to keep in the foreground the fact that we are constantly colonized and recolonized by the logic of the dominant system in our imaginations, in our desires, in our languages, and in our bodies. I also chose it because I am trying to ascertain whether decolonial thought, particularly as it circulates in English-speaking North America, can be a generative framework or is itself one that has by now been so deeply colonized that it is of no great help. I hope not, but I am not yet sure. At any rate, not everything that passes for "decolonial" or "decolonizing" is truly so, any more than everything that passes for "grace" is grace filled.

"There can be no discourse of decolonization, no theory of decolonization, without a decolonizing practice," says Silvia Rivera Cusicanqui.[27] She criticizes the "decolonialities" articulated in Northern Hemisphere academic circles—including those linked to Latin American academics living in North America—because of the ways they fall into essentialism, co-opt ideas from the South, develop language that "entangles and paralyzes their objects of study," create a new "world of references and counter-references that establish hierarchies," develop depoliticized discourses of alterity, and form "clientelist networks with indigenous and black intellectuals."[28] I take her vigorous critique as an important warning for (my) theology: this matter of decolonizing grace needs to be more than a linguistic gesture and it needs actively to resist an unwitting participation in patterns of recolonization.

If grace is decolonizing, decolonized, decolonial, it will entail a material *practice*, a sense that the grace Christian theologians speak of serves truly to liberate, to transform, to renew our lives and our structures. Decolonization is always more than a thought, a performative gesture, or a discourse.[29] "By their fruit you shall know them," as Matt 7:16 puts it. Yet in all its seriousness, grace is never grim. One of the things that Latin American liberation theology (and the theologies that are part of that genealogy) has had to learn through the decades—in order not to give up in the face of seemingly intractable problems—is that beauty and delight are an integral part of resistance to evil. Without music, dance, celebration, theology will never be liberating or decolonial. It will become bitter and self-righteous.

27. Rivera Cusicanqui, *Ch'ixinakax utxiwa*, 56.
28. See Rivera Cusicanqui, *Ch'ixinakax utxiwa*, 50–64.
29. See Rivera Cusicanqui, *Ch'ixinakax utxiwa*, 55.

Living with Grace

I find it instructive that research on how people experience grace has deep resonances with the dynamic, pneumatic flow I've been attempting to explore: "Grace is an ongoing, ever-present experience of acceptance from God, experienced in the moment-by-moment life and in relationships with one another and the divine."[30] Empirical studies of the experience of grace find that grace tends to be experienced as "receiving an unmerited free gift in response to failure or brokenness or as an encounter with goodness and beauty"; it is perceived as transformative "at the intrapersonal, interpersonal and/or situational level."[31] Though there is much that I value from our theological discussions of grace through the centuries, I worry that when they encourage detours into moralistic, individualistic, formalistic, or dualistic understandings, they rob the concept of grace of its subversive and liberating potential.

Grace itself as a theological concept is perhaps more ambiguous than I have depicted it in these pages. As Dale Irvin points out, "the ambiguity of grace as bestowing privilege has also to be acknowledged. The experience of grace has too often been associated with various forms of privilege, or election, to ignore its historical ramifications. The abundant life has been too often seen as being limited to those who are the recipients of grace, a limited number of human beings, those who are in Christ, those who constitute the 'us' over against 'them.'"[32] It is worth remembering that if it takes privilege to access grace, or if grace is synonymous with privilege, then it has lost the connection to Jesus of Nazareth and to the Spirit of Life and is not grace at all.

Additionally, even when theology simply "administers" lines of thought on grace that have been worked out and solidified through the centuries, it has "little to think about," as Boff points out. As an alternative, he proposes pondering our experiences of grace in the world: identifying with aspects of the theology of grace as it has been present in

---

30. Webster, "Experiences of Grace Among Christian Friends," 34–35. "Friends" here refers to Quakers. Webster states that whereas theologians tend to parse certain types of grace (such as common and salvific grace), this parsing did not seem helpful or necessary for most of the participants in his study; they experienced "just one grace and reveled in the fullness of its meaning for the present and the future" (29).

31. Schellekens, Dillen, and Dezutter, "Experiencing Grace," 360. This observation comes from a large qualitative study in Belgium of people aged 18–93, about 60 percent of whom identified as Christian.

32. Irvin, Response to Nancy E. Bedford, "Decolonizing Grace."

the tradition while at the same time creatively prolonging it. He suggests creating "an idiom and a line of reflection which will make us conscious of the divine grace in which we now live."[33] This sort of approach is what I had in mind in (experimentally) proposing "decolonizing grace" as a heuristic framework for the topic. Along those lines, I have attempted to "provincialize" discussions that approach grace in a binary manner in opposition to nature, sin, or the law, zeroing in instead on the pneumatological dimension of grace. I've also tried to avoid traditional taxonomies of grace or worries about predestination (single or double).

My meanderings through the topic of grace, as depicted above, suggest to me the following tentative principles with regard to the question of what it means to decolonize grace:

1. If it does not decolonize, then it probably is not grace.[34]
2. Whenever we pneumatologize grace, we will rediscover its decolonizing potential.
3. To de-pneumatologize grace is to colonize it; to decolonize grace means to pneumatologize it.

To "pneumatologize" grace in the sense I glean from the New Testament, Augustine, and other strands of the tradition, as well as from personal experiences and church life, does not mean to "spiritualize" it but rather to think of grace in terms of the wide, transformative work of the Holy Spirit in the way of Jesus. I agree with Segundo when he connects grace to the Spirit's creative work in the history of the universe,[35] expressing rather than minimizing the christological or trinitarian dimension of the doctrine.

My provisional conclusion is that grace is an expression of God's love, generosity, and compassion. We experience grace in life and in death, in personal and communal ways, in the smallest of quotidian gestures and in wider glimpses of change. The experience of grace is marked by thankfulness, delight, beauty, and the anticipation of the triumph of life, justice, and love over death, injustice, and hate. These are not optional dimensions of grace but rather an integral part of the

---

33. Boff, *Liberating Grace*, 5.

34. Needless to say, the "white Christ" or "white Jesus" of much of US Protestantism is not the One who brings grace and truth in the sense I am describing; the Jesus of white nationalism is a colonial and colonizing Jesus who brings dis-grace and untruths.

35. See Segundo, *Grace and the Human Condition*, 169–70.

way of Jesus and its liberating path of resistance to all manifestations of dis-grace. Grace is a transformative force: a gift from God and a vital mark of the presence of God's Spirit among us. The Spirit can be called the Decolonizing One.[36] Where the Spirit of the Lord is (2 Cor 3:17), there is decolonization, there is liberation, there is grace.

Bibliography

Augustine of Hippo. *The Confessions*. Translated by Maria Boulding. San Francisco: Ignatius, 2012.

———. *De correptione et gratia liber unus* [On reprimand and grace]. In *S. Aurelii Augustini Opera Omnia*. Editio latina. https://www.augustinus.it/latino/correzione_grazia/index.htm.

———. *De natura et gratia* [On nature and grace]. In *S. Aurelii Augustini Opera Omnia*. Editio latina. https://www.augustinus.it/latino/natura_grazia/index.htm.

———. *On the Free Choice of the Will, On Grace and Free Choice, and Other Writings*. Edited and translated by Peter King. Cambridge: Cambridge University Press, 2010.

———. *The Spirit and the Letter*. In *Selected Writings on Grace and Pelagianism*. Translated by Roland Teske, 217–94. New York: New City, 2011.

———. "Sermo 144." In *Sermones. S. Aurelii Augustini Opera Omnia*. Editio latina. https://www.augustinus.it/latino/discorsi/index2.htm.

Beachy, Alvin J. *The Concept of Grace in the Radical Reformation*. Nieuwkoop, Netherlands: B. de Graaf, 1977.

———. "The Grace of God in Christ as Understood by Five Major Anabaptist Writers." *Mennonite Quarterly Review* 37 (1963) 5–33.

Bedford, Nancy Elizabeth. "Looking Back and Looking Forward from the Margin of the Margins." In *Decolonizing Liberation Theology: Past, Present and Future*, edited by Nicolás Panotto and Luis Martínez Andrade, 243–56. London: Palgrave MacMillan, 2023.

Boff, Leonardo. *Liberating Grace*. Translated by John Drury. Maryknoll, NY: Orbis, 1979.

Burns, J. Patout. "Grace." In *Augustine Through the Ages: An Encyclopedia*, edited by Allan D. Fitzgerald, 393–96. Grand Rapids: Eerdmans, 2009.

Chakrabarty, Dipesh. *Provincializing Europe: Postcolonial Thought and Historical Difference*. Princeton, NJ: Princeton University Press, 2008.

Duffy, Stephen J. *The Dynamics of Grace: Perspectives in Theological Anthropology*. Collegeville, MN: Liturgical, 1993.

Haight, Roger. *The Future of Christology*. New York: Continuum, 2005.

Irvin, Dale. Response to Nancy E. Bedford, "Decolonizing Grace." American Theological Society meeting, April 1, 2023.

Kroeker, P. Travis. *Messianic Political Theology and Diaspora Ethics: Essays in Exile*. Eugene, OR: Cascade, 2017.

---

36. Dale Irvin's suggestion.

McGuckin, John Anthony. *The Westminster Handbook to Patristic Theology*. Louisville, KY: Westminster John Knox, 2004.

Phan, Peter. *Grace and the Human Condition*. Wilmington, DE: Michael Glazier, 1988.

Rivera Cusicanqui, Silvia. *Ch'ixinakax utxiwa: On Practices and Discourses of Decolonization*. Translated by Molly Geidel. Melford, MA: Polity, 2020.

Schellekens, Tine, Annemie Dillen, and Jessie Dezutter. "Experiencing Grace: A Thematic Network Analysis of Person-Level Narratives." *Open Theology* 6 (2020) 360–73.

Segundo, Juan Luis. *Grace and the Human Condition*. Translated by John Drury. Maryknoll, NY: Orbis, 1973.

Webster, Kyle T. "Experiences of Grace Among Christian Friends." DPsy diss., George Fox University, 2020.

8

Is a Messianic Theology of Science Possible? A Sketch

Douglas Harink

Is A MESSIANIC POLITICAL theology possible? Travis Kroeker's career-long efforts to answer the question have been fruitful and illuminating. My debts to his work in political theology are significant.[1] I am not aware that he has anywhere addressed directly the question of a theology of science. If we take "science" (as is often done) as a reified entity asserting its own metaphysical assumptions as truth, as distinct from the contingent assumptions, concepts, practices, and institutions that make up a loose, complex field of human inquiry and activity, there would be no reason for Travis to focus attention on science.[2] But if we take "science" as one sphere of diverse human interests and activities embedded in and shaped by complex social, institutional, economic, political, and cultural spheres of life,

---

1. See especially Kroeker, *Messianic Political Theology*. Travis's participation (along with some of his graduate and doctoral students) and co-leadership of a research group on "Saint Paul's Journeys into Philosophy" (2005–2008, culminating in the publication of Harink, *Paul, Philosophy, and the Theopolitical Vision*) contributed much to my own work in political theology. His influence is evident (and acknowledged) in my own recent effort in Pauline political theology, *Resurrecting Justice*.

2. Nevertheless, Kroeker's work often advances criticisms of the totalizing animations of modern science and especially technology, and offers a valuable starting point for projects like the present one. See, for example, "Messianic Ethics and Diaspora Communities: Upbuilding the Secular Theologically from Below"; and "Anabaptists and Existential Theology," in his *Messianic Political Theology*.

and contributing to these in important but not totalizing ways, it is not a stretch to try thinking messianically about science. This essay is an attempt to do so in a manner that in some measure follows and pays tribute to the overarching trajectory of Travis's work in political theology.

Travis's theological work has been fundamentally oriented by New Testament apocalyptic, the normative messianity of Jesus Christ, and the political-theological commitments that follow in the wake of these. Taking up these same orientations, I aim to embed the work of Christians in the sciences within a theological vision that runs deeper than the "science and religion" correlations currently on offer. This requires that I draw out the fundamental vision of reality disclosed in scriptural texts and unfold it with further conceptual range in such a way that scientific concepts and practices might be critiqued, comprehended, and clarified within a theological account rather than vice versa. Given the immensity of that task overall, I am impelled to describe what follows as no more than a sketch.

Apocalypse of the Real

It may seem odd to begin reflection on the theology-science relationship with the outrageous thought of biblical apocalyptic. What could be more offensive to the modern scientific mindset? But the thought is foundational and inescapable for Christians in the sciences.

"Apocalyptic" draws most Christians' attention to strange biblical texts in Ezekiel, Daniel, some Gospel passages (e.g., Mark 13), and especially the book of Revelation, and often fosters wild speculation on the "end times." Yet properly understood, these texts aim to provide a deeper vision of the Real—what's going on behind the scenes of nature and history as God works out God's purposes against the often death-dealing powers and trajectories of natural and historical "development." Thus, even the book of Revelation may yield important perspectives on scientific theories, aims, and practices within a theological vision. However, the basic form of apocalyptic theology that animates my project is learned from the apostle Paul, whose proclamation of the Real (the gospel) is rooted in the "apocalypse" of Christ to him (Gal 1:12) in the midst of his zealous pursuit of God's justice according to the Law of Moses. This apocalypse radically interrupted and "crucified" Paul's existing self (Gal 2:19–20) and cosmos (Gal 6:14), reconstituting them in the surpassing reality of "new creation"

(Gal 6:15). Seized by the New Real, Paul became its emissary in a world bound under the powers of Sin and Death.[3]

New Testament apocalyptic vision demands two things. First, apocalyptic declares the divine Absolute as revealed—"apocalypsed" in Pauline terms—as none other than the Personal One who interrupts, encounters, claims, and conscripts us as his own, sets us apart, and turns us toward himself as our beginning and end. So it was for Abraham and Sarah, Moses and Miriam, Isaiah, Jeremiah, Mary the Theotokos, and the apostle Paul. Second, existentially, the divine Absolute lays an absolute claim upon us: "that than which nothing greater can be thought" (Anselm) is the unconditioned condition of all being and thinking.[4] The Christian in science always already lives and moves within this Absolute condition, is claimed by it, and as Christian is called to be wholly given over to it in thought and practice. For Christians in the sciences, all aims, practices, theories, knowledges, and technologies must be understood and pursued as a living Yes to this One.

To be necessarily specific: the origin, orientation, and end of Christian understanding of all things is God's self-giving revelation (Gk. *apokalypsis*) in the incarnation, life, crucifixion, resurrection, ascension, and final coming of Jesus Christ and the sending of the Spirit upon the church. The fundamental grammar of this revelation is outlined in the Nicene and Chalcedonian definitions of the Trinity and Christology. This apocalypse is about divine initiative. If we have some understanding of the source, direction, and end of all things, it is because God graciously gives this understanding in the concrete, creaturely history of the Word-made-flesh and the Spirit, in which humans are given to participate. Further, this gift of understanding simultaneously exposes our incapacity to attain it from ourselves; human experience, insight, and reason did not lead humankind to the event of the incarnation. Jesus Christ is God's own timely, interruptive advent in cosmos and history for judgment and healing, the *apokalypsis* of the truth of God, humankind, and the cosmos. Finally, this divine event reveals that far from being predisposed to receive it, we are actively resistant and are in fact predisposed

---

3. This account of the apocalyptic Paul is informed primarily by the works of Ernst Käsemann, J. Louis Martyn, and Beverly Gaventa. My own brief accounts are offered in *Paul Among the Postliberals*, ch. 2; and *Resurrecting Justice*, 13–16.

4. I use the abstract word "Absolute" and Anselm's phrase here to signal the utter transcendence (beyond being), even impassibility and simplicity, of the Triune God. The abstractions are not substitutes for Father, Son, and Holy Spirit.

to acknowledge, bind ourselves to, and actively follow other immanent, finite principles and powers promising life, well-being, and the understanding of all things—that is, to live in untruth rather than in Truth. The Truth breaks into our enslaved, self-enclosed existences, claims us, and delivers us into the divine-human reality of Jesus Christ and the life-giving power of the Holy Spirit, evoking radical faith. This is the meaning of "Christian" for Christians in science, the existential place from which, in which, and toward which all their work proceeds.[5]

Messianic Creation

The apocalyptic event of the incarnation discloses, in the unity of divine and human natures in the person of Jesus and his form of life, something of the fundamental character of the relation of God the Creator to the creation. This is both a metaphysical and moral claim. The revelation of God in Jesus the Messiah gives understanding not only of the noncompetitive *ontic relation* of Creator and creature, but also of the *moral pattern* of the Creator in judging, healing, and redeeming creation through the Messiah's death, resurrection, and participation in divine life.[6] The nonviolent self-offering pattern of Jesus's life, crucifixion, and resurrection reveals "the grain of the universe."[7] Beyond all powers at work in the cosmos and history, the transcendent power of God is made known in the death and resurrected life of the Messiah in the Spirit. Again, while this may seem a strange thing to say to Christians in the sciences, their theories, methods,

---

5. Currently the most robust and compelling account of apocalyptically inflected theology is Ziegler, *Militant Grace*.

6. A definitive recent argument for the noncompetitive ontic relation of God and creation (or theological compatibilism) is made by Tanner, *God and Creation*. Other important figures advancing this understanding include Katherine Sonderegger, John Webster, and Rowan Williams. At some stage in my journey of teaching a science-theology course, I began to use the story of the Burning Bush ("the bush was blazing, yet it was not consumed," Exod 3:2) as a touchstone for explicating the noncompetitive ontic relation of God and creation. Along the way, I discovered that in Orthodox iconography the event of the Burning Bush is taken up as a figure of the Theotokos; in some icons they are superimposed—the Burning Bush is the Theotokos. The Burning Bush is also central to Sonderegger's understanding of the God-world relation (and other Christian doctrines); see her *Systematic Theology*, 1:80–85.

7. The phrase comes from John Howard Yoder ("people who bear crosses are working with the grain of the universe") and is taken up as the title of Stanley Hauerwas's published Gifford Lectures, *With the Grain of the Universe*. See the frontispiece of Hauerwas's book for the fuller quote from Yoder.

practices, and ends must be attuned to discerning and witnessing to Jesus Messiah as "the heart of creation."[8] How is *this one*, in full union with all dimensions of created reality, the clue to everything in creation that the sciences investigate, discover, manipulate, and technologize? How does faith in the reality of Jesus Messiah as the God-Man liberate scientific work from the reductive physicalisms and naturalisms presupposed in modern sciences? Christians in the sciences are called to discern and attend to dimensions of creaturely reality that their secular counterparts methodologically or willfully ignore, not in order to shut down scientific inquiry but as a way to keep it truly open to the Real. Such faith constantly reminds them that they and their work are always and only human: finite, broken, and radically dependent on that which they study. The modern co-optation and absorption of the sciences into all-consuming economic-technocratic visions, in which human mastery of nature and the use of all things created is the goal, is fundamentally challenged by the messianic way of Jesus. There aren't any metaphysically and morally neutral research programs. Will Christian scientists learn from the Messiah rightly to see, honor, and sacrificially serve not only other human persons, but all non-human creatures—each in its own right and according to its own inner mystery—as their "reasonable worship"?

Scriptural Hylomorphism

Central to the scriptural testimony is that the eternal Word of God, the eternal Son, is the One from whom, through whom, and for whom all creation comes into being.[9] Creation is the work of the Holy Trinity,

---

8. See Williams, *Christ the Heart of Creation*. Williams aims to make Chalcedonian Christology (the noncompetitive relation of divine and human natures in the one person of Jesus Christ) the touchstone for understanding the Creator-creature relation. Williams's probing christological explorations of the noncompetitive relation of Creator and creature are illuminating in ruling out many problematic ways of thinking about God and God's power in relation to the realms of scientific study. However, the actual messianic life and way of Jesus as God's Messiah in first-century Judea and his defeat of the powers of Sin and Death on the cross is not the guiding clue to Williams's theological metaphysics. Rather: "While the relation between Jesus and the eternal divine Word . . . is unique, it can only be understood in connection to a general conception, a metaphysical model, of how the finite and infinite relate to one another" (xiii). Does the "general conception" end up at the cross? Perhaps in some sense. But an apocalyptic understanding of the cross includes a more radical critique of power(s), including many notions of divine power, than a general conception offers.

9. The core texts are, of course, John 1:1–18, Col 1:15–23, and Heb 1:1–4.

which, in Christian retrospect, is also hinted in the first chapter of Genesis. Creation is the beginning of the creaturely history of the Word, culminating in the Word-made-flesh. Intrinsic to this claim is the "wording" of all things.

We begin with *creatio ex nihilo*.[10] However we interpret Gen 1:1–2, this doctrine is essential to understanding the God-world relation. Whatever state of *being* is intended by *tohu wabohu* (the formless void) and *tehom* (the deep—together, "the primordial chaos substrate"[11]) in Gen 1:2, it is none other than the creation *ex nihilo* of God. Theologically (if not grammatically), the hiatus between Gen 1:1 (God as Creator of everything) and 1:2 (whatever else besides God there is) is absolute, crossed only by the overflowing life and outgoing will of the Trinity as Creator.

We might detect another hiatus between Gen 1:2 and 1:3, that between the silence of God (as hovering Spirit) over *mere being* (*tohu wabohu, tehom*, which, however, seems neither static nor inert matter—Gen 1:2 hints at movement and powers) on the one hand, and the speaking of God and *creaturely being* on the other. Creaturely being is mere being formed by the call of God to be some thing or things. This is not Aristotle, but it may be discerned as a scriptural version of hylomorphism. Any existing thing is formed being and as such distinguishable from other things, and the forms of things are being's answer to the gracious, evocative Word of God "Let there be . . ." All things are thus "worded," and only are as worded: word (*logos*) is intrinsic to creation as a whole and all creaturely things; the words spoken to being by the Word are the forms of things. But this implies *morphe* not as the protological aspect of things (as, say, eternal ideas or built-in "information") but as eschatological, as the ongoing answering of being to the call of God to be this or that thing, not wholly defined in advance and never completed before the new creation. That answering comes to its *telos* in the Sabbath—the eschaton. If we wish to think in terms of the causes of things, here we have all four: material, efficient, formal, and final. Christians engaging the objects of scientific research may for practical reasons (and oftentimes dangerously) attend only to the first two causes, but they will have to

10. The interpretation of Gen 1:1 remains contested. Does it signify an absolute beginning, or a relative beginning with a pre-existing chaotic state (v. 2)? The interpretation is not decisive for the doctrine of *creatio ex nihilo*, which is developed in Christian tradition on a variety of scriptural and theological grounds beyond Gen 1:1–2. An outstanding collection of biblical, theological, historical, and scientific reflections on the doctrine is offered in Anderson and Bockmuehl, *Creation ex nihilo*.

11. Anderson, "*Creatio ex nihilo* and the Bible," 19.

understand those objects as abstractions from the real, truncations that lend themselves more readily to manipulation and technologization but not to fullness of understanding.[12] For Christian understanding of the real, the formal and final causes are determinative; all things are called by the Word into the fullness of their formal truth in living union with the Triune God—that is what things *are*. Attention to this must shape the aims and practices of the sciences in fundamental ways.

We might speculatively take this thought a step further. There is no creaturely being without "soul," each according to its own thingness. We might say this first about mere being, the primordial chaos *ex nihilo* of Gen 1:2, where the *tehom* is nevertheless full of motion and depth and ever attended by the *ruach* of God. The formless primordial deep of being is not exhausted by the divine calling into being of creaturely things. In itself, as attended by *ruach*, it remains the deep—untamed, unruly, even threatening and deadly, the unforming power at the edges of worded creaturely being, always available to the forming divine Word but not always formed.[13] It's what we call "nature," when by that we indicate what lies beyond human organization and control (disease, death, and disaster, for example), even though many "natural disasters" now often occur as a result of human impacts. Beyond the thin surface of things under human comprehension and control we become aware of the blurry edges between worded creaturely being—being called into form—and the unformed powers of the *ruach*-attended primordial deep.[14]

But all created things are also soulish, each in its own way, as worded and called toward their fulfillment; all things are thereby responsive, participating in and moved by the Word that calls them. From a scriptural-theological account of creation there is no reason to think otherwise; that non-human creatures of themselves proclaim God's glory is no mere metaphor.[15] In keeping with scriptural emphases on creation through Wisdom,

---

12. Ocean degradation, species decline and extinction, climate change, and other ecological disorders are some of the results of scientific description and practice as abstraction, without reference to formal and final causes of creaturely being as worded.

13. This is a different account of the meaning of *tehom* and *tohu wabohu* than that given by Karl Barth in his doctrine of *das Nichtige* in *Church Dogmatics* III/3. I would give a more anthropocentric account of Satan, the powers, evil, and sin than Barth does. For an outstanding recent account of Barth on these matters (across the *Church Dogmatics*), see Kelly, *Defeat of Satan*.

14. Images from the James Webb Space Telescope help us see this point.

15. An instructive theological discussion of the soulishness of all creatures may be found in Radner, *"Anima Mundi, Anima Popularum"*: "For a Christian or Jew to

the Word, and the Son, Christians are compellingly drawn toward understanding all created reality as living, conscious, telic—soulish—in some sense, or rather, in multitude senses appropriate to the untold multitudes, varieties, and hierarchies of created things. This truth evokes a humbler approach to scientific research, less driven toward mastery and use, more attuned to insight, wonder, honor, and mystery.[16]

Powers and Orders

In the ancient milieu of Scripture, "nature" was not its own entity operating in a self-contained way according to natural "laws." Nature—if the designation applies—was a complex mix of powers, sometimes in harmony, sometimes in conflict, at times beneficial to human flourishing, at times destructive. There were no clear demarcations between divine and natural powers, though perhaps not a simple identification of them either. Gods, spirits (benevolent and malevolent), humans, and the various dimensions of cosmic reality were interwoven into fluid, complex, dynamic, interacting fields of energy and relationships. Of course, spacio-temporal patterns and regularities in nature were observed, studied, accounted for in various ways (scientific inquiry is not simply "modern") and used to human benefit. But these were not considered manifestations of natural "laws," that is, as universal structural features intrinsic to cosmic reality, existing independent of the gods. They were part of the interplay of powers.

---

speak of something with a body and a soul, is to say that God graciously grants identity to *any* creature. Hence, in Scriptural terms, the breadth of created things including rocks and waters are 'living' in a fundamental way, capable of 'singing' praise to God (cf. Pss 96–98; Isa 44:23; Luke 19:40)" (195, emphasis original). Thinking "soul" in a metaphysical key, Leidenhag, in *Minding Creation*, provides a robust critique of philosophical and theological "emergentism" and an equally robust "welcome" of contemporary panpsychism on the way to her own version of Christian panpsychism in keeping with theological orthodoxy and creation *ex nihilo*. Arriving at a somewhat similar destination, but more adventurously through varieties of modern sophiology (occult, Orthodox, and Catholic), Martin, in *Submerged Reality*, argues for a Wisdom-infused, eschatologically oriented understanding of creation and the need for a corresponding "poetic metaphysics" in order to "see" creation as it is and is becoming. These metaphysical ventures may be helpful supplements in advancing a Christian theological vision against physicalist reductionisms.

16. Practically speaking, of course, an attitude of scientific humility and wonder cannot make it into research funding proposals, where the only thing that counts is useful technological outcomes.

Modern science (Newtonian physics, Darwinian biology) changed everything about this picture. In the past four centuries the European and Western world has come to imagine cosmic reality in terms of the "laws" of nature, structurally intrinsic to the physical world, universal, exceptionless, and fundamentally describable in terms of mass, movement, and mathematical relationships—all independent of any account of divine or spiritual agency. So it has remained until recently.

A new account of things is emerging. The success of modern science (and it has been successful according to its own self-understanding and aims) seems to be built on the idea of natural laws as described above. But it only seems so. In truth, the real-world advances in the sciences (from physics and biology to sociology and economics) depend on a "motley assembly" of models and methods that often employ an equally motley assembly of not always compatible theoretical constructs.[17] The highly abstracted theoretical constructs of universal natural law (particularly in physics) depend substantially on the rule of *ceteris paribus* (other things being equal)—that is, on theoretically bracketing out all conditions but one affecting an object, conditions that are nevertheless always actually operative upon the real-world objects and systems that practicing scientists work with.[18] In other words, "natural laws" cannot simply be descriptively mapped onto actually existing things in the world, or vice versa. They are imagined ideal states of affairs rather than living cosmic reality, which is simultaneously well-ordered, "dappled," and unruly on all fringes because multiple powers are always at play. Theoretical constructs, like the ancient gods, are often useful in imagining cosmic reality insofar as they are intrinsically related to the powers of nature, even as they transcend those powers in some way, but the relation of theories to powers remains mysterious and not itself subject to scientific description. Aware of this, Christians in the sciences, engaging a "motley assembly" of theories, models, and methods, may yet muddle through to new knowledge and understanding of "dappled"

---

17. The phrase "motley assembly" is from Cartwright, "Dethronement of Laws," 38. The essays in Cartwright and Ward, *Re-thinking Order*, which address physics, biology, sociology, and religion, are essential reading for coming to understand nature not in terms of universal and exceptionless laws but "as a realm of diverse powers, potencies, and dispositions, a 'dappled world.' There is order in nature, but it is more local, diverse, piecemeal, open, and emergent than Newton imagined." *Re-thinking Order*, back cover. The phrase "dappled world" is from Cartwright, *Dappled World*.

18. See Cartwright, "Dethronement of Laws," 33–36; and Horst, "From Laws to Powers," 165–66.

nature as their way to honor and respectfully and humbly manage some of its "powers, potencies and dispositions."

Powers and Disorder

If we accept theologically on the one hand that the primordial chaotic condition of mere being remains as background to the creative Word calling things into being—things being formed in response to that call—and on the other hand that things are only fully formed by their end, as sharing in divine life, then their being thus on the way to their fulfillment requires their continuing responsiveness to and participation in the Word's call. For human things (beings) this participation in its fundamental form is trust—trust in the One who calls from beyond being, trust that this One graciously gives them life and all things and moves them toward fulfillment. Human persons and peoples become idolaters when their trust gravitates toward the powers of nature—the wild animal in the Garden, the allure of purely immanent goodness, beauty, and truth, the rational capacity to attain wisdom apart from the divine commandment (Gen 3:1–6). The turn away from the Word-beyond-Being to the word of immanent unruly being as the power of life—this turning away as sin—is the beginning of evil. In sin, the powers of nature are separated in human imagination from the Power beyond nature and trusted to bring humankind to its "natural" end.[19] And so they do. Apart from the Word that calls and forms and fulfills, the end is death, "passing away," the return to mere primordial being. Neither gods nor the highest theoretical constructs—great powers though they may be—can save from that end. Yet for human beings formed by the Word's gracious call, there remains another *telos* ever before us, the end beyond mere being for which we yearn but which we have no inherent capacity to attain. We strive against our "natural" end as death, aligning with (through the mastery of technique) and giving allegiance to as many immanent powers as we can in this struggle, and warring against other human beings and nature itself. Scripture calls this alliance with the powers of nature enslavement to Sin and Death, the

19. I signal with "natural" the timeworn theological discussion of nature and supernature and pitch my tent among those who would argue that our supernatural end—sharing in divine life—is in fact always already the very condition of our creation by the Word from the beginning. In other words, the supernatural end is the natural condition of humankind (and other creatures); the "natural" end in death, as return to mere being, is in fact unnatural for worded beings.

über-powers that reign in every sphere of human existence, including the sciences. Spurred on by economic, political, and societal forces, Christians, like others in the sciences, are tempted to trust their capacity for theoretical comprehension, methodological mastery, and technological deployment of natural powers to bring about the salvation of humankind. STEM (science, technology, engineering, and mathematics) is one of the most compelling, all-consuming, and enslaving idols of our time, its worship one of the clearest indicators of humankind's failure to hear and obey the call of the forming, fulfilling Word of life.

Divine Presence and Power

As various genealogies of our secular age have demonstrated, there has been an overwhelming loss of the sense of divine presence and power in the world. However the trajectory of that loss is traced, the rise of modern sciences is at the heart of the story. The contributions of the likes of Isaac Newton, Charles Darwin, Adam Smith, and Karl Marx can, it seems, fully account for the powers and movements of cosmic and historical reality. There is no need for the God hypothesis.

Some theological responses to this loss attempt to engage modern science directly, on its own terms, and adjust theological grammar to the theoretical languages of the natural and social sciences.[20] More recently, however, there has been a return to classical theism, with its doctrines of divine aseity, simplicity, impassibility, invisibility, and so on. At the heart of these doctrines is the radical ontological distinction of God from all that is not God. A certain priority is given to "negative theology," the importance of declaring what God is *not*: God is not an entity among other entities, not a power among other powers—not the greatest, not the highest, not the most powerful, not the most enduring. God is not on any scale of being, duration, or power, but beyond them absolutely.[21] God as God *is* Being, Eternity, Movement, and Power in the inexhaustible mystery of Triune Love. God's *relation* to all that is not God—expressed as creation *ex nihilo*—is not causal, temporal, or spatial; it is

---

20. Varieties of process theology, open theism, panentheism, and some political theologies come to mind. For the theological failures of efforts to accommodate theology to scientific discourses, see Buckley, *At the Origins*; and Milbank, *Theology and Social Theory*.

21. Steenbuch, *Negative Theology*, provides an excellent brief historical account of negative theology from Moses, Plato, and Philo to Radical Orthodoxy.

Grace, Gift, Love, Word, Spirit, the eternal and infinite source, power, condition, and context of all that is. God *reveals* this relation: the "I AM that I AM" in utter aseity *is* the Love that arrives in time to rescue the children of Abraham, Isaac, and Jacob; *is* the Word that calls forth and forms created things; *is* the Word made flesh in Jesus of Nazareth; *is* the Spirit that raises Jesus from the dead. As currently practiced, the sciences refuse this revelational reality and have structured their theories, methods, and practices in fundamental rejection of it. Creation, incarnation, resurrection are unavailable within the closed worlds of reductive physicalisms and theological emergentisms.

Apocalyptically, messianically speaking, God's invisibility is God's radical, "simple," undivided presence to all things. God's power is God's "holy humility" in relation to all things.[22] These divine attributes cannot become the subject of scientific discourse, cannot be wrested into its categories, for God is not another thing or another power among creaturely things and powers. Christians in the sciences must avoid attempts to "find" and point to God among, or even at the edges of, all the creaturely things and powers it studies, even invisible powers. The first purpose of science is to praise the God beyond all things and powers. For Christians in the sciences, anything and everything at all, as creatures destined for new creation, partakes of the divine apocalypse, the revelation of the unconditioned, gracious presence and power of God beyond all things, from whom and in whom and for whom all things exist. Christians as "theological scientists" studying creaturely things are ever breaking out into praise and resolving into silence, along with geckos, gorillas, and galaxies.

---

22. The phrase "holy humility" is from Sonderegger's account of divine omnipotence in *Systematic Theology*, 1:151–332. My discussion of God's presence and power is deeply indebted to Sonderegger. Her rejection of the language of God as cause—even Prime Cause—is especially helpful and apropos of this discussion: "Omnipotence cannot be a species or form of causality because the most general definition of cause—to bring something about—entangles the Divine Being, in its very Power, with creation, or *per impossibile*, with other gods. . . . God's very relation to the world cannot be a species of a larger category, even the broadest forms of cause or 'bringing about.' *God is His own relation to the world: there is no other*" (178–79; emphasis added). I must add that God as God's own relation to the world is manifest most fundamentally in the crucifixion and resurrection of Jesus.

Participatory Realism: Science as Spiritual Practice

Cosmic reality seems to be available to human rational probing, description, explanation, and manipulation. Such realism is the core assumption of all modern natural sciences. Concepts, equations, models, and methods seem somehow to connect reasoning to the real. But while this is a core, usually unexamined, assumption in the sciences, its truth has been questioned from the beginning of philosophy. In the current atheistic context of reductionist physicalism, this assumption is more questionable than ever. How is it that a thought, a vocalization, or a set of signs (a number, a letter, a sentence, or equation—more broadly, language), generated by electrical pulses across synapses in the brain, sometimes inscribed on a surface, connects to or makes available a thing in the world? And why *this* vocalization and not that, why *these* signs and not those? Why and how have we agreed on which ones? Is the real available to us without them, and if not, where is the real? Is it "out there" or is it in the language? What is truth? These are the puzzles of philosophical realism and its opposite, idealism, and other variations such as pragmatism. They seem distant from ordinary science textbooks, classrooms, and labs, but Christians in the sciences do well to think about them.

The rough-and-ready or naive realism behind the instrumentalism of quotidian practicing scientists betrays a faith in the validity of the relation between minds and things that bears critical scrutiny. This is not the place for such scrutiny.[23] Instead, I make a few claims that seem important for Christians thinking about truth in sciences. First, all science is intrinsically linguistic (requiring widely accepted concepts, vocalizations, and signs), which is to say science is hermeneutical. Science seeks to understand things and relations with and through language, indeed, never without language, including such highly specialized languages as mathematics. Equations and sentences are not identical with the things they are about, yet the things they are about are simply unavailable and incommunicable apart from equations and sentences. There is no science without language. Further, there is no language apart from massive complexes of shared experiences, practices, and agreements among populations, minimally among a population of scientists in a given field. And those populations and their shared languages are embedded in and affected by multitudes of

---

23. A recent, exceptionally (excessively?) thorough treatment of these questions and critical analyses of various figures and proposals regarding them, along with a compelling Christian understanding, is offered by Pickstock, *Aspects of Truth*.

environments, relationships, powers, and interests: geographical, cultural, societal, economic, political, military, and so on—manifest especially in which scientific endeavors receive funding.

The real arrives as language. Modernity is troubled by this. Isn't science about coming to know the truth of things "as they are," "out there," independent of the all-too-human mess of language and its users? If there is nothing "out there" available to us that is not always already "languaged," what is truth in science? What do we know?

To these questions I propose a Christian response rooted in the conviction of creation by God the Word. The Word calls out to mere being, "Let there be . . . ," and things are formed. The in-forming of things is their participatory movement into the Creator's call. Apart from the language of the Word there are no things. Language is intrinsic to the existence of things as soul to body; things *are* insofar as they are *spoken* by and share in the divine Word. As being languaged by the Word, we humans participate in creaturely reality more deeply and truly through language than through any other aspect of our being. Equations, models, sentences are less descriptions that correspond to things "as they are" than they are attentive, even loving, participations in "worded" things, bringing things more fully into manifestation and their anticipated reality. As Catherine Pickstock puts it,

> In order for there to be truth, the connection between things and spirits . . . must be more than arbitrary. Truth must, in some sense, be *supposed* to be there. It must be analogical, really relational, horizontally participatory and teleological. To know must be an event in the life of that which is known, bringing it to fruition. . . . If there is truth, if things and spirits are connected, then one need no longer speak of a strange "correlation," but of a mysterious "conformation."[24]

Seen this way, the sciences themselves might be considered spiritual practices: not the examination and exploitation of inert, passive, soulless "objects," but disciplined intellectual participation in and relation to living things within living wholes, seeking out not only their spatio-temporal relations and causes but also their form and final good. And the final truth of things, apart from which they are not truly known, is not simply immanent to those things but is their participation in the Eternal: in the creating power of the Word, the liberating

24. Pickstock, *Aspects of Truth*, 256–57.

power of the crucifixion, and the resurrecting, new-creating power of the Spirit.[25] To know things in their truth is to know things as they have been apocalypsed in the Messiah, in whom we share through the Spirit and faith. For Christians, this kind of "theological science" is their "rational worship." It is how their sciences become more, much more, than they are currently constrained to be.

Conclusion

I have attempted to sketch some aspects of an apocalyptic-messianic theology of science. For Christians in the sciences, the theories, methods, and practices of the sciences have their place within convictions about the nature of the real: the Real as the Triune God, and the real as creaturely being and things called into being as creatures by the divine Word. Christians confess reality in its truth to be revealed—apocalypsed—in the event of the incarnation, crucifixion, resurrection, and exaltation of Jesus Christ and the sending of the Spirit. This demands that Christians move beyond trying to correlate the findings of scientific inquiry with Christian convictions (or worse, explain those convictions within the terms of the sciences). It requires a grasp of the real shaped ontically and morally by the fundamental theological claim of the Gospel and existential commitment to dwell within that claim in every aspect of scientific aims, inquiries, and practices.[26]

Bibliography

Anderson, Gary A. "*Creatio ex nihilo* and the Bible." In *Creation* ex nihilo: *Origins, Development, Contemporary Challenges*, edited by Gary A. Anderson and Markus Bockmuehl, 15–35. Notre Dame, IN: University of Notre Dame Press, 2018.

Anderson, Gary A., and Markus Bockmuehl, eds. *Creation* ex nihilo: *Origins, Development, Contemporary Challenges*. Notre Dame, IN: University of Notre Dame Press, 2018.

Book Symposium on Paul Tyson, *A Christian Theology of Science. Modern Theology* 40 (2024) 678–742.

Buckley, Michael J., SJ. *At the Origins of Modern Atheism*. New Haven, CT: Yale University Press, 1987.

---

25. Pickstock, *Aspects of Truth*, 257–58.

26. For a recent attempt to formulate a robust theology of science along these lines, see Tyson, *Christian Theology of Science*. See also the critical Book Symposium on Paul Tyson, *Christian Theology of Science*, with response by Tyson, in *Modern Theology*.

Cartwright, Nancy. *The Dappled World: A Study of the Boundaries of Science*. New York: Cambridge University Press, 1999.

———. "The Dethronement of Laws in Science." In *Re-thinking Order: After the Laws of Nature*, edited by Nancy Cartwright and Keith Ward, 25–52. London: Bloomsbury Academic, 2016.

Cartwright, Nancy, and Keith Ward, eds. *Re-thinking Order: After the Laws of Nature*. London: Bloomsbury Academic, 2016.

Harink, Douglas. *Paul Among the Postliberals: Pauline Theology Beyond Christendom and Modernity*. Grand Rapids: Brazos, 2003.

———, ed. *Paul, Philosophy, and the Theopolitical Vision: Critical Engagements with Agamben, Badiou, Žižek, and Others*. Eugene, OR: Cascade, 2010.

———. *Resurrecting Justice: Reading Romans for the Life of the World*. Downers Grove, IL: IVP Academic, 2020.

Hauerwas, Stanley. *With the Grain of the Universe: The Church's Witness and Natural Theology*. Grand Rapids: Brazos, 2001.

Horst, Steven. "From Laws to Powers." In *Re-thinking Order: After the Laws of Nature*, edited by Nancy Cartwright and Keith Ward, 157–83. London: Bloomsbury Academic, 2016.

Kelly, Declan. *The Defeat of Satan: Karl Barth's Three-Agent Account of Salvation*. London: T. & T. Clark, 2022.

Kroeker, P. Travis. *Messianic Political Theology and Diaspora Ethics: Essays in Exile*. Eugene, OR: Cascade, 2017.

Leidenhag, Joanna. *Minding Creation: Theological Panpsychism and the Doctrine of Creation*. London: T. & T. Clark, 2021.

Martin, Michael. *The Submerged Reality: Sophiology and the Turn to a Poetic Metaphysics*. Kettering, OH: Angelico, 2015.

Milbank, John. *Theology and Social Theory: Beyond Secular Reason*. Oxford: Blackwell, 1990.

Pickstock, Catherine. *Aspects of Truth: A New Religious Metaphysics*. Cambridge: Cambridge University Press, 2020.

Radner, Ephraim. "*Anima Mundi, Anima Popularum*: The Soul of Israel and the Church in the Hierarchy of Salvation." In *Covenant and the People of God: Essays in Honor of Mark S. Kinzer*, edited by Jonathan Kaplan et al., 193–203. Eugene, OR: Pickwick, 2023.

Sonderegger, Katherine. *Systematic Theology*. Vol. 1, *The Doctrine of God*. Minneapolis: Fortress, 2005.

Steenbuch, Johannes Aakjaer. *Negative Theology: A Short Introduction*. Eugene, OR: Cascade, 2022.

Tanner, Kathryn. *God and Creation in Christian Theology: Tyranny or Empowerment*. Oxford: Blackwell, 1988.

Tyson, Paul. *A Christian Theology of Science: Reimagining a Theological Vision of Natural Knowledge*. Grand Rapids: Baker Academic, 2022.

Williams, Rowan. *Christ the Heart of Creation*. London: Bloomsbury Continuum, 2018.

Ziegler, Philip G. *Militant Grace: The Apocalyptic Turn and the Future of Christian Theology*. Grand Rapids: Baker Academic, 2018.

9

Miracles and Matter
Toward a Messianic Theology of Creation

Justin D. Klassen

In Thomas Merton's final speech before his untimely death in 1968, he told his audience, "Christianity is against alienation. Christianity revolts against an alienated life."[1] I have long appreciated this statement as a distillation of the Christian imagination. The foundational claim that the eternal wisdom of God is made flesh in Christ, that we might know divinity in the faces of neighbors and enemies, and in all created things, is a clear revolt against any alienating conception of beatitude. If our ultimate origin and end is irrevocably present to and in creation, there is no cause to separate salvation from the healing of what God has made, no reason to look elsewhere to find home.

From a different point of view, however, Merton's statement might seem patently indefensible. There is ample evidence to suggest that the modern Christian imagination has been a potent vehicle of alienation. A year before Merton's death, Lynn White Jr. wrote that ecological degradation would only get worse unless we abandoned Christian conceptions of God and creation.[2] For White, Christianity's relentless focus on the divine-human relationship, to the exclusion of what human beings share with all creatures, was a key cause of modern humanity's alienation from

1. Merton, *Asian Journal of Thomas Merton*, 335.
2. White, "Historical Roots of Our Ecologic Crisis."

materiality. Five and a half decades later, self-described Christians are among the least likely to recognize climate change as a moral problem, ostensibly owing to their belief that God alone is in control of the climate.[3] In practical terms, to worship such a God is to be assured of the authorization of one's every whim, since any ecological consequences will occur in God's exclusive domain. Whatever is meant by "salvation" here has nothing to do with the entanglements of earthly life.

This sort of alienation from the material world prompts many of my students to abandon Christianity. Climate change is part of the picture, but their concerns extend to everyday experiences of joy and pain as well. Life as they know it brims with beauty and suffering, the depths of which are scarcely mentioned by modern people of faith. They seek concrete ways to repair social injustices, habits that promote mental health, practical ways to enrich their friendships and resist tech addiction, and avenues to creativity. But the Christians they are familiar with would rather police what Rowan Williams calls the furniture of their imaginations[4] than attend urgently to the world's fragile beauty or to their own material flourishing. Worshiping the Christian God therefore seems less like a balm than an abstraction and a waste of time, "thoughts and prayers" that heal nothing and nobody.

The implication of this critique is that worship ought to be measured by enacted commitments, not bumper stickers. And here my students, many of whom are religiously unaffiliated "nones," demonstrate their surprising agreement with a crucial lesson of messianic political theology. Travis Kroeker explains that messianic ethics "must take seriously the theological terms of the way of life of a people: what it worships and therefore what shapes its judgments about what is most important."[5] Relating worship to our "judgments about what is most important" implies that all of our doing is apocalyptic, in the sense that it discloses materially what we treat as sovereign, for good and for ill. People can say they worship or don't worship all kinds of things; the real question is, What do their actions reveal about their judgments? How do those judgments inflict or heal the wounds of alienation? While they are unlikely to appeal to the Bible positively or at all, there is a sense in which the nones' objection to alienating forms of worship functions as a messianic critique of modern Christianity.

3. Alper, "4. Religious Groups' Views on Climate Change."
4. Williams, *Tokens of Trust*, 6.
5. Kroeker, "Whither Messianic Ethics?" 55.

This unexpected alignment highlights the abiding relevance of apocalyptic messianism in an age of ecocrisis. While apocalyptic theology has a reputation for emphasizing the irreducible otherness of God and the consequent "perpendicularity" of revelation, what its vision of faith shatters is not the empirical experience of ordinary life but the alienating devotion to gods of violence manifest in our contemporary ecological crisis. As I will outline in what follows, the apocalyptic appeal to Christ found in messianic ethics, while radically opposed to prevailing conceptions of reality, effects a humble return to our creaturely senses, to the empirical world of matter and its miraculous goodness. It is a resounding revolt against alienation.

Ecocrisis and Worship

After completing my doctorate, my first teaching post was at a liberal arts college in Texas. I remember explaining to students that apocalypse means "uncovering," not the fiery finale of all things described by literalist interpreters of Revelation on television and Christian radio. Now it strikes me that there might be less of a difference than I implied between these definitions of apocalypse—end and disclosure. Maui is scorched earth.[6] Salmon are disappearing from their familiar runs in coastal rivers.[7] Entire ecosystems are falling prey to shortsighted human cravings.[8] Anthropogenic warming continues to narrow zones of habitability increasingly colonized by the rich.[9] Economists are sounding the alarm that growth, our functionally unquestionable aim, may soon prove elusive.[10] The end is indeed nigh—maybe not the end of everything, but certainly the end of this way of being. What is being disclosed by, and in, this ending?

Messianic political theology suggests that this moment reveals nothing less than the nihilistic violence of our favorite gods. The primary challenge of this claim is that most so-called secular North Americans do not think of their economic and political commitments as religiously inflected. At the same time, many churchgoers prize their fidelity to the

6. Bogel-Burroughs et al., "How Fire Turned Lahaina into a Death Trap."
7. Einhorn and Whittaker, "California Salmon Stocks Are Crashing."
8. Cuadros, "Has the Amazon Reached Its 'Tipping Point'?"
9. Borenstein and Jordans, "World on 'Thin Ice' as UN Climate Report Gives Stark Warning."
10. Andreoni, "Economists Would Like a Word."

biblical God without interpreting therein a necessary reconfiguration of their lives politically and economically. In other words, for both parties, our participation in the political and economic status quo is not valid territory for theological investigation. This tacit agreement is a tremendous boon to the established order and to those who benefit from it most directly. And this is precisely where messianic political theology presses its point: when we fail to acknowledge societal arrangements as manifestations of spiritual commitments, we effectively render those arrangements omnipotent. For all practical purposes, we worship them.

I remember experiencing the magnitude of this interpretive shift on a personal level. I was raised in an evangelical Protestant milieu where faith referred to an inner sphere of correct belief. Its political implications extended to holding positions on certain moral issues but not to cultivating genuinely alternative forms of social life. Faith in Christ justified a believer to God in the heavens but meant little in terms of who or what had sovereignty over one's daily choices. When I came to McMaster University, conversations with Travis illuminated another way of thinking about faith, as "a politics of 'counter-sovereignty,' based on the sovereignty of weakness displayed in the crucified Messiah."[11] From this angle, worship is inherently political and politics is always about worship, because how we live together is inescapably shaped by our attributions of sovereignty—our "judgments about what is most important." In biblical terms, it is worship that redounds to either destruction or life. What we treat as sovereign can lead us toward either wholeness or nothingness.

The material effects of societal arrangements therefore tell us something about the quality of our spiritual judgments. The destructiveness of contemporary global economic arrangements, inflicted on human beings and on the whole of creation, is or at least should be obvious at this point. "Our ways of life are killing people," Cynthia Moe-Lobeda explains in *Resisting Structural Evil*. "Moreover, through myriad forms of ecological degradation we are disrupting a fundamental quality of God's garden—its life-generating capacity. We are *uncreating*."[12] The fact that corrective action seems slow and difficult, if not impossible, reveals our firm and even religious attachment to shared judgments about what is most important. Our society "generally promotes the excessive consumption and wealth accumulation enabled by prevailing

---

11. Kroeker, "Whither Messianic Ethics?" 54.
12. Moe-Lobeda, *Resisting Structural Evil*, xvii; emphasis original.

economic arrangements as *a good life*."[13] Living a "good life," so defined, is what is most important to us. Measured by the empirical effects of this judgment, we worship a god defined by the pleasures of control and domination above kinship and cooperation. The fires of Hawaii and the disappearing salmon of Oregon and the climate-induced global migration crisis reveal this god as a god of death.

Messianic political theology makes a particular claim about the apocalypse of true, life-giving sovereignty in Jesus, arguing that the one the Bible calls anointed is the prism through whom all judgments about what is most important are revealed in their truth and consequences. Jesus, in this sense, is both the lens that clarifies the wounds inflicted by bad judgments about sovereignty and the healing balm for those very wounds. Even so, abundant data show precipitous declines in religious affiliation and literacy in recent decades. We are, from a certain point of view at least, a society that has given up on worship. To preach Jesus against mammon in such a context is to risk adopting the persona (non grata) of the street-corner crank. Therefore, what messianic ethics must also clarify is the fact that nothing solidifies our commitment to gods of violence and destruction like the presumption that we have no gods at all.

Modern Dogma

William Cavanaugh's argument in *Migrations of the Holy*, following Carl Schmitt, is that secularization "is not the stripping away of the sacred from some profane remainder. Rather, the state takes over the theological underpinnings of the church, and casts them in terms that are only implicitly theological."[14] At least since the end of World War II, the meaning of our fidelity to the nation-state has become increasingly economized. As goes the economy, so goes the nation-state. Richard Norgaard, Jessica Goddard, and Jalel Sager argue that the rise of modern economic theory is rooted in the emergence of social sciences that sought to explain human actions and their proper ends ("what is most important") without reference to the transcendent—in other words, without any reliance upon dogma.[15] For example, Adam Smith's *Wealth of Nations* "initiated a train of reasoning that provided new, plausible, and implementable roles for

---

13. Moe-Lobeda, *Resisting Structural Evil*, 4; emphasis added.
14. Cavanaugh, *Migrations of the Holy*, 96.
15. Norgaard et al., "Economism and Ecological Crisis," 404.

markets and government."¹⁶ The premise that markets freed from regulatory constraints would guide themselves invisibly yet naturally toward equilibrium was justified with reference to growth, whose quantifiability gave it the sheen of objectivity.

This idea began to take hold while the increased burning of fossil fuel energy was leading to rapid industrialization, population growth, and major ecological disruption. In other words, massive transformations in human relationships to neighbor and creation took place at the same time that religious accounts of societal flourishing were being superseded by ostensibly more transparent and "rational" logics. "The whole process was regulated by the norms of the market, by new ethical stances that privileged today's production, even greed, unbalanced by the needs of future generations."¹⁷ The assumption was that if greed was generative of quantifiable economic growth, then its morality could not be relevant—at least not as an objective matter.

Accepting this shift was not automatic or immediate. During the nineteenth century, mainstream teachers of economics were often trained in theology, too. As such, some tempered the new theories with reference to the established wisdom that treating wealth as humanity's highest good is spiritually and psychologically ruinous. Greed might be an engine of GDP growth, but that fact alone cannot make it a life-giving disposition. We know from the way economics is taught today, however, that this tension between what we might call the instrumental and moral sides of economic theory was not to last. "At the end of the nineteenth century," as Richard B. Norgaard, Jessica J. Goddard, and Jalel Sager explain, "younger scholars, trained in universities rather than theology schools, sought to distance themselves from moral questions and become more scientific, objective, and 'professional.'"¹⁸ Moral questions were seen as qualitative and thus nonrational, lacking in "real" explanatory power. "Objective and professional" came to mean looking at the numbers and only the numbers.

The irony is that all of this is premised on an inherently moral claim, the claim that moreness is goodness, or at least the only kind of goodness we can consider in public reasoning. Another irony is that modern economic theory's putative objectivity has insulated it from

---

16. Norgaard et al., "Economism and Ecological Crisis," 404.
17. Norgaard et al., "Economism and Ecological Crisis," 405.
18. Norgaard et al., "Economism and Ecological Crisis," 406.

criticism and therefore led to its failure as a science (i.e., a discourse inherently subject to questions and challenges). Norgaard, Goddard, and Sager show that modern economics is founded upon assumptions that today must be accepted *dogmatically*, lest one risk charges of immorality, treason, and sacrilege. Economism rationalizes "how greed is good, in opposition to long-standing, religiously rooted moral teachings stressing care for others," defines "the growth of GDP as progress, human destiny, and social transcendence,"[19] and renders these assumptions de facto unquestionable. Any proposal to regulate the petrochemical industry to protect the environment or to order the pharmaceutical industry toward the common good is treated first and foremost as a threat to "the economy," which is to be measured only by the logic of economism—that is, GDP growth. The effective implication is that such growth, which has no moral content beyond a bigger number, is sacred and unquestionably real. "Incorporating virtues of care and stewardship in today's public economies comes up against economism, which has powerfully inscribed mathematical formalism as a prerequisite to policy choices."[20] Under these terms, "better" can never trump "more."

For all their purported objectivity, of course, economism's premises are manifestly bad. Their moral shabbiness as guiding principles, their flimsiness as a trustworthy description of "what is most important" if one would lead a fulfilling and healthy life, is utterly clear. This is why few if any would call it wise to teach one's children to worship the absolutes which in public life we nonetheless agree to live by as if their mathematical rectitude were a sure sign of divinity. Ray Anderson was the CEO of a carpet company in 1994 when he suddenly recognized this absurdity. Following the perfectly legal arrangements of our global economic system had made him a professional "plunderer." Anderson later described it as his spiritual awakening, a "spear in the chest" moment.[21] This, precisely, is what must be disclosed or "apocalypsed": the fact that much of our common life demands a spiritually debasing fidelity to a bad absolute, a false god. We never gave up on worship; we simply gave our god the facade of objectivity so we could pretend we're not making judgments at all. In this, we adopted the most alien and hostile of deities, an unquestionable sovereign that cannot but spoil the goodness of creation.

19. Norgaard et al., "Economism and Ecological Crisis," 409.
20. Norgaard et al., "Economism and Ecological Crisis," 409.
21. Vitello, "Ray Anderson, Businessman Turned Environmentalist."

A Violent Metaphor

Economism is one example of the broader modern tendency to elevate purely immanent rationality to a position of supreme authority. Kroeker suggests that the root of this tendency is the mechanized view of reality that came to dominate the Western mind in the wake of the Scientific Revolution. The story that prevails today says that we *know* the world in a deeper way than ever before because we have learned to construe it in terms of rational causality. We assume that seeing the world through the lens of this metaphor—as a machine that functions similarly to a logical argument or mathematical equation—is to know it without metaphors at all. Rather than myths, feelings, intuitions, and so forth, we modern human beings have learned to trust only quantifiable data, which we tell ourselves is the key to accessing the world's own deep logic. Advances in human technological power, which arise through the application of the mechanistic metaphor to creation, have done much to convince us of the validity of this shift from metaphor to ontology.

Clearly there *are* practical benefits to looking at the world as a rational machine. Modern medicines and treatments, bridges and skyscrapers, airplanes and text messages all arise from its application. As a tool, the lens is useful. Yet it became something more than a tool. In *The Death of Nature*, Carolyn Merchant argues that the Scientific Revolution was not only about developing new uses for the mechanistic metaphor but justifying it as ontology. "The rejection and removal of organic and animistic features and the substitution of mechanically describable components would become the most significant and far-reaching effect of the Scientific Revolution,"[22] she writes. For Merchant, it makes sense to describe the shifts this way—as expressions of a will to reject and remove other metaphors—because the shifts occurred in a context of fear. "Fear that nature would interdict her own laws, that the cosmic frame would crumble, and that chaos and anarchy would rule lay just beneath the sheen of apparent order."[23] The mechanistic metaphor's promise of order and predictability in an uncertain world made it seem a safe harbor for familiar fears. The world is ultimately an equation we can manipulate and control. Illuminating this existential appeal helps to destabilize the metaphor's pretense of objectivity. As such, we can ask, with Kroeker, "To what extent is our technoscience guided by a morally laden *logos* of nature that denies its

22. Merchant, *Death of Nature*, 125.
23. Merchant, *Death of Nature*, 126.

own moral judgments and assumptions as such (by assuming that the mechanistic metaphor is objective rational description)?"[24]

To answer this question, we should consider the moral concomitants of the Scientific Revolution—the domination of nature, women, and people of color. It serves the epistemological status quo very well to imagine that the championing of scientific rationality as we know it has only an accidental relationship to the destructiveness of colonialism. Yet it is not accidental that Francis Bacon's proposed innovations in methods of scientific investigation coincided with a societal backlash against women's independence. "Like wild chaotic nature," Merchant writes, "women needed to be subdued and kept in their place."[25] Indeed, any form of human existence that did not appear to submit to the mechanistic rationality of the leading men of the day became a legitimate target of coercive power. "Because women's physiological functions of reproduction, nurture, and childrearing are viewed as closer to nature, their social role is lower on the cultural scale than that of the male."[26] Similar assessments were made of non-European cultures, which, not manifesting the preferred rationality of the colonizer, were not even cultures at all but so many examples of unreformed chaos. The hope was that "a new experimental method designed to constrain nature and probe into her secrets would improve and 'civilize' society."[27] In other words, the logic of colonialism and that of the Scientific Revolution reflect each other in ways that ought to make us more skeptical of the latter than we might prefer. It is domination all the way down.

From the standpoint of messianic ethics, the issue is not the mechanistic metaphor per se, but our existential relationship to it. The assertion of its objectivity is rooted not in empirical discovery but in a fantasy of control that is spiritually ruinous. Thus Kroeker argues that Christian faith, as "a politics of counter-sovereignty," must relativize the metaphor by affirming reality's excess of rationally transparent causality: "The belief in resurrection puts the scandal of miracle at the very heart of reality: God creates the world *ex nihilo* at each moment; the world is not an immanent becoming according to causal laws of nature but is rather the gift of divine spirit."[28] When we read "miracle," it is tempting

24. Kroeker, *Messianic Political Theology*, 164.
25. Merchant, *Death of Nature*, 132.
26. Merchant, *Death of Nature*, 143–44.
27. Merchant, *Death of Nature*, 148.
28. Kroeker, *Messianic Political Theology*, 162.

to imagine that we have flown to an immaterial and alien realm. Yet here is the paradox: the "scandal" Kroeker appeals to is not a call to abandon empiricism, to forsake material creation and its tangibility in the name of a remote God. Instead, becoming open to "the scandal of miracle" means attending humbly to the world, which we did not author and thus do not command. It involves the simple act of admitting that our logics of creation are always metaphorical and inevitably reflect contestable judgments about what is most important. When we witness that some of those judgments generate violent and destructive outcomes, this act of admission becomes a spear in the chest, an awakening.

Kroeker writes that "our only possible redemption from such violent colonial politics lies in remembering again that we did not make the world, nor therefore do we measure it."[29] This redemption is messianic because it occurs through the form of the anointed one, who renounces control and enters into communion with creation. Dominating modes of relationship are transformed by Messiah Jesus's apocalyptic judgment about what and who is truly sovereign. This judgment "takes its ethical bearings from the non-possessive biblical vision of a creation in which human creatures dwell in the world vulnerably, in a manner that opens it up to being made new by the ever-new agency of the sovereign Creator."[30] To dwell in the world vulnerably means, in the first place, to acknowledge that the world's truth, rooted in God, exceeds human understanding and control. This is by no means a polemic against the human quest for truth and understanding but a reminder that genuine knowing cannot be found through a denial of our embodied creatureliness. The truth is not denied to us; it has been made flesh.

Empirical Miracles

Erazim Kohák, in his inimitable book *The Embers and the Stars*, develops a helpful and resonant account of truth and embodiment in philosophical terms. Kohák suggests that our modern sense of the world is mediated by "ideal constructs," which are efficient and orderly representations of reality. He offers the example of "clock time," which does not exist anywhere "out there" in nature. In actual fact, "it is the experience of the evening, lodged in the shadows about me and in the weariness of my arms,

---

29. Kroeker, *Messianic Political Theology*, 141.
30. Kroeker, *Messianic Political Theology*, 142.

which is the primordial given. Only secondarily do we designate it by a clock reference or acknowledge it in an internal time consciousness."[31] Of course clocks exist, and the referent of clock time is "real" in that sense, but ontologically it is secondary. For the sake of efficiency, clock time construes each second according to a common measure, while the primary thing, our embodied *experience* of time, is less ideally ordered. Kohák knows it would be impractical to navigate our days with only our perceived energy or fatigue as referents, of course. "For the sake of managing our environment purposively—say, of dispatching rockets to the moon or of assembling a body of persons for a lecture on temporality—such a natural time reference is, admittedly, not overly effective."[32] Just as the mechanistic metaphor for the natural world can be put to good use, so too is clock time a tool properly fitted to certain tasks. The problems arise only "when we attribute an ontological significance to it, treating it no longer as a construct contingent upon and restricted by prior purpose but as a description of the true nature of reality."[33]

The key problem with this attribution is that it downgrades the priority of lived experience, which becomes merely "subjective." In truth, our sensate experience has "all the hardness of the real, a logic of its own—the rhythm and vigor of fatigue, of day and night, the cycle of the seasons in the life of nature and humans alike. Its stages, though personal, are not in the least arbitrary."[34] The orderliness of the ideal construct tempts us to assert its primacy, because order promises control, or at least the semblance of stability amid the flux of time. It is comforting to assume that constructs we have authored are in fact the sovereign arbiters of reality, but here we take comfort in an alienating fiction. "It is what we are accustomed to treating as 'objective reality'—the conception of nature as a system of dead matter propelled by blind force—that is in truth the product of a subject's purposeful and strenuous activity."[35] Kohák does not mean that all is lost when we conceptualize and symbolically represent reality, nor that we should return to some mute and prehuman state. His point is that when we treat as objective the description of nature "as a system of dead matter," we become less than fully human. For it is always on the basis of our sensate materiality that we are able

---

31. Kohák, *Embers and the Stars*, 16.
32. Kohák, *Embers and the Stars*, 16.
33. Kohák, *Embers and the Stars*, 17.
34. Kohák, *Embers and the Stars*, 16.
35. Kohák, *Embers and the Stars*, 6.

to conceptualize in the first place. Humanity was not made for the ideal construct, but the ideal construct for humanity.

My argument is that messianic ethics rests on a similar claim. The point of Kroeker's statement that "the world is not an immanent becoming according to causal laws of nature but is rather the gift of divine spirit"[36] is not to reject our empirical sense of the physical world for the sake of a religious abstraction. It is, rather, to deactivate the power of any abstraction (e.g., "the economy") to obscure the miracle of our creatureliness. It is a revolt against alienation. One could read this, from Kohák, in the same light:

> We need to suspend, for the moment, the presumption of the ontological significance of our constructs, including our conception of nature as "material," and look to experience with a fresh eye, taking as our datum whatever presents itself in experience, as it presents itself and only insofar as it presents itself, using the totality of the given as the starting point, the justification and the ultimate test of all speculative claims.[37]

We need, in other words, to dwell in the world humbly, as creatures, that we might apprehend the miraculous precisely in the empirical.

In like manner, Kroeker's messianic appeal to "the scandal of miracle" at each moment of the world's becoming is a call to communion with creation rather than a leap away from it. It is a theology of creation whose Messiah-mediated theocentrism is not some alienating appeal to an unconcerned abstraction but a critical disclosure of our wounding fidelity to gods of violence. We have hidden this fidelity in our purportedly civilized rationalism and economism, but it is now disclosed in its destructive consequences. The invitation of a messianic imagination is to wake up and discover in our humble creaturehood the healing gift of life, and to participate in the miracle by advocating for those who suffer and desire flourishing.

Conclusion

In one of the first seminars I took with Travis in graduate school, we read apocalyptic political theology, beginning with Karl Barth's *Epistle to the Romans*. "Faith beholds life and existence where the man of the world

---

36. Kroeker, *Messianic Political Theology*, 162.
37. Kohák, *Embers and the Stars*, 22.

sees nothing but death and non-existence; and contrariwise, it sees death and non-existence where he beholds full-blooded life," Barth writes.[38] To interpret God's participation in creaturely reality as such an upending interruption could suggest an alienating form of theism. I remain grateful to Travis for showing me, among many other lessons, a different way to read the disruption—namely, as the disclosure and clearing away of thoughtless assent to destructive logics, for the sake of creation itself. Mechanistic metaphors masquerade as objective reality. The reason we judge them sovereign is that they do not demand humility in the face of mystery. They leave us in charge. But in this way, they also keep us alienated from the possibility of communion with our fellow creatures. They pay us the compliment of making us possessors of creation, but the flattery is ultimately hollow, since we too are creatures. Domination leaves no one unscathed. In Kroeker's words, "The *logos* become flesh provides a different account of the causality of reality, one that (Paul claims) sets us free from the subjugating *nomoi* of worldly powers and authorities that have blinded human eyes to true reality and its (hidden, mysterious) causes."[39] This is not a logic puzzle, as it sometimes seems in Barth and others. Instead, it is a way of seeing what is right in front of you via a humility that enlivens and generates rather than destroys. It is an affirmation of ordinary experience as the locus of miraculous goodness, a profound and consoling revolt against an alienated life.

Bibliography

Alper, Becka A. "4. Religious Groups' Views on Climate Change." In *How Religion Intersects with Americans' Views of the Environment*. Pew Research Center, November 17, 2022. https://www.pewresearch.org/religion/2022/11/17/religious-groups-views-on-climate-change/.

Andreoni, Manuela. "Economists Would Like a Word." *New York Times*, March 31, 2023. https://www.nytimes.com/2023/03/31/climate/economic-growth-climate-change.html.

Barth, Karl. *The Epistle to the Romans*. Translated by Edwyn Clement Hoskyns. London: Oxford University Press, 1968.

Bogel-Burroughs, Nicholas, et al. "How Fire Turned Lahaina into a Death Trap." *New York Times*, August 15, 2023. https://www.nytimes.com/2023/08/15/us/hawaii-maui-lahaina-fire.html.

---

38. Barth, *Epistle to the Romans*, 141.
39. Kroeker, *Messianic Political Theology*, 162.

Borenstein, Seth, and Frank Jordans. "World on 'Thin Ice' as UN Climate Report Gives Stark Warning. " *AP News*, March 20, 2023. https://apnews.com/article/un-climate-change-report-ipcc-guterres-science-30d8451c0f3fb7b8a857e3ed4fd01172.

Cavanaugh, William T. *Migrations of the Holy: God, State, and the Political Meaning of the Church*. Grand Rapids: Eerdmans, 2011.

Cuadros, Alex. "Has the Amazon Reached Its 'Tipping Point'?" *New York Times Magazine*, January 4, 2023. https://www.nytimes.com/2023/01/04/magazine/amazon-tipping-point.html.

Einhorn, Catrin, and Max Whittaker. "California Salmon Stocks Are Crashing. A Fishing Ban Looks Certain." *New York Times*, April 3, 2023. https://www.nytimes.com/2023/04/03/climate/salmon-fishery-closed-california.html.

Kohák, Erazim V. *The Embers and the Stars: A Philosophical Inquiry into the Moral Sense of Nature*. Chicago: University of Chicago Press, 1987.

Kroeker, P. Travis. *Messianic Political Theology and Diaspora Ethics: Essays in Exile*. Eugene, OR: Cascade, 2017.

Kroeker, P. Travis. "Whither Messianic Ethics? Paul as Political Theorist." *Journal of the Society of Christian Ethics* 25 (2005) 37–58.

Merchant, Carolyn. *The Death of Nature: Women, Ecology, and the Scientific Revolution*. New York: Harper & Row, 1989.

Merton, Thomas. *The Asian Journal of Thomas Merton*. Edited by Naomi Burton et al. New York: New Directions, 1975.

Moe-Lobeda, Cynthia D. *Resisting Structural Evil: Love as Ecological and Economic Vocation*. Minneapolis: Fortress, 2013.

Norgaard, Richard B., et al. "Economism and Ecological Crisis." In *Routledge Handbook of Religion and Ecology*, edited Willis Jenkins et al., 402–11. New York: Routledge, 2017.

Vitello, Paul. "Ray Anderson, Businessman Turned Environmentalist, Dies at 77." *New York Times*, August 11, 2011. https://www.nytimes.com/2011/08/11/business/ray-anderson-a-carpet-innovator-dies-at-77.html.

Williams, Rowan. *Tokens of Trust: An Introduction to Christian Belief*. Louisville, KY: Westminster John Knox, 2007.

White, Lynn. "The Historical Roots of Our Ecologic Crisis." *Science* 155 (1967) 1203–7.

10

The Speed of Christian Patience

PAUL G. DOERKSEN

UNDERSTANDING THE CHRISTIAN PRACTICE of patience necessarily begins with reflection on God's patience with creation, including divine patience with humanity. Karl Barth argues that God provides time and space for humans to become what they were created to be, to live in faithful response to the free love of God, even in the permitting of sin and rebellion without delivering immediate judgment, though it may well be justified.[1] God's patience extended toward humanity suggests strongly that God's work includes a dimension of taking time with creation, a way of working with the world that takes into account the nature of that created world as finite and even circumscribed. The world is the place of God's incarnation and redemption, and the fact "that He does not grow weary of it implies patience at the roots of His creation."[2] God's creation and desiring of earthly life is itself a revelation of his patience, for only through that patience can it thrive. Put another way, God's love does not desire in a short time what can only be realized in a long time—it allows play, abundance, and even apparently superfluous folly, all of which suggests that "life without patience is impossible. For patience bears with the imperfect, uses restraint in dealing with the

---

1. I'm drawing on Karl Barth's famous formulation in his treatment of God's perfections, here wisdom and patience. Barth, *Church Dogmatics* II/1, 408.
2. Guardini, "God's Patience," 19.

defective, spares the unfortunate and surrounds them with that deep-seated concern which is not only compassion, but also a sense of sharing with them a common destiny."[3]

God's patience implies that humans also have been given time to be patient. However, the connection between divine and human patience must be attended to carefully, since the practice of human patience cannot be said to be based on some straightforward imitation of God's patience. Seeking to conform human striving to God's action and attitude toward the world seems to identify an analogy that is not necessarily present in the relationship of God and human. Rather, human patience is called for and made possible by God's covenant of grace with humanity.

> God's patience, one must even say, awaits a *dis*-analogous response. We are not asked to do the impossible: correspond ourselves to the God who has time and space, and who gives time and space to us, by giving God time and space to act in freedom and obedience. Nor, for that matter, are we asked to exercise restraint or to take on the responsibility of incarnating God's patience. Our task is otherwise: to move towards and purposefully to inhabit the Kingdom which is the in-breaking gift of the patient God.[4]

Divine patience takes time, and human patience, even though not directly analogous to divine patience, seeks to make good on God's patience. That is, I want to show that God's mode of action in the world, understood as taking time and giving time, calls forth this making good on God's patience extended toward us. Put another way, creaturely temporality produces an ethical relationship to that temporality.[5] God's gifts give us time in which to relate to God and learn to be fully human by taking time with our moral development, with others, and with creation, resisting what we might call the "absolutism of the present," embracing a certain kind of modesty and patience in accepting the limits of human existence.[6]

Discussions of the practice of patience, whether divine or human, often reflect close correlations between patience and slowing down in response to concerns about the hurried pace of current society, setting up a kind of binary discourse in which patience understood as slowness is

---

3. Guardini, "God's Patience," 23.
4. Jones, "On Patience," 288.
5. Quash, "Making the Most of the Time," 97.
6. Quash, "Making the Most of the Time," 98.

pitted against impatience characterized as haste. Despite the considerable merit in such discourse, we should be careful not to make the mistake of believing that all slowness is constructive and that all haste is destructive. To be committed to slowness itself or to reject all haste as a matter of principle is to embrace a distorted notion of the practice of Christian patience. Instead, an embrace of the practice of patience, made possible by God's patience toward the created world, while indeed often slow is not a commitment to a singularly slow pace. Therefore, I will call for an embrace and practice of *urgent patience*, which seeks to move at a faithful pace, made possible by God's patience toward us. My argument proceeds along the following lines. First, I will establish the positive dimensions of a correlation between patience and slowness, but without pushing that correlation to the point of equation. Then, I bring to view the present dangers of haste, while arguing that we should resist the temptation to pit slow against fast in absolute terms. Therefore, I consider the potential dangers in slowness and the potential benefits of haste, and conclude with the argument that we should be committed to patience, not to a particular pace, and so I put forward the notion of urgent patience, which can be practiced at various paces without giving way to impatience or to the destructive possibilities of slowness or haste.[7]

The Importance of Slow

It is no hard task to find encouragement to slow down in our fast-paced world, whether this means participating in the Slow Food movement, Slow Church, or other such initiatives.[8] John Swinton contributes an important and theologically substantive discussion to this issue of divine and human patience as they relate to temporality, slowness, and a faithful understanding and practice of "pace." He argues against modern understandings where time is "perceived as morally neutral and instrumental, a blank sheet onto which humans can inscribe their histories."[9] Instead, Swinton claims, a mode of time exists within the world that is perceived by understanding God's time for creation.[10] Swinton argues that to have

---

7. I take the term "urgent patience" from Scott, "Church and the Urgent Patience of Christ."

8. See, for example, Honoré, *In Praise of Slow*; Matties, "Slow Food"; and Kenneson, *Practicing Ecclesial Patience*.

9. Swinton, *Becoming Friends of Time*, 42.

10. Swinton, *Becoming Friends of Time*, 49.

the same attitude as Christ means we need to allow God's time to come upon us, emphasizing the reception of something given to us by God. As God's time is received, we enter a specific relationship with time. To be humble, contingent, obedient, and faithful requires that we inhabit God's time in ways that match the nature of the time within which we live. If time is indeed a gift, this inevitably and absolutely changes our relationship to it, meaning that we cannot attempt to master time.[11] Rather, Swinton advocates becoming friends of time. Drawing on 2 Pet 3:8–9, Swinton presses the case for what he calls "the Three Mile an Hour God."[12] God is a God who takes time to do things, and the love of God is inexorably slow, which redefines our understanding of the meaningful nature of slow. Swinton explicitly connects the speed of love to patience, love, and wisdom. Such ways of being in the world are radically different from those that seem to dominate our times. God's time welcomes friendship and is slow, patient, kind; it is a way of being in the fullness of time that is not determined by productivity, success, or linear movement toward radically individualistic goals. It is a way of love, a way of the heart that produces qualities such gentleness, perseverance, and love: these are the qualities of people who have become friends of time.

> The ideas of slowing down; taking Sabbath, finding Sabbath moments; learning to be gentle, patient, and perseverant; coming to know what it means to become friends with slowness, and becoming friends of time (the practises of timefullness) are not easy to understand or to value in a world filled with clocks and meaningless evolutionary history. However, if in God's coming kingdom "slow is the new fast" and if gentleness and vulnerability are the new modes of transformative power, we find ourselves in a quite different world that holds to a different perception of time.[13]

Swinton's work, with its focus on a theology of disability, rehabilitates the notion of slowness, rescuing it from being used as a pejorative descriptor of people with disabilities. In Swinton's use of the term, slowness becomes a positive and constructive challenge to take up in our understanding of God's "speed," as well as the work of humans in the world in which we find ourselves. Swinton's embrace of slow goes beyond some

---

11. Swinton, *Becoming Friends of Time*, 64.

12. Swinton takes this notion from Koyama, *Three Mile an Hour God*, especially 3–8.

13. Swinton, *Becoming Friends of Time*, 83; the longer argument is found on 68–83.

notion of simply recapturing so-called natural ways of being in the world, such as a farmer waiting for the crop.[14]

Swinton's reframing of slowness as a constructive, faithful way of being in the world provides guidance not only for his theology of disability but more broadly for faithful Christian discipleship. Against the suggestion that slowness might be seen as passive, being friends of time provides a way to get beyond having to choose between being active and passive, as working slowly can be understood as participation in faithful activity but at a pace that does not seek to control people or events. In addition, to frame slowness as faithfulness, as being a friend of time, resists the notion that slowness amounts to something like a loss of initiative; that waiting, for example, is only preparation for action rather than part of what it means to be a faithful disciple.

The Dangers and Violence of Haste

Recognizing a positive correlation between patience and slowness leads us to confront a related dynamic, namely, that haste should be recognized as a potentially destructive force, one that denies patience and indeed is antithetical to the practice of patience. The embrace of slowness, as seen above, is often accompanied by warnings against the dangers of haste—slow is good, haste is bad. We see this in Swinton: "The time of the clock has taught us to pay attention to the realm of time in ways that are grasping, utilitarian, instrumental, focused, selfish, and ultimately idolatrous."[15] Theologically understood, inordinate speed or impatience, moving at a speed that is faster than is faithful, must be considered at its heart a sinful resistance to God. This can also be seen in John Calvin's insistence on connecting patience to Christ's example and describing impatience as unfaithfulness: "We must bear patiently, since impatience would be insolence against God."[16]

Jeffrey Vogel, drawing on Irenaeus's account of patience, argues that the human propensity to take what can only be given, to grasp what can only be graciously bestowed is at the heart of the haste of sin, seen originally in Adam and Eve's hurry to grasp what could only be given. "In the

---

14. I am using "natural" here in the way Kierkegaard uses that term in his discussion of patience. Kierkegaard, *Eighteen Upbuilding Discourses*, 160–63.
15. Swinton, *Becoming Friends of Time*, 57.
16. Calvin, *Institutes of the Christian Religion*, 2:711.

Genesis story, Adam and Eve are shown trying to take what God was going to give them anyway once they could keep it. In their impatience, they cut themselves off from the life of God, by forsaking the very condition necessary to participate in it."[17] This original haste is the root of sin: it is a desire for closure, a wish to be done with waiting, which is different from the work of Christ, whose central role in Irenaeus's theology is to be the one who receives from God, undoing the disobedience of Adam and reorienting humanity to God. Put another way, "If it is haste that alienates human beings from God, insofar as it leaves them ill-disposed to receive divine life, a fitting salvation would have to undo this impatience."[18] And so Vogel argues that Jesus's consent to receive from God "reversed the haste of sin," constituting a refusal of haste, "a rejection of the temptation to lunge and grasp at premature completion."[19]

Kelly Johnson, in her essay "Hurry and the Willingness to Be Creatures," warns against haste, arguing that we hurry but we don't change. Our hurry is a manifestation of anxiety about time, a fear of losing or wasting it. "The moral problem of a hurried culture is not its love of speed, but its collective evasion of the truth about ourselves and our world; we are creatures, living in an unfolding time whose purposes we did not create."[20] Johnson shows that modernity has attempted to use time as raw material, as commodity, even arguing that time became for Western European society "the seedbed of global capitalism" in an attempt to maximize its utility, wherein time "became an item for exchange, rather than an aspect of creaturely life."[21] Seen this way, hurry becomes a social practice, useful as evasion and necessary for maintaining our place in the world of empty, objective time.[22] Not having an ethical dimension to our temporality allows for the cultivation of the delusion that we both know and can shape temporal events to our liking, which engenders the danger of instrumentalization of time, which is a denial of appropriate "metachronical modesty" and results in "frantic unrest [which] is the unrest of those who think they have to save themselves."[23]

17. Vogel, "Haste of Sin, the Slowness of Salvation," 448; the longer argument is found on 443–59.
18. Vogel, "Haste of Sin, the Slowness of Salvation," 451.
19. Vogel, "Haste of Sin, the Slowness of Salvation," 454.
20. Johnson, "Hurry and the Willingness to Be Creatures," 12.
21. Johnson, "Hurry and the Willingness to Be Creatures," 13.
22. Johnson, "Hurry and the Willingness to Be Creatures."
23. Quash, "Making the Most of the Time," 99, 100, 114. A further case can be

In a recent influential social-scientific study, Hartmut Rosa provides a nuanced account of the dangers of speed within modernity, captured in the term "social acceleration."[24] Rosa asserts that the constitution of society and social process is radically temporal in nature, a fundamental dimension that much of social-scientific analysis has largely ignored. He identifies in these analyses a pervasive "forgetfulness of time" and a focus instead on structural differentiations, cultural rationalization, individualization of personality, and domestication of nature, all of which are treated as static. To address this forgetfulness, Rosa, who understands modernity as the "perception of the progressive dynamization and shortening of periods of time associated with events, processes, and changes," analyzes social processes by paying attention to the effect of time, especially with respect to social acceleration, which unfolds in waves, produces shifts in social arrangements, and encounters resistance and countertendencies.[25] Rosa highlights three dimensions of acceleration: (a) technical acceleration, which is goal directed, evident especially in the fields of transportation, communication, and production; (b) acceleration of social change, seen in the escalation of the rate of social change in structures, knowledge, social practices, and social orientations; especially important here for Rosa is the concern for the shortening periods of time defined as "present"; and (c) acceleration of the pace of life, in which we experience a lack of time and an increasing number of episodes of action per unit of time.[26] Rosa is also interested in the relationships among these dimensions. That is, the processes of acceleration in the three dimensions interact in such a way as to create an unstoppable feedback loop.

---

made for the importance of recognizing the dangers inherent in speed or haste, and the significance of the practice of patience for resisting those dangers, especially the danger of violence. This notion of the violence inherent in speed owes much of its currency to the philosophical work of Paul Virilio, which has been taken up in a theological key by Chris Huebner. Huebner's concern centers on Virilio's analyses of violence in the contemporary world, analyses that he draws into theological conversations focused especially on Christian understandings and practice of peace. "Virilio highlights the epistemological and political prioritization of speed, as exemplified in related technological developments involving the commodification of knowledge as information and the rapid and wide-ranging developments in the techniques of surveillance. Because of the largely unquestioned triumph of these forms of power, Virilio argues that violence has come to organize the very way we act or think." Huebner, "Patience, Witness, and the Scattered Body of Christ," 57.

24. Rosa, *Social Acceleration*.
25. Rosa, *Social Acceleration*, 299, 300.
26. Rosa, *Social Acceleration*, 301.

Technical innovations represent a powerful instigator of social change, which creates compulsions to adapt, while accelerated social change represents a forceful driver of increases in the pace of life. "Therefore, social acceleration has become a self-reinforcing process in modernity. It places the three domains of acceleration into a reciprocal relationship in mutual escalation that takes on a circular form and is almost entirely impervious to social or political interventions."[27]

Rosa's analysis of social acceleration leads him to identify several societal dangers within modernity that are directly related to speed. Among other concerns, he claims that acceleration of the pace of life results in fear of missing out and a compulsion to adapt, creating a life consisting of a rapid succession of episodes without the ability to transform lived events into genuine experience. Social acceleration also raises the problem of attempting to become infinitely fast so as not to miss out, essentially attempting to live several lifetimes in one, which is doomed to failure. The increase of realized options also multiplies the number of realizable options, thus failing to address the "missing out" problem.[28]

Further, Rosa connects these acceleration dynamics to military and state-centered competition for the conquest, control, and defense of territories. All of this acceleration in its various dimensions and connections results in a "frenetic standstill." Says Rosa, "The dialectical inversion of acceleration and movement into rigidity and standstill, which is, so to speak, a leitmotif of my analysis of the modern acceleration process, culminates in a 'postmodern' political culture that dispenses with the claims to autonomy and identity that have always characterized the project and ethos of modernity ... *a condition where nothing remains the same but nothing essentially changes.*"[29] Living in this kind of a world produces significant alienation, which results from living in the condition of frenetic standstill.[30]

The embrace and practice of slowness as a way of recognizing the ethics of temporality, of resisting grasping attempts at control, of acknowledging the importance of receiving gifts, of making good on God's patience, of becoming friends of time—all of these factors help us to recognize and resist the dangers exposed when considering the effect of haste; dangers such as the logic of violence, programmatic

---

27. Rosa, *Social Acceleration*, 308; quotation on 309.
28. Rosa, *Social Acceleration*, 307–11.
29. Rosa, *Social Acceleration*, 314; emphasis original.
30. Rosa, *Social Acceleration*, 318.

immediatism, a lack of faith and trust in God. We have the strong impression that slow and fast are to be pitted against each other in absolute terms (slow = good; speed = bad). A further obvious implication, then, would be that we ought to commit ourselves to practicing slowness and avoiding speed. However, it is not the case that slow is intrinsically good and speed intrinsically destructive. Rather, it is Christian patience to which we ought to commit ourselves; patience, which is often slow, can also act in urgency. Put another way, patience has a variety of tempi. Slow can and does have a shadow side, and speed or haste can be deployed in constructive ways; my claim is not for an embrace of slowness in general or rejection of speed in general, but an embrace of Christian patience that includes faithful urgency.

The Danger of Slow Violence

To embrace a belief in the violence of haste may occlude the possibility of seeing the dangers that lurk in a commitment to slowness, which seem to be more difficult to identify, since slowing down carries with it so many constructive possibilities. Yet there is a dynamic at play here in which something with seemingly great promise may also disguise its own destructive possibilities. For example, William Cavanaugh sees this kind of danger in the proliferation of consumer choices and the so-called free market, which seem to offer endless freedom of choice, but in reality that "freedom" covers over "depredations of naked power."[31] Freedom, seen by many as an unmixed good, especially when "conceived as an absence of interference," offers "no common ends to which our desires are directed. In the absence of such ends, all that remains is the sheer arbitrary power of one will against another."[32] This dynamic of a surface appearance of some good that disguises a destructive shadow side is also seen in slowness. Here the danger is that of slow violence, a term that has been given significant currency in the work of Rob Nixon, who develops the notion to mean "a violence that occurs gradually and out of sight, a violence of delayed destruction that is dispersed across time and space, an attritional violence that is typically not viewed as violence at all . . . neither

---

31. Cavanaugh, *Being Consumed*, 28. Thanks to Grant Poettcker for bringing Cavanaugh's argument to mind.

32. Cavanaugh, *Being Consumed*, 2.

spectacular nor instantaneous, but rather incremental and accretive."[33] As Jill Didur claims, Nixon's book "represents an important engagement with the problem of making visible the uneven burden and long-term social, cultural, political, and environmental effects of such (environmental disaster) events."[34] Nixon distinguishes between slow violence and structural violence, arguing that the former has a "wider descriptive range in calling attention . . . to broader, more complex descriptive categories of violence enacted slowly over time."[35] In her review of *Slow Violence*, Lindsay Dillon observes that "Nixon emphasizes change and movement, the extensive temporalities, slow-moving mutations, and imperceptible ecological transformation that are constitutive of modern power structures, through which, as he puts it, 'time becomes an actor.'"[36]

One obvious implication of Nixon's work is a shift from understanding violence as being situated primarily in the military realm; rather, violence does its work in many quotidian dimensions of life that are often ignored in the search to understand and address violence. In a recent article, Laura Lysen and Paul Martens deploy the interpretive insight of Nixon's work in a theological key by examining the practices of the apparel industry. In the course of their examination, they seek to address a too-narrow view of violence as limited to the military sphere, arguing that the near-invisible systemic and slow violence of exploitative economic arrangements and systematic environmental degradation implicates all of us.[37] The authors frame their argument within the debate between neo-Anabaptists and neo-Augustinians regarding intentional and discreet actions such as policing and war.[38] Lysen and Martens are at pains to show that both sides need to be much more cognizant of the fact that they are all involved in violence that destroys both friend and enemy, that they must come to grips with the violence that is endemic to what either or both of them consider to be peace. Both sides are culpable of the kind of violence that has its primary life in day-to-day destructiveness, in a politics of death whose logic is to consume until there is nothing left, a dynamic seen in many quotidian dimensions of life and put on display here with a probing study of the violence and

33. Nixon, *Slow Violence*, 2.
34. Didur, "Provincializing Ecocriticism," 585.
35. Nixon, *Slow Violence*, 11.
36. Dillon, Review of *Slow Violence*, 830.
37. Lysen and Martens, "How Can We Love Our Enemies?" 462.
38. Lysen and Martens, "How Can We Love Our Enemies?" 462, 463.

exploitation that make up the apparel industry. The argument contained in this article serves as a dire warning that slow violence is of great concern across ideological and theological lines, and that obfuscation of any violence, fast or slow, reduces our capacity to see and repent of the kind of violence that is not primarily military in nature.[39] Paying close attention to the reality of slow violence is especially important for those traditions that oppose military violence, given the temptation to believe that such resistance constitutes a full-fledged rejection of violence and embrace of peace. The exposure of slow violence puts the lie to any self-righteousness on the part of peacemongers.

The Practice of Urgent Patience

Just because God does not hurry does *not* mean that we never should act with urgency. It is useful to make a distinction between moving quickly and hurrying, if the latter carries with it a sense of recklessness, a lack of attention, a grasping. As Kelly Johnson puts it nicely, "Grace can move quickly, but it does not hurry."[40] Hurrying carries with it the sense of a social practice that allows for moving too quickly to be able to confront what we must confront; hurrying allows for evasion of the truth about ourselves and the world, substituting quick action for patient practice. However, if that is the case, the problem isn't really the love or deployment of quick action, it's the collective evasion of truth by following a pace that restricts us from seeing what needs to be seen. The use of speed itself isn't always cause of destruction, but rather the use of speed to avoid truth and to grasp what cannot be controlled is the more fundamental problem. Christian patience is in fact delusionary if it is understood as "an invitation to escape from the tasks of large struggles against gargantuan and fast-moving whirls of destruction."[41]

The real problem is that slowness can also be instrumentalized in ways that are destructive. That is, if slowness is used as a contingent way of achieving whatever goals one might have, a means to an end, then it may well be equally as dangerous as haste, although slowness may appear to be directly opposite to haste. If both speed and slowness are contingent

---

39. Lysen and Martens, "How Can We Love Our Enemies?" 474.
40. Johnson, "Hurry and the Willingness to Be Creatures," 14.
41. Coles, "Pregnant Reticence of Rowan Williams," 193.

means to ends, they may have more in common than first meets the eye. That is, haste can become constructive or violent, so too slowness.

Recognizing the constructive possibilities of haste is important, since doing so can reveal the temptation to romanticize slowness.

> The obvious solution to excessive hurry is "slowing down," and for those of us fatigued from living in a hurry, slowing down sounds very appealing. We harbor visions of gentle mornings of sunrise and birdsongs, long walks with loved ones, homecooked meals, and long restful sleep. . . . The romance of slowing down hides from us the reasons we do not want to slow down for long, the reasons we cling to our hurry.[42]

Johnson's observations here are important to acknowledge—that while hurrying reveals and expresses all manner of pathologies, the therapy is not simply slowing down, since that too can be another expression of the same dynamics of hurrying. The problem is evading "the truth about ourselves and our world: we are creatures, living in an unfolding time whose purposes we did not create."[43]

Slow is not synonymous with patience; sometimes violence relies on slowness. Not all speed is to be avoided, but hastiness often ignores truth and assumes that time is ours to control. So how can we express Christian patience? I contend that we need to recognize that Christian patience can move at various tempi, but whatever pace we choose to follow, slow *or* fast, ought to be shaped by our understanding of patience. Perhaps the way to express this is to say that we are called to the practice of *urgent patience*. In this regard, I have often thought of the father in the well-known parable we refer to as the Prodigal Son. Much is made of the father's hurrying in joy to embrace his wayward son who has come home. Fair enough, but we also ought to recognize that the final urgent sprint of that story is shaped by and comes only after and as part of enduring, waiting, watching, and hoping. The father distributed the share of inheritance against his own better judgment, he continued his work over the years, he worked side by side with his other son and employees, and all the time the working and the waiting were of a piece, a way of being which I am calling urgent patience.

Urgent patience, then, consists not only in expanding our recognition of the moral danger in speed to also seeing the dark possibilities

---

42. Johnson, "Hurry and the Willingness to Be Creatures," 16, 17.
43. Johnson, "Hurry and the Willingness to Be Creatures," 12.

of slowness. Urgent patience calls us to a way of being in the world as Christians; urgent patience describes a way of living with the other without reducing the importance of the Christian faith and practice; urgent patience offers us ways of setting the stage for living *with* long-term difference but *without* terminal division; urgent patience provides not just a way of taking a long time to make decisions but presses us into finding a way forward and getting on with life without first coming to some form of unified resolution.[44] Urgent patience acts as a sort of political and ethical capacity,[45] and encourages us to believe that because God has time, we also have time—to listen, to be vulnerable, to engage in important conflicts without becoming violent, to refuse to be driven by the speed that society seeks to impose on us, and to resist the notion that the world and other people are directly in our control; indeed to resist the notion that we are radically autonomous individual entities.[46]

Finally, insofar as the practice of urgent patience is possible in our lives and churches, and in the world in which we find ourselves, it is made so by "the love that waits, scandalous in its patience, (which) will finally be unreserved in its haste to welcome us into the feast of reconciliation. In the meantime, we wait in joyful hope."[47]

Bibliography

Barth, Karl. *Church Dogmatics*. Vol. II/1, *The Doctrine of God*. Edited by G. Bromiley and T. Torrance. Translated by T. Parker et al. London: T. & T. Clark, 2004.
Calvin, John. *Institutes of the Christian Religion*. Vol. 2. Edited by John McNeill. Philadelphia: Westminster, 1960.
Cavanaugh, William. *Being Consumed: Economics and Christian Desire*. Grand Rapids: Eerdmans, 2008.
Coles, Romand. "Letter of July 17, 2006." In *Christianity, Democracy, and the Radical Ordinary: Conversations Between a Radical Democrat and a Christian*, by Stanley Hauerwas and Romand Coles, 31–44. Eugene, OR: Cascade, 2008.
―――. "The Pregnant Reticence of Rowan Williams." In *Christianity, Democracy, and the Radical Ordinary: Conversations Between a Radical Democrat and a Christian*, by Stanley Hauerwas and Romand Coles, 174–94. Eugene, OR: Cascade, 2008.
Didur, Jill. "Provincializing Ecocritism." *Contemporary Literature* 53 (2012) 585–91.
Dillon, Lindsay. Review of *Slow Violence and the Environmentalism of the Poor*, by Rob Nixon. *Progress in Human Geography* 36 (2012) 830–31.

---

44. I acknowledge a series of fruitful conversations with Dr. Cheryl Pauls here.
45. Coles, "Letter of July 17, 2006," 42.
46. See my earlier essay: Doerksen, "Politics of Moral Patience," 454.
47. Johnson, "God Does Not Hurry," 81.

Doerksen, Paul G. "The Politics of Moral Patience." *Political Theology* 15 (2014) 454–67.

Guardini, Romano. "God's Patience." In *The Faith and Modern Man*, translated by Charlotte Forsyth, 15–32. London: Burns & Oates, 1953.

Honoré, Carl. *In Praise of Slow: Challenging the Cult of Speed*. Toronto: Vintage Canada, 2004.

Huebner, Chris. "Patience, Witness, and the Scattered Body of Christ: Yoder and Virilio on Knowledge, Politics, and Speed." In *A Mind Patient and Untamed: Assessing John Howard Yoder's Contributions to Theology, Ethics, and Peacemaking*, edited by Ben C. Ollenburger and Gayle Gerber Koontz, 56–74. Telford, PA: Cascadia, 2004.

Johnson, Kelly. "God Does Not Hurry." In *God Does Not . . . : Entertain, Play Matchmaker, Hurry, Demand Blood, Cure Every Illness*, edited by D. Brent Laytham, 63–81. Grand Rapids: Brazos, 2009.

———. "Hurry and the Willingness to Be Creatures." In *Attentive Patience*, edited by Robert Kruschwitz, 11–18. Christian Reflection series, Institute for Faith and Learning. Waco, TX: Institute for Faith and Learning at Baylor University, 2016.

Jones, Paul Dafydd. "On Patience: Thinking With and Beyond Karl Barth." *Scottish Journal of Theology* 68 (2015) 273–98.

Kenneson, Philip. *Practicing Ecclesial Patience: Patient Practice Makes Perfect*. Eugene, OR: Wipf & Stock, 2013.

Kierkegaard, Søren. *Eighteen Upbuilding Discourses*. Translated by Howard Hong and Edna Hong. Princeton, NJ: Princeton University Press, 1990.

Koyama, Kosuke. *Three Mile an Hour God*. London: SCM, 2021.

Lysen, Laura M., and Paul Martens. "How Can We Love Our Enemies When We Kill Our Friends? Shifting the Theological Debate Over Violence." *Modern Theology* 36 (2020) 462–77.

Matties, Gordon H. "Slow Food: Feasting Sustainably on Scripture." In *A University of the Church for the World: Essays in Honour of Gerald Gerbrandt*, edited by Paul Dyck and Harry Huebner, 211–30. Winnipeg: Carnegie Mellon University Press, 2016.

Nixon, Rob. *Slow Violence and the Environmentalism of the Poor*. Cambridge, MA: Harvard University Press, 2011.

Quash, Ben. "Making the Most of the Time: Liturgy, Ethics and Time." *Studies in Christian Ethics* 15 (2002) 97–114.

Rosa, Hartmut. *Social Acceleration: A New Theory of Modernity*. Translated by Jonathan Trejo-Mathys. New York: Columbia University Press, 2013.

Scott, Kevin F. "The Church and the Urgent Patience of Christ." *Scottish Bulletin of Evangelical Theology* 27 (2009) 5–23.

Swinton, John. *Becoming Friends of Time: Disability, Timefullness, and Gentle Discipleship*. Waco, TX: Baylor University Press, 2016.

Vogel, Jeff. "The Haste of Sin, the Slowness of Salvation: An Interpretation of Irenaeus on the Fall and Redemption." *Anglican Theological Review* 89 (2007) 443–59.

11

Labor of Love
Simone Weil's Kenotic Spirituality of Work

RACHEL MATHESON

IN HER FINAL MAGNUM opus, *The Need for Roots*, the French philosopher, activist, and mystic Simone Weil urged a reconsideration of contemporary notions of greatness. One of the main obstacles keeping her own time and place from becoming a civilization that was "worth something," she argued, was its "false" conception of greatness, which she characterized as an adoration of force and prestige and which she diagnosed as one of the contributing factors to the rise of totalitarianism and the modern "disease" of uprootedness.[1] Perhaps even more strikingly, she declared that the means for her country's social, political, and spiritual renewal could be found in the "spirituality of work."[2] Weil's meaning here is unclear, and she does not spell out the specifics of this claim anywhere in the text. I suggest that it is best understood by turning to her kenotic theology and her broader critique of force and sovereignty. While Weil's vision in *The Need for Roots* is meant to be broad and universal, she also develops a more specifically Christian (mystical) theology of work in the text, particularly near the end, where she articulates labor as a practice of self-effacement. I first briefly outline Weil's understanding of the religious significance of work, then turn to her

1. Weil, *Need for Roots*, 216.
2. Weil, *Need for Roots*, 97.

kenotic theology and the way she situates labor within a divine drama of fall and redemption. I argue that for Weil, work can become a practice of self-renunciation or *decreation*. After outlining the way labor effects this more personal transformation, I turn to the broader sociopolitical implications, demonstrating how Weil's characterization of work fits within her theological critique of sovereignty and her prioritization of the self-emptying Christ as a model for emulation.

Thought, Action, and the Spirituality of Work

Weil's life was marked by a formidable integration of intellectual pursuits and active engagement in the issues of her time. This is particularly true of her lifelong interest in labor; her writings on the subject are marked by their philosophical rigor while being equally grounded in practical specificity inspired by her own experiences. Born in 1909 to a French Jewish family, Weil was educated at the prestigious École Normale Supérieure in Paris, after which she began working as a schoolteacher at a *lycée* in the small village of Roanne. There, she became actively involved in the trade union movement of the region. Never one simply to theorize, she applied for a one-year leave of absence from her teaching position in 1934–35 to gain firsthand experience of factory work and to better understand the conditions of the working class. She spent approximately ten months in three different factories as an unskilled laborer. The experience was marked by discouragement and exhaustion, and she emerged "in pieces, soul and body," her sense of dignity crushed through humiliation and affliction.[3] Still, her interest in labor was not diminished, and she continued to reflect on how the conditions of work might be less oppressive and more dignified for the rest of her life.

Following the Nazi invasion of Paris in 1940, Weil traveled south with her family, where she spent a brief period as a farm laborer. It was here that her compositions and notebook entries on labor became increasingly inflected with religious concerns, informed by a series of mystical experiences that shaped the final years of her life. More and more she viewed work as not only the primary means of acting within the world but also a point of contact with the divine. These ideas are taken up again in *The Need for Roots*, where she develops what she called the "spirituality of work" as a crucial element in her vision for the future of France. Weil

3. Weil, *Waiting for God*, 25.

wrote the text while she was living abroad, having fled occupied France with her family, first for America and then England. In London, she found work with France Libre, a French political group that established a government-in-exile in London led by General Charles de Gaulle and which was working with the resistance against the puppet Vichy government in France. Weil penned the text hurriedly in some of the final months of her life as her contribution to a vision of her country after German defeat, but she never saw her vision come to fruition. Tired and overworked, she died of tuberculosis in a sanatorium in Ashford, Kent, in 1943, her condition believed to have been exacerbated by her desire not to eat more than the food rations being distributed in France.

In Weil's final text, she envisions labor as a central component in the reconstitution of France. A civilization based on the "spirituality of work," she writes, would give human creatures "the very strongest possible roots in the wide universe" and be a remedy to the state of uprootedness that she felt characterized her time.[4] Weil refers not just to geopolitical uprootedness but also to moral and spiritual uprootedness, and therefore urges the need for social, political, economic, but also spiritual remedies. Indeed, the crucial preamble to the text, what Weil calls the "Profession of Faith," delineates the scope of what she was trying to accomplish in explicitly religious terms. There is a reality outside this world, she begins, a reality beyond space and time that every human heart longs for.[5] She proposes labor as a means of becoming "rooted" again in that reality. Weil believed that long ago, physical labor had been a religious activity in which the bodily movements of one's craft or trade were a direct expression of religious faith,[6] and she sought to recover its sacred aspect so that quotidian life could again be infused with the transcendent. A "spirituality" of work was something she felt could be broadly agreed upon, even creating unanimity across creeds and political affiliations,[7] and she envisioned it as an antidote to the sufferings of her day because of the way it would orient and "root" society in a shared transcendent reality.

For work to be transformed in this way, however, it would have to undergo major reforms in the way it is organized. In her earlier analysis of the causes of oppression in labor Weil had argued, like Karl Marx, that the division of labor into intellectual and manual work has

4. Weil, *Need for Roots*, 97.
5. Weil, *Selected Essays*, 219.
6. Weil, *Need for Roots*, 292.
7. Weil, *Need for Roots*, 97.

been degrading and alienating, since it reduces workers to "things" who thoughtlessly carry out the actions required by those who command. Modern industry, with its mass production and specialization, has reduced the worker to an increasingly passive role, in which they become dominated slavishly by another's will.[8] In *The Need for Roots*, her analysis takes on a religious dimension: "If we go to the heart of things, there is no true dignity without a spiritual root and consequently one of a supernatural order."[9] In her suggestions for reform she sought to bring more dignity to work by infusing it with thought, but perhaps most importantly, she argued that "this world and the world beyond, in their double beauty, should be present and associated in the act of work."[10] Through the contemplation of divine truths, specific to each sort of work and impressed on the mind through habit, every physical movement would become a means of connection to the divine. As Simone Kotva has argued,[11] Weil's spirituality of work envisioned labor as a way of cultivating and exercising the faculty of attention.

At the end of *The Need for Roots*, however, the character of her remarks on work changes dramatically, and she suggests that labor is "the most perfect form of obedience," that it "does violence to human nature," and even that it is a "daily death." She turns to the Genesis account to frame labor within the context of the Fall, writing in a far more explicitly theological mode. The abrupt shift in tone makes it difficult to understand how her descriptions of labor here are connected to the rest of the text and to her previous comments on the spirituality of work. Yet her language bears resemblances to passages in some of her religious essays and notebooks, especially in the way she identifies labor as a means of relinquishing the "I." Attention to the resonances with her broader kenotic theology and her concept of decreation helps to clarify the final, puzzling pages on labor as a more specifically Christian mystical theology of work, but also illuminates how Weil was positioning labor as an alternative to the greatness of power and might in the rest of the text.

---

8. Weil, *Oppression and Liberty*, 41.
9. Weil, *Need for Roots*, 94.
10. Weil, *Need for Roots*, 95.
11. Kotva, *Effort and Grace*, 150–51.

Labor and Kenotic Theology

Weil never mentions the kenotic hymn in *The Need for Roots*, yet it informs much of her later religious thought and is especially important to understanding her challenging characterization of labor as humble obedience and death. Situating Weil's brief, suggestive intimations about work within her kenotic theology reveals the way she locates labor within a much larger, cosmic drama of divine love, fallenness, and reintegration. Weil's account of the divine prioritizes God's self-limitation and relinquishment of divinity rather than power and sovereignty. She describes the Creation, Incarnation, and Passion as a single drama of cosmic scope, inspired by the kenotic hymn of Phil 2:6–11, in which Christ's descent is expressed as a movement of self-emptying love and servitude:

> On God's part creation is not an act of self-expansion but of restraint and renunciation. God and all his creatures are less than God alone. God accepted this diminution. He emptied a part of his being from himself.... God permitted the existence of things distinct from himself and worth infinitely less than himself. By this creative act he denied himself, as Christ has told us to deny ourselves.[12]

The God who appears in the pages of Weil's notebooks and essays is described primarily in terms of this renunciation, restraint, and distance rather than as a being who commands wherever there is power to do so. Concerned about the kinds of triumphalism that could arise from focusing too exclusively on Christ's Resurrection, she stresses the descending motion of the first half of the kenotic hymn with its language of servitude and obedience to death, lingering on the Crucifixion rather than the exaltation of the passage's second half.[13] So central is the kenotic hymn of Philippians to her understanding of Christian faith that she confesses in a letter that it is "what compels me to believe."[14] For Weil, it is the relinquishment of power that demonstrates God's divinity and expresses the depth and magnitude of divine love.

---

12. Weil, *Waiting for God*, 89.

13. Christine Hof has suggested that kenosis is the central and unifying theme in Weil's philosophy. She notes that there is a profound link between Weil's first use of the term decreation and kenosis, in that the term appears only a few pages after her first citation of the hymn. Hof, *Philosophie et kénose*, 49.

14. Weil, *Letter to a Priest*, 35.

Weil situates human creatures within this drama as beings who have moved away from God because of an imagined sense of their own divinity. In her reading of the Genesis narrative, the distance between God and creatures is caused by Adam's assertion of the self that claims freedom and existence outside of God, a sin that humans continue to reenact.[15] The problem for Weil is one of the self, which always has a tendency to expand like a gas that grows to occupy the whole space open to it.[16] Just like God, who is both outside the universe and at the very center of it, every person imagines they are situated at the center of the world.[17] It is this imagined self, with all its illusions of power and mastery, that must be renounced: "God has conferred upon [the human being] an imaginary likeness to his power, an imaginary divinity, so that he also, although a creature, may empty himself of his divinity."[18] According to Weil, we possess nothing in the world except the gift of the ability to say "I," and it is this that must be offered back to God in the only truly free act we can perform.[19] To imitate Christ, we must therefore emulate his self-limitation and kenotic descent through a process of decreation, a term Weil employs to designate the relinquishment of the "I," offering it back to God in a posture of radical self-dispossession.

At the end of *The Need for Roots*, Weil situates labor explicitly within this greater narrative of human fallenness and redemption by turning to the Genesis account of the Fall. Weil believes it is a mistake to read in the text the "slightest hint of disdain" for work, arguing that interpretations that regard labor as simply a subsequent and necessary evil misunderstand the purpose of punishment.[20] Instead, she sees labor as a means of purifying the self that causes the distance in the first place and as a means of cultivating a lost obedience, bringing the will back into conformity with God's will: "Man placed himself outside the current of Obedience. God chose as his punishment labor and death. Consequently, labor and death, if Man undergoes them in a spirit of willingness, constitute a transference back into the current of supreme Good, which is obedience to God."[21] Weil admits that while at times there may be a superabundance of energy for

15. Weil, *First and Last Notebooks*, 218.
16. Weil, *Notebooks*, 198.
17. Weil, *Waiting for God*, 99.
18. Weil, *Waiting for God*, 99.
19. Weil, *Notebooks*, 336–37.
20. Weil, *Need for Roots*, 292.
21. Weil, *Need for Roots*, 296.

the work at hand, at other times there is only exhaustion, strain, anxiety, and disgust.[22] Labor is a daily practice of obedience, since one carries out the motions of work whether one feels sad or happy, tired or energetic.[23] It is performed, that is, not because of daily whims or desires but as a form of regular, habituated obedience dependent on a prior consent that is then renewed at the beginning of each day.

Earlier in the text, Weil suggests that a "spirituality of work" is something that does not imply any particular religious affiliation and that could be understood and agreed upon broadly within society,[24] but here she puts labor in specifically theological terms. While I suggest the kenotic hymn is in the background of how she was thinking about labor as obedience, she also refers more explicitly to Paul's words in Heb 5:8–9 ("yet learned he obedience by the things which he suffered, and was made perfect"), pointing to Christ as the ultimate model of obedience and the reversal of Adam's disobedience.[25] Passages such as these that emphasize Christ's suffering have sometimes been understood as a call to emulate Christ's pain and sacrifice, but Weil was very careful not to glorify affliction in work. Throughout her life she sought ways of making labor less degrading and more dignified, pressing for specific reforms toward this end in *The Need for Roots*. Yet her account is not an idealizing attempt to eliminate the burden of work entirely, as she argues Marx attempted to do in his dream of returning to the Garden and regaining "the happiness of Adam and Eve before the fall."[26] Weil admits that a certain degree of pain and fatigue is always involved in one's work and that efforts to remove suffering entirely are delusional at best, and at worst, recreate postures of mastery. She carefully notes suffering is an aspect of labor, but she never claims it should be sought. The aim is obedience, not affliction.

When performed with a Christ-like posture of obedience, labor can become a spiritual exercise, a practice of submission through which both the mind and body are brought back into conformity to God's will. Gavin Flood puts it well when he suggests that Weil develops an "asceticism of work," in which work consciously performed can be a form of detached acceptance, an *ascesis* or exercise in eradicating the private will

22. Weil, *Need for Roots*, 297.
23. Weil, *Need for Roots*, 298.
24. Weil, *Need for Roots*, 97.
25. Weil, *Need for Roots*, 296. This quotation is Arthur Wills's translation of Weil's rendering of Hebrews.
26. Weil, *Oppression and Liberty*, 42.

and replacing it with divine will.[27] In her notebooks, Weil indicates this in a brief note about what must have been a planned essay on precisely this topic: "Titles. 'Work as a spiritual exercise.' 'Work as a mystical experience.' 'Work as poetry.'"[28] Weil's mystical sensibility is revealed in the way she articulates labor here and in *The Need for Roots* as a means of effacing the self and becoming a channel through which God works in the world. To become obedient in this way is to emulate the passivity of matter and become perfectly receptive to divine will.

Weil puts this in more provocative terms when she likens labor to a "daily death."[29] On the final page of *The Need for Roots* she writes:

> Consent to suffer death, when death is there and seen in its nakedness, constitutes a final, sudden wrenching away from what each one calls "I." Consent to perform labor is of a less violent nature. But where it is absolute, it is renewed each morning throughout the entire length of a human existence, day after day, and each day it lasts until the evening, and it starts again on the following day, and this goes on often until death.[30]

This is no bodily death but a death of the ego, and it takes place not as a single event but as a continual practice within daily life. If approached intentionally, Weil seems to be suggesting, labor can become a form of decreation, in which the ego is renounced through the consent to take up one's daily tasks.[31] Though she does not put it in these terms in the text, the implication is that as the "I" withdraws, one moves from obscuring God's light to incarnating love through one's work.

If work is like a death and "does violence to human nature," however, what differentiates it as an exercise in decreation from the oppressive forms of work that Weil compares to slavery? The difference is an important one that rests on consent and the ability to freely offer the self. Whereas one is an unwilling submission and subjugation to force, the other is a voluntary relinquishment of one's will to power in emulation of the servitude of Christ. In a crucial passage from one of her religious essays, Weil articulates these different forms of obedience:

---

27. Flood, *Ascetic Self*, 38. Flood gives an excellent account of some of the ambiguities in the way Weil thinks about subjectivity. See also Kotva, *Effort and Grace*.

28. Weil, *Notebooks*, 79.

29. Weil, *Need for Roots*, 297.

30. Weil, *Need for Roots*, 297–98.

31. Robert Chenavier has called work the "decreative activity" par excellence for Weil. Chenavier, *Simone Weil*, 451.

"Among men, a slave does not become like his master by obeying him. On the contrary, the more he obeys the greater is the distance between them. It is otherwise between man and God. If a reasonable creature is absolutely obedient, he becomes a perfect image of the Almighty as far as this is possible for him."[32] While in human relationships of domination the slave's obedience to the master's will only reinscribes the difference between them, it is the opposite with obedience to God. Part of Weil's critique of the many forms of modern-day enslavement is that they deprive others of their ability to voluntarily renounce the "I" and therefore rob them of this expression of self-giving love.[33] Those who keep others in subjection by exercising force and cruelty deprive them of both liberty and obedience, since they are no longer granted the ability to consent to the authority to which they are subjected.[34] In this sense, Weil's own experience of work in the factories was not one of consented decreation but of imposed affliction. To become the "perfect image of the Almighty" through obedience for Weil means that one more closely resembles God by *not* engaging in the race for power and by refusing to use force over others. The kenotic hymn thus has far wider implications for Weil's theology of work than individual transformation.

Weil's Critique of Greatness

I return now to Weil's claim that the contemporary form of true greatness lies in a civilization founded upon the spirituality of work in order to suggest the ways in which that labor becomes part of Weil's larger religious and sociopolitical critique of sovereignty. In *The Need for Roots*, she frames this as an incisive criticism of what she calls the prevalent idea of "greatness" (*grandeur*). Weil associates contemporary ideas of greatness with prestige, might, and conquest. She demonstrates how this form of "false greatness" is apparent in the fascist regimes of her time, and especially Hitler's in totalitarianism as well as in France's own history of colonialism. She presents a ruthless condemnation, not just focusing on these more apparent displays of force but also revealing the less obvious and more insidious ways that greatness as might permeates all of culture

---

32. Weil, *Waiting for God*, 115.
33. Weil, *Waiting for God*, 115–16.
34. Weil describes both obedience and liberty as two of the "needs of the soul." *Need for Roots*, 14.

by being idolized in literature, public institutions, and history lessons that are always told from the perspective of the vanquishers.[35]

This "cult of grandeur" is greatness as empire. More specifically, Weil traces its roots to the Roman Empire, arguing that Hitler's will to domination and his dreams of political expansion and conquest are vestiges of the dominant Roman ideology.[36] But Rome's influence is not only evident in the political realm for Weil; she also criticizes its contribution to the idolization of might and a misguided worship of sovereignty in Christianity, writing that when Christianity became associated with the Roman Empire, God was turned into a counterpart of the emperor—that is, a Roman slaveholder with sovereign rights over another's life.[37] She insists that the Roman sense of power continues to hold sway within Christianity: "The Roman spirit of imperialism and domination has never loosened its hold over the Church sufficiently for the latter to be able to abolish the Roman conception of God."[38] Weil is deeply suspicious of any form of Christianity that claims to be centered on Christ while effectively worshiping power or prestige, and she tries to reveal the ways that this continues to permeate attitudes about the divine and the attributes we worship.

Weil held that the peoples of Europe were desperately in need of an alternative model of greatness, one of a "spiritual order" rather than the "old, old lie of world conquest."[39] The reconstruction of France would have to be built upon a different foundation than that of empire, with very different aspirations for the future and an alternative model of greatness. It is in this context that she claims that "the contemporary form of true greatness lies in a civilization founded upon the spirituality of work."[40] The "vocation" of her time, she argues, is to create a civilization founded upon the spiritual nature of work, and that "such a vocation is the only thing great enough to put before the peoples instead of the totalitarian

---

35. Weil, *Need for Roots*, 222.

36. Weil compares this to France's own colonization project: "Even in our own time, it would certainly be difficult to deny that we have made and are still making use of methods similar to Rome's in conquering and ruling our colonial empire; and many Frenchmen would be more inclined to boast of this than to deny it." *Selected Essays*, 134.

37. Weil, *Need for Roots*, 268.

38. Weil, *Need for Roots*, 274.

39. Weil, *Need for Roots*, 97.

40. Weil, *Need for Roots*, 97.

idol."[41] This is where Weil's kenotic theology is illuminating, in that it reveals a model that does not revolve around building up the self but losing it, does not valorize displays of the will to power or greatness as might but self-emptying service and attention to one's neighbor. It centers not on a slave-owning king but a suffering servant.

As a practice of decreation, labor can become a means of relinquishing the self and its hunger for power, but this does not merely have a personal, inner disposition as its end goal for Weil. Rather, as kenotic practice it cultivates a different way of being in the world and of relating to others. As Deborah Nelson puts it, "Decreation is a theology of nonsovereignty; for Weil, the sovereign individual can only ever be a fantasy, one that is maintained with all the forms of self-delusion, self-aggrandizement, and hubris that create oppression."[42] One who clings to the sense of their own divinity will have a distorted vision of reality and is more likely to oppress others because of the false perception of their superiority. Moreover, as Christine Hof has noted in her analysis of the kenotic motif in Weil's philosophy, part of the subversive function of the hymn is that it calls into question the very foundations on which human organizations and systems are based. In Christ's kenosis, she writes, there is a de-centering of sovereignty that can liberate humankind from the thirst for power, disrupting the meaning that human beings have given to the divine.[43] Within the more specific context of labor, a theology of work that is informed by the kenotic hymn is one that demands continual reflection on how power is being exercised, seized, and expressed. It contests the valorization of mastery and might and calls into question the structures and forms of work that seek to dominate others.

How did Weil understand this more concretely in terms of labor? An example from her life illustrates the way the kenotic hymn inspired her own aspirations to participate in the war efforts as a frontline nurse. At the time that Weil was writing *The Need for Roots*, she was also attempting to put forward a proposal for an organization of courageous volunteer women nurses who would administer first aid on the front lines of battle.[44] Their primary purpose would be to save the lives of

41. Weil, *Need for Roots*, 95–96.
42. Nelson, *Tough Enough*, 29.
43. Hof, *Philosophie et kénose*, 74–76.
44. The plan was included in a letter written from New York to Maurice Schumann on July 30, 1942. Weil included an extract from the *Bulletin of the American College of Surgeons*, which suggested that according to the American Red Cross, the greatest proportion of deaths in battle were the result of the shock, exposure, and loss of blood that required immediate treatment on the battlefield. Weil's proposal is a clear attempt to

injured soldiers, but Weil also envisioned the nurses as a moral inspiration for the injured, the general public, and even the opposing side. She refers to Hitler's successful ability to stoke the imagination through visual displays of heroism, most notably in the special forces of the SS who first parachuted to places such as Crete.[45] Weil insists that the Allies cannot simply duplicate such acts, whose heroism originated in brutality and corresponded to the spirit of the regime. Instead, she envisions a striking visual symbol as a counterpart to Hitler's parachutists that would be rooted in an entirely different inspiration. The sight of a small group of women caring for the wounded on the front line "would be a spectacle so new, so significant, and charged with such obvious meaning, that it would strike the imagination more than any of Hitler's conceptions have done."[46] Rather than a courage that springs from the will to power and destruction or prestige, theirs would be of a "more difficult and rarer kind,"[47] rooted in a radical alternative sense of greatness as self-emptying servitude and love.

Weil's project of frontline nurses never gained traction, but it illustrates her vision of an embodied response to the problems of her time through a vocation inspired by the kenotic hymn. In a notebook entry, Weil describes what it is to emulate this movement of self-emptying love: "One must strip oneself of the imaginary sovereignty of the world in order to reduce oneself to the point one occupies in space and time."[48] Unlike the disincarnating tendency of the imagination, which makes us "kings and masters of the world in thought," the privilege of labor is that under the right conditions, it can be a practice of relinquishing the self and its false divinity in order to attend to the tasks, people, and place of our specific point in time. The alternative sense of greatness that she only alludes to in *The Need for Roots* might also be described by the words of Matt 20:26–28, which she mentions in several passages of her notebooks: "Whoever wants to become great among you must be your servant, and whoever wants to be first must be your slave—just as the Son of Man did not come to be served, but to serve, and to give his life as a ransom for many" (NRSV). For Weil, the greatness of labor is revealed paradoxically when it is a willing

---

consider how such loss of life might be avoided, although her proposal was purportedly met with this reaction from Charles de Gaulle: "But she is mad!" Pétrement, *Simone Weil: A Life*, 514.

45. Weil, *Seventy Letters*, 149.
46. Weil, *Seventy Letters*, 151.
47. Weil, *Seventy Letters*, 150.
48. Weil, *Notebooks*, 213.

descent of mutual servanthood that allows the growing of common roots through shared work and its attendant suffering.

Conclusion

Weil sought a new sanctity for her time, an alternative vision of greatness that would not be rooted in power or prestige but in the radical call to participate in the mystery of divine love through one's daily work. If undertaken as a form of consented obedience in which the "I" is relinquished—that is, as a practice of decreation—Weil believed that one's labor could move from obscuring divine love to incarnating it in the world through daily acts of attentive service and care.

Bibliography

Chenavier, Robert. *Simone Weil: Une philosophie du travail*. Paris: Les éditions du cerf, 2001.

Flood, Gavin. *The Ascetic Self: Subjectivity, Memory and Tradition*. Cambridge: Cambridge University Press, 2004.

Hof, Christine. *Philosophie et kénose chez Simone Weil: De l'amour du monde à l'Imitatio Christi*. Paris: L'Harmattan, 2016.

Kotva, Simone. *Effort and Grace: On the Spiritual Exercise of Philosophy*. London: Bloomsbury, 2020.

Nelson, Deborah. *Tough Enough: Arbus, Arendt, Didion, McCarthy, Sontag, Weil*. Chicago: University of Chicago Press, 2017.

Pétrement, Simone. *Simone Weil: A Life*. Translated by Raymond Rosenthal. New York: Pantheon, 1976.

Weil, Simone. *First and Last Notebooks*. Translated by Richard Rees. Toronto: Oxford University Press, 1970.

———. *Letter to a Priest*. Translated by A. F. Wills. New York: Routledge Classics, 2002.

———. *The Need for Roots: Prelude to a Declaration of Duties Toward Mankind*. Translated by Arthur Wills. New York: Putnam, 1952.

———. *The Notebooks of Simone Weil*. 2 vols. Translated by Arthur Wills. London: Routledge and Kegan Paul, 1956.

———. *Oppression and Liberty*. Translated by Arthur Wills and John Petrie. London: Routledge, 2001.

———. *Selected Essays: 1934–1943*. Translated by Richard Rees. Eugene, OR: Wipf & Stock, 1962.

———. *Seventy Letters: Personal and Intellectual Windows on a Thinker*. Translated by Richard Rees. Eugene, OR: Wipf & Stock, 1964.

———. *Waiting for God*. Translated by Emma Craufurd. New York: HarperCollins, 2001.

12

Paul's Apocalyptic Doctrine of Justification

STEPHEN WESTERHOLM

IN HIS *DE DOCTRINA Christiana*, Augustine asks what interpreters of Scripture should do when they encounter texts that permit more than one interpretation.[1] Any reading, he advises, must conform to the "rule of faith"; of those that do, the interpreter should adopt that which best fits the progression of thought (3.2.2). Students of Scripture should "make every effort to arrive at the intention of the author through whom the Holy Spirit produced that portion of scripture." On the other hand, provided a reading "does not clash with right faith, and is supported" by other passages in Scripture, it need not be rejected. After all, if the Holy Spirit, who "produced" the text, "provided" a wording that admits more than one interpretation, we should make the most of Scripture's "abundant and generous provision" (3.27.38).

Augustine's counsel is worth bearing in mind when we approach so controversial a topic as Paul's understanding of justification. In what follows, I shall indeed "make every effort" to arrive at Paul's own intentions.[2] I focus on Rom 1:17, where Paul introduces the subject, searching for the interpretation that, while consistent with what he says elsewhere, best

---

1. This article is dedicated to Travis Kroeker, my friend and colleague of many years, with whom I share a deep appreciation of the work of Kierkegaard, Kohák—and Paul.
2. Cf. Meyer, "Primacy of the Intended Sense."

fits the progression of his thought in Romans. Such is the task, if not of every reader of Scripture, at least of the biblical scholar. At the same time, readers of Paul today ought, like Augustine, to be open to readings other than that intended by the apostle. Texts take on new meaning in changed circumstances and with new interpreters.[3] Though limitations of space prevent their consideration here, I am well aware that, particularly in the last half century or so, other interpretations of Romans 1:17 and of the term "justification" have been proposed; furthermore, the substance of several of these alternatives is, to my mind, fully consonant with Paul's thought even where they are not, to my mind, what Paul intended in Rom 1:17. Here, however, I must confine myself to the simple question, What does Paul mean when he writes, "The righteousness of God is revealed in the gospel . . . as it is written, 'The one who is righteous based on faith shall live'"? To be "righteous [Gk. *dikaios*] based on faith" is to be "declared righteous," or "justified [Gk. *dikaioutai*]"—and in the process "the righteousness [Gk. *dikaiosynē*] of God is revealed." Brief discussion of the apocalyptic character of his doctrine will follow its definition.

The "Righteousness of God" in Context

I begin with the progression of Paul's thought, allowing it to determine the boundaries within which his understanding of the "righteousness of God" in Rom 1:17 must be found.[4]

1. Since Romans 1:17 begins with "for" (Gk. *gar*), the revelation of God's righteousness must represent the means by which God effects "salvation" (1:16): the gospel is "the power of God that brings salvation . . . *for* through the gospel the righteousness of God is revealed." Paul's argument in Romans makes clear that salvation is accompanied by forgiveness of sins (4:6–8), the gift of the Spirit (5:5), adoption into God's family (8:15), and other divine blessings. But like the words "salvation" and "Savior" in English, the Greek *sōtēria* and *Sōtēr* imply deliverance *from* danger. Romans 5:9 speaks of "salvation from [divine] wrath"; from 1:18—3:20, it is evident that the same deliverance is intended in 1:16–17 (note also 1 Thess 1:10, 5:9).

---

3. Cf. the nuanced discussion of Meyer, "Tricky Business."
4. All quotations from Scripture are my own translation.

2. The "salvation" brought by the revelation of God's righteousness is neither automatic nor universal; it comes to "everyone who *believes*," Jews and gentiles alike—though "first to the Jew and also to the Greek" (1:16).

That said, Paul does not glorify "believing" (Gk. verb *pisteuō*) or "faith" (Gk. noun *pistis*) as such. The faith Paul speaks of has a definite object—and derives its efficacy from that object: God (Rom 4:24; 1 Thess 1:8), who has acted in Christ to reconcile the world to himself (2 Cor 5:19); or, simply, Christ (Gal 2:16; Phil 1:29); or (as in Rom 1:16) the proclaimed gospel (also Rom 10:16; 1 Cor 15:11). We may, in principle, distinguish belief in some proposition (e.g., Rom 6:8, 10:9) from confidence in someone or something believed to be trustworthy (e.g., Rom 4:5, 4:24). But when Paul speaks, in Romans 10:9–10, of belief *that* God raised Jesus from the dead as a belief "with the heart," he shows that in the case of the gospel, the two cannot be separated: a "heart" belief is something more than (although it includes) an acknowledgment of true statements. Indeed, Paul can speak of the "obedience of faith" (Rom 1:5): if the gospel brings deliverance from the wrath occasioned by human rebellion against God (1:16–32), then faith in the gospel necessarily means laying down one's arms and submitting to God's rightful claim on one's life and obedience.

Such faith, by its very nature, is that of an individual: "to ev-er*yone* who believes" (Rom 1:16). When the gospel is proclaimed, some believe, others do not (2 Cor 2:15–16). Different responses to Paul's message divided servants from masters (1 Tim 6:1–2; Phlm 10–11), spouses from each other (1 Cor 7:12–13; cf. Matt 10:34–35). To be sure, those who believed became part of the community of believers; moreover, the scope of Paul's message in Romans extends beyond that community to include the redemption of all creation. Still, in the present age, God's new creation, like Paul's Epistle to the Romans, begins with the "salvation" of individuals who respond in faith to the gospel (cf. 2 Cor 5:17). And "the righteousness of God" is seen in their salvation.

3. The thesis of Rom 1:17a is restated ("as it is written") in Paul's quotation (v. 17b) from Hab 2:4: "The one who is righteous by faith shall live."[5] The righteousness of God is at work where people are "righteous by faith."

---

5. Alternatively, "The righteous shall live by faith." In Paul's context, however, the

A number of scholars today read the quotation messianically: "the One who is righteous" is Christ. They then proceed to interpret "by faith" as a reference to Christ's "faithfulness." But although Christ is indeed referred to elsewhere in the New Testament as "the righteous one" (Acts 3:14, 7:52, 22:14), in each of these cases, the context makes the reference to Christ unmistakable; nothing in the context of Rom 1:17 suggests such a reference.[6] Here, "by faith" (Gk. *ek pisteōs*) is naturally taken to refer to the faith of "everyone who believes" (Gk. *panti tō pisteuonti*) in 1:16.[7]

4. Paul returns to the thesis of Rom 1:17 at 3:21-22. The intervening material, 1:18—3:20, treats the condition from which the revelation of God's righteousness brings deliverance.

When Paul speaks, in Rom 1:16, of "salvation," he means (as we have seen) deliverance from God's "wrath." That conclusion is confirmed by the progression of his thought in verses 17-18: the revelation of God's righteousness brings deliverance from God's wrath, "for the wrath of God is revealed from heaven against all the ungodliness and unrighteousness of human beings who, by their unrighteousness, suppress the truth" (v. 18)—a subject on which the apostle then expands at great length.

At the very outset of Paul's argument, he makes clear that human beings *ought* to show godliness and righteousness in their manner of living, and that they are subject to God's judgment when they do not. The obligation is implicit in all Paul's writings; here, uniquely, he spells out its nature and source.

As those alive to the reality before them cannot but wonder at and praise great art, music, courage, or beauty, so human beings,

---

issue is not how the righteous person should live but with what righteousness a person may find "salvation"; namely, that obtained through faith. Moreover, elsewhere in Romans, references to "the righteousness of faith" (4:11, 4:13), "righteousness based on faith" (9:30; 10:6), faith being counted as righteousness (4:5, 4:9), etc., suggest that Paul understands Habakkuk's words in the sense adopted here.

6. Note, furthermore, that when Paul quotes the same Habakkuk text in Gal 3:11b, the *oudeis* of v. 11a ("*no one* is found righteous") requires a generic understanding of *ho dikaios* in v. 11b: that *no one* is found righteous by the law is clear because, according to Scripture, one (i.e., *anyone*) is righteous by faith. See the pointed remarks of Wolter, *Der Brief*, 1:127n131; and the detailed argument of Oropeza, "Justification by Faith," 116-21.

7. Watson observes that when the "generic individual" who has faith (Rom 1:17) "becomes specific and acquires a name" in Rom 4, that name "is not Jesus Christ but Abraham." *Paul and the Hermeneutics*, xlii.

living in a world suffused with God's goodness and glory (Ps 33:5; Isa 6:3), are bound to praise him; indeed, how "impoverished" are those who live their lives "without ever having wondered over God, without ever, out of wonder over God, having lost [themselves] in worship!"[8] For Paul, such failure is not only impoverishing but inexcusable (Rom 1:20), since "what is knowable about God" is plain to all through his "works." "The world is charged with the grandeur of God" (Gerard Manley Hopkins). If people attend to God's creation, they cannot but intuit ("perceive") God's "eternal power and divine nature" (1:19–20). It is only *right*, then, that they acknowledge the truth of their situation by giving God due "honor" (1:21); their lives are built on a lie, out of step with reality, and, in the end, unsustainable when they refuse to do so.

Beyond that, human beings themselves are born, not of their own will, into a world not of their making and in which everything about them as well as their own physical and mental well-being is largely out of their control (life on earth is never *safe*)—and dependent on God. In the words of the hymn, "All that borrows life from Thee is ever in Thy care"; in the words of Paul, "from him and *through* him . . . are all things" (Rom 11:36a). It is only *right*, then, that people acknowledge the truth of their situation by giving God appropriate "thanks" (1:21)—and they live a lie when they do not. In refusing to honor and thank God as they ought, they "suppress" the most fundamental "truth" of their existence (1:18). As a result, their thinking, falsely based however sophisticated the superstructure ("they purported to be wise" [v. 22]), inevitably becomes vain, and their hearts are darkened (1:21). In all that matters most, they become "foolish" (1:22).

Paul then proceeds to show that humanity's refusal to acknowledge its Creator finds inevitable expression in rejection of creation's divinely given moral order (Rom 1:26–31). "Unrighteousness" has its roots in "ungodliness" (1:18). And as the "salvation" of which Paul speaks in 1:16 is "for every*one* who believes," so the sins Paul lists here as provoking God's judgment are not impersonal, systemic wrongs in which my part can be but little, but evils rooted and rotting in each of our hearts: vices like jealousy, spite, gossip, slander, faithlessness to one's commitments, and indifference where compassion

---

8. Kierkegaard, *Christian Discourses*, 132.

is called for. These may not seem egregious in our eyes, but they are more than sufficient to show that the innocence of Eden is lost to us all. Such things ought *not* to be, and people (Paul says) know as much (he develops the point in 2:14–15); but they flaunt God and his judgment by doing them anyway, and, by their approval, encourage others to dismiss *their* compunctions as well (1:32).

God's "wrath" is brought to bear against such sin—the very *goodness* of God cannot brook the corruption of his creation—both now and at the final judgment. Human accountability at God's final judgment remains the subject throughout Rom 2:1—3:20 (2:5–13, 2:16, 2:27, 3:19–20), a section that ends with Paul's declaration that the "whole world" will find itself culpable before God (3:19) (though judgment, be it noted, remains individual [2:5–6; cf. 14:10–12]). In chapter 1, however, Paul sees divine judgment at work already in the present (1:18): human beings are "handed over" as captives to the very sins they embrace (1:24, 1:26, 1:28; cf. 3:9). Inasmuch as those vices are the products of their own desires and passions, humans are, to be sure, willing captives, scarcely aware of their confinement. But captives they remain, locked into the pursuit of desires that, satisfied, never satisfy but demand further gratification; and their end is death (1:32, 6:16–23).

5. From the divine judgment ("wrath") of which Paul speaks in Romans 1:18—3:20, the revelation of God's righteousness of which he speaks in 1:17 brings deliverance. At 3:21–22, he restates and adds detail to the original thesis. According to 1:16–17, the revelation of God's righteousness is of benefit to those who believe, and it is revealed *ek pisteōs eis pistin*. At 3:22, Paul identifies Jesus Christ as the object of their faith,[9] and the terms he uses in doing so suggest

---

9. Gk. *dia pisteōs Iēsou Christou*. The phrase expands upon the *ek pisteōs* ("by faith") of Rom 1:17. Gk. *pistis* may mean "faithfulness" as well as "faith," so that a number of recent interpreters render the phrase "by the faithfulness of Jesus Christ" (taking "Jesus Christ" as the one who shows faithfulness rather than as the object of faith). So, for example, the commentaries of Johnson, *Reading Romans*; Longenecker, *The Epistle to the Romans*; and Wright, "The Letter to the Romans." This reading is by no means un-Pauline in its essence (although Paul speaks rather of Jesus's "obedience" than of his "faithfulness" [cf. 5:19; Phil 2:8]); Rom 3:24–25 makes clear that the righteousness of faith is, indeed, viable only because of what Christ has done.

Still, Christ's "faithfulness" does not appear to be what Paul intends in his references to "the righteousness of faith." As Lev 18:5 articulates the fundamental principle of "the righteousness of the law" (Rom 10:5; Gal 3:12), so a generalization of Gen 15:6 articulates the fundamental principle of "the righteousness of faith": "*x* believes God,

how we should understand the ambiguous *ek pisteōs eis pistin* in 1:17: "*through* faith in Jesus Christ *for* all who believe" (so 3:22); "*by* faith *for* faith" (i.e., based on faith, for all who believe [1:17]).[10] At 1:17, the revelation of God's righteousness is seen when people are found "righteous by faith" (v. 17b, quoting Habakkuk)—and those so found "righteous" are otherwise subject to God's wrath because of their "ungodliness and unrighteousness" (1:18). In chapter 3, the revelation of God's righteousness (v. 21) is seen when those who "have sinned and lack God's glory" (v. 23) are "found righteous[11] *through the redemption that comes through Christ Jesus*" (v. 24); and they are "found righteous *as a gift by God's grace*"—though what is a gift for them cost the Son of God his life: in the plan of God and

---

and it is credited to *x* as righteousness"—where *x* represents Abraham, who believed God's promise, *and* believers in the One who raised Jesus from the dead (4:3, 4:9, 4:24). Throughout Rom 4, the "faith" of which "the righteousness of faith" speaks is that of Abraham and his spiritual descendants who "believe" and to whom God credits righteousness (4: 3, 5, 9, 11, 12, 13, 16, 17, 18, 20). Note, further, that the Greek verb (*pisteuō*) that is cognate with *pistis* means "believe" or "trust," not "show faithfulness"; and in Paul's discussions of righteousness by faith, the noun "faith" is repeatedly that shown by one "who believes" (i.e., "faith" here represents the nominalization of the verb "to believe"; cf. Cirafesi, "*Echein pistin* in Hellenistic Greek," 12–15; Jensen, "*Pistis* and *Pisteuō* in Romans 4:5," 6–9). Thus, the "faith" on which "the righteousness of God" is based in Rom 1:17 and 3:22 is that of "everyone who believes" in 1:16 and of "all believers" in 3:22 (also Gal 2:16). The faith by which, according to 5:1, "we have been found righteous" is that of 4:24: *not* the faithfulness of Jesus but the faith of "those who believe [Gk. *tois pisteuousin*] in the One who raised Jesus our Lord from the dead." In 10:4, Christ is the "end of the law for *righteousness* for *everyone who believes*"; and in 10:6–10, the "faith" at issue in "the righteousness of faith" (v. 6) is, again, that of believers who "believe with the heart" and whose faith leads to "righteousness" (v. 10; cf. v. 9). Thus, when Paul speaks of those who are "righteous *ek pisteōs*," he consistently means "righteous by [their] faith," not "righteous by the faithfulness of Christ"; and when, in a context where the granting of righteousness is the issue, Paul supplies a genitive after *pistis* (*Iēsou Christou, Iēsou, Christou*), he is not introducing a notion foreign to his other discussions of that righteousness (the faithfulness of Christ) but merely identifying the object of the faith that (he everywhere says) leads to righteousness.

10. Cf. Calhoun, *Paul's Definitions*, 208; Watson, *Paul and the Hermeneutics*, 45; Wilckens, *Der Brief*, 1:88.

11. Gk. *dikaioumenoi*. In the active voice, and in a forensic or quasi-forensic context, the verb *dikaioō* means "find innocent," "find righteous," "acquit" (e.g., LXX Exod 23:7; Deut 25:1; 3 Kgdms 8:32). In the opening chapters of Romans, the last judgment is in view (2:13)—a judgment where only those "found righteous" obtain "salvation." Using the language of Gen 15:6, Paul speaks interchangeably of being "found righteous" or of being "credited with righteousness" (note the equivalence in Rom 4:5). Note that the verb *dikaioō*, "find righteous," is traditionally rendered "justify" in English, and the noun *dikaiosynē* rendered "justification." "Justification by faith" thus refers to God's "finding righteous" ("justifying") sinners who believe the gospel.

through the shedding of Christ's blood, Christ atoned for their sins so that God could rightly find guilty people righteous (3:25–26).

The "Righteousness of God"

We turn now to the crucial phrase in Rom 1:17, "the righteousness of God is revealed." But we do so bound by constraints imposed by the context in which it occurs: the righteousness of God is revealed when, because Christ's death atoned for their sins, God "finds righteous" those individuals who believe in Christ—whether Jew or gentile—even though as sinners they are otherwise subject to his judgment.

What, precisely, then, *is* "the righteousness of God"? The phrase means different things in different contexts even within the Pauline corpus; we must search for usages that correspond to what, in Rom 1:16—3:26, the righteousness of God is said to accomplish. Two usages seem relevant.

1. Paul speaks in Rom 5:17 of those who receive from God "the gift of righteousness." According to Phil 3:9, Paul wants to be "found"—at the last judgment, the same setting where being "found righteous" is crucial in Rom 1–3—having a "righteousness from God" (Gk. *ek theou*), a righteousness that is Paul's "through faith in Christ" (cf. "through faith in Jesus Christ" [Rom 3:22]). If we understand the genitive *theou* in Rom 1:17 as a genitive of origin or source, then "the righteousness of God" in 1:17 is the same as that spoken of as "*from* God" in Phil 3:9 and identified as the "gift of righteousness" in Rom 5:17: a gift of righteousness that God grants believers in Jesus Christ and that stands them in good stead before the divine tribunal. Such an understanding fits perfectly the progression of Paul's thought in 1:16—3:26.[12]

2. In Rom 9:30—10:10, "the righteousness of God" means the righteousness that God approves, namely, that of faith. There, Paul refers to "righteousness by faith" (Gk. *ek pisteōs*) (9:30, 10:6) as the path taken by gentile believers—but not by Jews who fail to acknowledge "the righteousness of God" (10:3): "the righteousness of God" is thus identified with righteousness "by faith." Along these

---

12. For this view, see further Irons, *Righteousness of God*, 311–36, and the literature there cited.

lines, "the righteousness of God" in 1:17 may be understood as the divinely ordained and approved path to righteousness. Note, too, that in Rom 10, "the righteousness of God" (v. 3), which is that "of faith" (v. 6), is contrasted with "the righteousness of the law," whose path to righteousness is spelled out in the principle "the one who does [the law's commands] will live by them" (v. 5, quoting Lev 18:5). Similarly, "the righteousness of God" (Rom 3:21–22), which is "through faith in Jesus Christ" (3:22), is contrasted with the law whose demand for works as a path to righteousness has not been met (3:20, 3:28; cf. "apart from the law, the righteousness of God has been brought to light" [3:21]). In the end, "the righteousness that God approves" seems the most satisfactory understanding of "the righteousness of God" in Rom 1:17a: the same phrase is reproduced in 10:3, and there, as here, it carries the same sense of being based on faith and contrasted with the path of the law.[13]

An "Apocalyptic" Doctrine?

"Apocalyptic" is a slippery word, meaning different things to different people and in different contexts. But what Paul says about the righteousness of God and justification is "apocalyptic" at least in the sense that it is the subject of a divine revelation (Gk. *apokalypsis*): Paul says that the "righteousness of God is revealed [Gk. *apokalyptetai*] in the gospel." In what sense, "revealed"?

The Greek verb *apokalyptō* often refers to the disclosure of information (indeed, of mysteries) hitherto unknown (Matt 11:25; 1 Pet 1:12). That can hardly be the case here, however, since Paul claims that the righteousness of God "revealed" in the gospel was already the subject of an oracle of Habakkuk; furthermore, righteousness by faith was spoken of in Genesis 15:6 (Rom 4:3). A similar problem arises in Galatians, where, after noting that Abraham was justified by faith (Gal 3:6), Paul speaks of faith's "coming" as simultaneous with the coming of Christ, bringing to an end the period in which the law served as

---

13. Cf. Lightfoot, *Notes on Epistles*, 250; Watson, *Paul and the Hermeneutics*, 43–44. Paul speaks of believers as those who are *now* "found righteous by faith" (Rom 3:24, 28), those who "*have been found* righteous by faith" (5:1), and those whom, at the future judgment, God *will find* righteous by faith (3:30; Gal 5:5)—on the assumption that, throughout their lives, they will persevere in and give obedient expression to the faith with which they began (Rom 11:20, 11:22; 1 Cor 15:1–2; Gal 5:6; Col 1:22–23).

"guardian" (Gal 3:23-25). The point appears to be that although even before Christ's coming, God found sinners righteous by faith, he did so (at the time, passing over their sins) because, in the divine plan, Christ's death would atone for sins committed before, at the time of, and after his redemptive work (Rom 3:25-26). Though the path to righteousness through faith was open already for Abraham, its viability depended, for believers of all ages, on Christ's death "for our sins" spoken of in the gospel (1 Cor 15:1-3). To say that God's righteousness "is revealed" thus refers here not to the disclosure of hitherto unknown information, but to the coming into effect on the stage of human history of what, in the plan of God, had been prepared from eternity (cf. 1 Pet 1:5). The path to righteousness through faith depends on and "is revealed in" (i.e., becomes effective with) the gospel of Christ's redemptive work.[14]

That said, it is true that deliverance from the wrath to come counts as an "apocalyptic" theme on most definitions of the term.

Concluding Reflections

The world as we know it is not the world as God made it or meant it to be. Paul (together with all of Scripture) finds the cause of its corruption in the sin of its moral inhabitants. Human beings, created with a capacity to appreciate and affirm what is beautiful, good, and true, and to acknowledge the Source and Creator of all, have chosen to suppress the truth. Rejecting God and defying creation's moral order, they live—by the providence and grace of God, be it noted—as though in a world of their own making, free to do as they choose.[15] Such falsehood, in a moral world, is disastrous in the short term, unsustainable in the end. God, who has the last word, will make all things new, while that which is old and corrupt lies under his condemnation, its judgment pending.

Pending judgment, with its dual outcomes, and entrance into God's eternal kingdom were central themes in the proclamation of Jesus and remained so in the message of Paul. From 1 Thessalonians (likely Paul's earliest epistle), we see that from Paul's initial visit to their city, the Thessalonians had learned all about deliverance from the "wrath to come" (cf. 1 Thess 1:10, 5:9). A similar picture emerges from Paul's Corinthian

---

14. For this understanding of the verb "is revealed," see, for example, the commentaries of Moo, *Letter to the Romans*; Schlier, *Der Römerbrief*; and Wolter, *Der Brief*.

15. Cf. Kohák, *Embers and the Stars*, 67-109.

correspondence. Wherever he goes, Paul says, his concern is to bring "salvation" to his hearers (1 Cor 1:18, 1:21, 9:19–22) lest they share in the "condemnation" that awaits the "world" (1 Cor 11:32) and its "perishing" inhabitants (1 Cor 1:18; 2 Cor 2:15, 4:3). It is first in Galatians, however, that the language of "righteousness" (or "justification") becomes prominent (though see 1 Cor 1:30, 6:11; 2 Cor 5:21), as Paul responds to the demand that gentile believers be circumcised (and thus, in effect, become Jews) if they are to be delivered from "this present evil world" and the curse that hangs over its sinful inhabitants (Gal 1:4, 3:10). Christ bore that curse (3:13) so that sinners may be "found righteous [justified] by faith" (2:16, 3:11–12). (Note that Paul says that he and Peter, too, needed to be "justified by faith" [Gal 2:15–16]; the need for justification is not limited to gentiles.) Thereafter, justification becomes part of Paul's theological repertoire, figuring largely in Romans and Philippians. (In Phil 3:9, Paul again speaks of the "righteousness" in which he himself, a "Hebrew of Hebrews" [v. 5], wants to be "found.") Hence, though the *language* of "justification by faith" was first adopted in response to issues arising in Paul's gentile mission, its *substance*—deliverance from divine judgment through faith in the gospel—was a focus of that mission from the start, and it was no less relevant for Jews than for gentiles.[16]

Jews and gentiles alike, we are all (such is Paul's argument from Rom 1:18—3:20) a part of what is wrong with this world and subject to its condemnation. Yet God has abandoned neither us nor his world. In the fullness of time, Christ, the innocent, holy One, bore the bane of all our sin so that we might be forgiven, delivered ("saved") from God's wrath, and "found righteous" by his judgment; so "justified," we may have a part in the eternal life of the world made new, God's kingdom. It is all a gift of grace; but in receiving the grace of God, we are necessarily abandoning the lie that we are gods ourselves and submitting, in faith, to "the One who raised Jesus our Lord from the dead: Jesus, who was handed over to death for our offenses and raised again for our justification" (Rom 4:24–25).

Bibliography

Augustine. *Teaching Christianity: De Doctrina Christiana*. Translated by Edmund Hill. Hyde Park, NY: New City, 1996.

Calhoun, Robert Matthew. *Paul's Definitions of the Gospel in Romans 1*. Tübingen: Mohr Siebeck, 2011.

---

16. Westerholm, *Justification Reconsidered*, 1–22.

Cirafesi, Wally V. "*Echein pistin* in Hellenistic Greek and Its Contribution to the *pistis Christou* Debate." *Biblical and Ancient Greek Linguistics* 1 (2012) 5–37.

Irons, Charles Lee. *The Righteousness of God: A Lexical Examination of the Covenant-Faithfulness Interpretation*. Wissenschaftliche Untersuchungen zum Neuen Testament 2.386. Tübingen: Mohr Siebeck, 2015.

Jensen, Aaron Michael. "*Pistis* and *Pisteuō* in Romans 4:5: Neglected Evidence for 'Faith in Christ,' and a Re-Detheologizing of the *Pistis Christou* Debate." *Journal for the Study of Paul and His Letters* 8 (2018) 5–19.

Johnson, Luke Timothy. *Reading Romans: A Literary and Theological Commentary*. New York: Crossroad, 1997.

Kierkegaard, Søren. *Christian Discourses*. In *Christian Discourses: The Crisis and a Crisis in the Life of an Actress*, translated by Howard V. Hong and Edna H. Hong, 1–300. Princeton, NJ: Princeton University Press, 1997.

Kohák, Erazim. *The Embers and the Stars: A Philosophical Inquiry into the Moral Sense of Nature*. Chicago: University of Chicago Press, 1984.

Lightfoot, J. B. *Notes on Epistles of St. Paul from Unpublished Commentaries*. London: Macmillan, 1904.

Longenecker, Richard N. *The Epistle to the Romans: A Commentary on the Greek Text*. New International Greek Testament Commentary. Grand Rapids: Eerdmans, 2016.

Meyer, Ben F. "The Primacy of the Intended Sense of Texts." In *Critical Realism and the New Testament*, 17–55. Allison Park, PA: Pickwick Publications, 1989.

———. "A Tricky Business: Ascribing New Meaning to Old Texts." *Gregorianum* 71 (1990) 743–61.

Moo, Douglas J. *The Letter to the Romans*. 2nd ed. New International Commentary on the New Testament. Grand Rapids: Eerdmans, 2018.

Morgan, Teresa. "Faith in Dialogue." *Journal for the Study of the New Testament* 40 (2018) 299–311.

Oropeza, B. J. "Justification by Faith in Christ or Faithfulness of Christ? Updating the *PISTIS CHRISTOU* Debate in Light of Paul's Use of Scripture." *Journal of Theological Studies* 72 (2021) 102–24.

Schlier, Heinrich. *Der Römerbrief*. 2nd ed. Herders Theologischer Kommentar zum Neuen Testament. Freiburg: Herder, 1979.

Watson, Francis. *Paul and the Hermeneutics of Faith*. 2nd ed. London: Bloomsbury T. & T. Clark, 2016.

Westerholm, Stephen. *Justification Reconsidered: Rethinking a Pauline Theme*. Grand Rapids: Eerdmans, 2013.

Wilckens, Ulrich. *Der Brief an die Römer*. Study edition. 2 vols. Evangelisch-Katholischer Kommentar zum Neuen Testament 6. Neukirchen-Vluyn: Neukirchener, 2010.

Wolter, Michael. *Der Brief an die Römer*. 2 vols. Evangelisch-Katholischer Kommentar zum Neuen Testament 6. Vol. 1: Ostfildern: Patmos, 2014; Vol. 2: Göttingen: Vandenhoeck & Ruprecht, 2019.

Wright, N. T. "The Letter to the Romans: Introduction, Commentary, and Reflections." In *The Acts of the Apostles; Introduction to Epistolatory Literature; The Letter to the Romans; The First Letter to the Corinthians*, 393–770. Nashville: Abingdon, 2002.

Exploring Literary Revelations

13

Apocalyptic Reversal and the Struggle for Honor

BRUCE K. WARD

AN APOCALYPTIC AGE SUCH as ours is in dire need of a properly apocalyptic thought, an apocalypticism that is neither fundamentalist nor romantic, neither merely literalist nor merely figurative, and which takes human history seriously. This imperative has prompted contemporary secular philosophers such as Alain Badiou and Giorgio Agamben to mine the messianic texts of the New Testament for insight. Christian theologians, however, have been more reluctant to take up the challenge, likely out of fear of being tarred with the fundamentalist brush. Indeed, as P. Travis Kroeker has pointed out, foundational theological figures such as Saint Augustine have been conventionally read as *anti*-apocalyptic. Kroeker himself has made a powerful case for Augustine's apocalypticism, regarding it as foundational for a messianic political theology that is rooted in the Gospels and Paul while still offering a critical resource for our own apocalyptic time.[1] Through his revision of the conventional reading of Augustine, he shows us what apocalyptic thought can and should be. Another resource on which Kroeker draws for his development of a contemporary messianic political theology is a foundational modern figure, the Russian novelist Fyodor Dostoevsky. While I am not sufficiently versed in Augustine studies to comment on

1. See, for instance, Kroeker, *Messianic Political Theology*, ch. 3.

the impact of Kroeker's work in that field, I can say that his reading of Dostoevsky within the apocalyptic stream emanating from Paul and Augustine constitutes an original, indeed groundbreaking, interpretation of the Russian writer as a prophet of messianic community.[2]

What relation does this messianic community bear to actual human history and politics? Kroeker's answer to this might appropriately be expressed in the contrasting images from the book of Revelation (5:5–10), to which he refers frequently in his reading of *The Brothers Karamazov*: the "conquering Lion" and the "suffering Lamb."[3] The former image is in accord with the expectations of the "powers and principalities," the structures of worldly sovereign authority that dominate history but are already passing away; the latter image signifies the unexpected inbreaking of a new community transformed through penitential suffering. Kroeker characterizes this confrontation, whether in Augustine or Dostoevsky, variously as an "agonistic apocalyptic contrast," a "scandalous collision," and an "apocalyptic reversal."[4]

In what follows, I want to reflect more closely on these concepts of *agon* (the ancient Greek term for "contest"), *scandal*, and especially *reversal* in regard to the relationship between the historical power structures of the Lion and the messianic community of the Lamb—or, in other terms, between the non-Christian and the Christian within history. My reflection will bear upon this question particularly: To what extent does the *reversal* of fallen history presuppose that its structures be *accepted*? Or to put the question more provocatively: Can one imagine the Lamb entering into a duel with the Lion?

The provocation, I hasten to add, comes from Dostoevsky himself. The question of how the Christian living in messianic time should relate to those (whether calling themselves Christian or not) living in worldly time was a central preoccupation of Dostoevsky's apocalypticism. It is given dramatic artistic expression in his treatment of that *agon* of *agons*, the duel. We find dramatizations of the duel ritual almost everywhere in Dostoevsky. In the major post-Siberian works, beginning with *Notes from Underground* and ending with *The Brothers Karamazov*, there is only one novel, *Crime and Punishment*, in which a duel is not imagined,

---

2. See, for instance, Kroeker, *Messianic Political Theology*, 90–96; Kroeker and Ward, *Remembering the End*, chs. 4 and 6.

3. For instance, Kroeker and Ward, *Remembering the End*, 14, 16, 186.

4. Kroeker, *Messianic Political Theology*, 57, 60; Kroeker and Ward, *Remembering the End*, 16.

threatened, discussed, or undertaken. In the image of the duel, Dostoevsky fashioned a literary vehicle of remarkable compression and power for what he wanted to say, both descriptively and prescriptively, about the relation of the suffering Lamb to the conquering Lion.

The concept and practice of the duel arose from what Charles Taylor has called "the ethic of honor and glory," one of those two or three frameworks of moral value that have dominated Western history.[5] The honor ethic is usually treated as an historical artifact, now superseded by capitalist commerce and the liberal equality that goes along with it. Yet while the warrior societies based on the honor ethic have long been consigned to the dustbin of history, it is not so obvious that the ethic itself, along with its corollary concepts of dignity and reputation, has met the same fate. As Taylor insists, "This goes on being an important dimension of our life in modern society, and the fierce competition for this kind of dignity is part of what animates democratic politics."[6] Insofar as the generalized respect due to each human being as such does not account for the respect due to human beings in relation to the circumstances of their social environment, the need for honor must, as Simone Weil argues, always be considered a "vital need of the human soul."[7]

Given the importance of the honor ethic within the dominant Western historical structures and frameworks of meaning, it isn't surprising that the question of honor would be a focal point in the "collision" between conquering Lion and suffering Lamb. In what follows, I will delineate the three aspects, or moments, of this collision already noted above—*agon*, scandal, and reversal—in connection with Christian thinkers who were on the side of the Lamb, while nonetheless called by their sense of justice to give the honor ethic its full due. The movement from *agon* to scandal to reversal—from Augustine, the ancient Roman theologian, to Pierre Corneille, the seventeenth-century French playwright, to Dostoevsky, the nineteenth-century Russian novelist—is not meant to imply a progressive development of insight, or even a clear line of successive influence. It is more the case that Dostoevsky's image of the duel is so compressed that, as I hope to show, what is at stake in his apocalyptic reversal can be more fully illumined by some prior acquaintance with Augustine's and Corneille's treatments of the honor ethic.

---

5. See Taylor, *Sources of the Self*, 14–45.
6. Taylor, *Sources of the Self*, 25.
7. Weil, *Need for Roots*, 19–20.

Agon: Augustine

The honor ethic in the West is Homeric in origin, and although severely criticized by the Platonists and Stoics, it continued to flourish within Graeco-Roman civilization, reaching arguably its most (vain)glorious manifestation in the Roman Empire. The *agon* between the conquering Lion and the suffering Lamb comes under extended philosophical-theological scrutiny in book 5 of Augustine's *City of God*. According to Kroeker, Augustine here exposes the "warrior ethic of glorying in power" as "rooted in a lie about divine glory and power" that reflects "the love of power rather than the power of love."[8] A close reading of Augustine's critique of Roman honor, however, reveals certain nuances that, if they do not run counter to his general condemnation, at least mitigate it, and in interesting ways. He observes that in the earlier Roman period, before the onset of imperial decadence, a distinction was made between "right" and "wrong" ways of pursuing honor and glory. Roman honor, as embodied in a figure like Cato, was not merely a matter of winning human praise, by fair means or foul, but of winning "the good opinion of enlightened judges." Presumably, "enlightened judges" would be able to see through appearances brought about through deceitful means. For Augustine, this ambition for attaining glory "by the right path" is, of course, inferior to the virtue of the Christian conscience, which is not dependent on merely human testimony but seeks "the glory which comes from God alone." But it is still superior to a pursuit of glory based solely on greed or the *libido dominandi*. Indeed, as Augustine observes, the "love of praise," in the right way, even "counts as a virtue because it checks greater vices." One might ask, with Augustine, how often still does the concern for reputation, the desire to be well thought of by others, restrain "greed for money and other faults"?[9]

Moreover, and here Augustine directs himself to fellow Christians, the Roman honor ethic at its best not only restrained baser vices but inspired acts of remarkable self-sacrifice. In order to illustrate this point, he draws from Roman letters, from Virgil, Sallust, Plutarch, and Livy, examples of selfless deeds inspired by the love of honor: the putting of one's country ahead of one's own family (Brutus); the putting of one's country ahead of one's own life (Curtius); the putting of one's sworn word, even to an enemy, ahead of one's life (Marcus Regulus);

---

8. Kroeker, *Messianic Political Theology*, 55. See also Taylor, *Sources of the Self*, 214.
9. Augustine, *Concerning the City of God* 5.12, 5.13, 5.19.

the undertaking of voluntary poverty for the sake of one's country (the leaders of the early republic). Although Augustine dwells at length on such examples, there is no reason to see in this a lingering admiration that betokens an inner conflict between the former Roman rhetorician and the Christian convert. As he says, these Roman figures, by the very fact that they are still known, "have received their reward in full." Very different is the "reward of the saints." Augustine's point is that the "saints" are also called upon to exhibit a virtue analogous to that of the best Romans: "If we do not display, in the service of the most glorious City of God, the qualities of which the Romans, after their fashion, gave us something of a model, in their pursuit of their earthly city, then we ought to feel the prick of shame."[10]

Augustine does not repudiate the concept of honor and its attendant glory so much as he seeks to *redirect* it, in the manner of Scripture itself, throughout which, it need hardly be said, divine honor and glory are prominent motifs.[11] One aspect of this redirection concerns the Christian's relationship to God, in seeking "the glory that comes from God alone" rather than from other human beings. The other aspect concerns the Christian's relation to the non-Christian. According to Augustine, the Christian who "despises" the flattering judgment of others nevertheless remains concerned with the question of reputation. Why? Because "if he is a truly good man, he does not regard the salvation of his fellow-men as of no importance . . . he loves even his enemies . . . and he wishes them to be reformed so that he may have them as fellow-citizens, not of the earthly city, but of the heavenly. . . . As for those who praise him . . . his ardent concern is that praise should rather be given to him from whom man receives whatever in him is rightly deserving of praise."[12]

If I understand Augustine correctly here, he is arguing that in response to all those examples of Roman virtue he has cited, the Christian should also offer an example. It should be an example that non-Christians can appreciate in such a way as to direct their attention away from the human example toward God, a kind of "teaching moment."

---

10. Augustine, *Concerning the City of God* 5.15, 5.16, 5.18.

11. And not only divine honor; see, for instance, Paul's exhortation to Roman Christians to "outdo one another in showing honor" (Rom 12:10 NRSV). For a remarkable genealogical tracing of the movement in the other direction, from the glory of divine *oikonomia* to the political apparatus, especially "public opinion," of human governing, see Agamben, *Kingdom and the Glory*, especially ch. 8.

12. Augustine, *Concerning the City of God* 5.14, 5.19.

Skandalon: Corneille (as Interpreted by Charles Péguy)

What might be considered Augustine's redirection or "radicalization" of Roman honor[13] has important implications for interpreting the duel in relation to Dostoevsky's apocalypticism. Before turning to the Russian novelist, though, let us pause along the way with the French playwright Corneille. According to Taylor, in Corneille "the ethic of honor and glory [received] one of its most inspiring expressions,"[14] demonstrating its resilience even long after the critiques of Plato, the Stoics, and Augustine. Corneilleian honor would resonate strongly with the youthful Dostoevsky.[15]

The conflict between honorable duty and passionate love was a favorite, indeed almost the only, subject of Corneille's great plays, a number of which were set in ancient Rome. The last of these, *Polyeucte*, took as its subject the historical martyrdom of Polyeuctus, an Armenian nobleman who converted to Christianity during the persecutions of the emperor Decius in the third century. In Corneille's play, Polyeucte's very public opposition to Roman paganism—he enters the temple and casts down its idols—requires that he be judged and punished with death by the Roman military commander of the province of Armenia, Severus, a soldier-aristocrat close to the emperor's court. It is a characteristic Corneilleian complication that Severus is in love with the woman to whom Polyeucte is engaged, Pauline, who has remained a pagan. Before dying, Polyeucte entrusts Pauline to the care of his judge.

Most commentary on the play focuses on how the romantic triangle dramatizes the conflict between love and honor, but it can be read also as a dramatization of the "scandalous collision" between Christian and non-Christian. This is the focus of the remarkable commentary on the play by the twentieth-century Catholic poet and essayist Charles Péguy, who addresses the confrontation between the soon-to-be-martyred Polyeucte and his Roman judge, Severus. For Péguy, the confrontation represents a "prodigious spiritual duel," a collision of values in which there is no cheating by the author to give one side the advantage over the other: "In

---

13. See John Milbank on Augustine's "radicalization" of Roman honor in *Beyond Secular Order*, 236.

14. Taylor, *Sources of the Self*, 214.

15. See Ward, *Dostoevsky's Critique of the West*, 17. In a letter written when he was nineteen, Dostoevsky included Corneille among the European authors such as Homer, Shakespeare, and Schiller who most enthralled him.

the duel of thought . . . each of the theses presents itself in its exactitude and its fullness."[16] Corneille's balanced presentation of each side of the agonistic contrast between Lion and Lamb, each in its own "exactitude and fullness," is of paramount importance for Péguy as a model for the relation between Christian and non-Christian. The Christian "doesn't despise the world . . . doesn't debase the world in order to elevate himself . . . those who take on height by leaving the world while debasing the world, don't elevate themselves. They remain at the same height."[17]

The figure of Severus as presented by Corneille, devoted to justice and duty as he understands them, could easily occupy a place among those Romans cited by Augustine as positive examples, even to Christians. In this, Corneille, like Augustine, gives the temporal its due. Severus, a Stoic, might not have the gods he deserves, but still he deserves to be honored, even admired by Polyeucte as a high type of antique greatness.[18]

Yet this doing justice to the temporal does not alter the nature of the confrontation as a spiritual duel, an agonistic collision. As a follower of the suffering Lamb, Polyeucte is prepared to die a martyr's death at the hands of Severus, but he also wishes Severus "to be reformed" so that he may have him as "a fellow-citizen, not of the earthly city, but of the heavenly," to recall Augustine's words. If this is the case, then Polyeucte wishes to have an impact on Severus, he cares about what Severus thinks of him, about what reputation he has in the estimation of Severus. He wants to be honored by Severus, not for his own sake but to draw Severus's attention toward "him from whom man receives whatever in him is rightly deserving of praise."[19] From this point of view, it is not enough that Polyeucte have truth on his side, that he be "right" before God, in defiance of the world, for if Severus could see and appreciate that, he would already be a Christian. Somehow, Polyeucte must appear "right" before Severus and according to the values of Severus. Just as Polyeucte might regret that the admirable Severus is not a Christian, Severus should regret that Polyeucte did not remain a pagan. As Péguy puts it:

> This regret for Polyeucte . . . is the only vulnerable point there may be in Severus's heart . . . for it is the only point of recourse we have there against habit . . . . Severus is a man habituated

---

16. Péguy, *Notes on Bergson and Descartes*, 113.
17. Péguy, *Notes on Bergson and Descartes*, 136.
18. Péguy, *Notes on Bergson and Descartes*, 139.
19. Augustine, *Concerning the City of God* 5.14, 5.19.

to everything and particularly to everything pagan, and upon whom the Christian has no point of leverage—except he is not habituated to this . . . that a man like Polyeucte could have become a Christian.[20]

This is where the agonistic collision becomes also a "scandalous" one.

Severus is scandalized not so much by the image of the slain Lamb as by the image of Polyeucte, a man no less honorable than himself, who is also, regrettably, a Christian. Severus's regret is more than mere disappointment that Polyeucte did not remain a pagan. It is a "point of anxiety,"[21] the anxiety of a thoughtful person whose moral framework is brought into question by the presence of a contradiction: between the noble, courageous bearing of his prisoner, and what he believes a follower of the crucified Lamb should be like.[22] Severus was expecting to be offended by what he encountered, to be scandalized, in the bad sense.[23] Instead, what happens, according to Péguy's reading of the play, is a *skandalon* (that is, "stumbling block") "in reverse . . . in the good sense," for the scandal constitutes a "rupturing of habit" and therefore a possible point of opening, "the only point through which we can hope that grace could ever pass."[24] This scandal "in the good sense" is more a matter of reputation, of "image" than of truth, though it remains no less rooted in

---

20. Péguy, *Notes on Bergson and Descartes*, 145.

21. Péguy, *Notes on Bergson and Descartes*, 146.

22. Neither Corneille nor Péguy elaborate on what the pagan Severus's preconceived image of a Christian would have been. Most likely it would have been similar to that of the Roman historian and statesman Tacitus, who in his *Annals of Rome* described the followers of Christ as captive to a "shocking" and "shameful" superstition, which inspired among them "hatred of the human race." Quoted in Huttunen, *Early Christians Adapting to the Roman Empire*, ch. 2. Or we might consider Nietzsche's description of the scorn of the noble Roman faced with "the *corruptest* form of corruption. . . . These stealthy vermin which, shrouded in night, fog, and ambiguity crept up to every individual and sucked seriousness for *real* things . . . out of him, this cowardly . . . and honeyed crew. . . . This underhanded bigotry, conventicle secrecy, gloomy concepts such as hell, such as the sacrifice of the innocent, such as the *unio mystica* in blood-drinking, above all the slowly stirred-up fire of vengefulness, of Chandala revengefulness." And so on. See Nietzsche, *Twilight of the Idols and The Anti-Christ*, 193.

23. For biblical references to a *skandalon* in the bad sense, see Matt 18:6–7 and Rom 14:13. Péguy seems to have Matthew in mind when he writes: "*Nolite scandalizare*. For the same reason that one must not scandalize the children, one must not scandalize the pagans and infidels. They also are ignorant; and consequently in a certain sense innocents. . . . They do not have that terrible privilege of being able to sin like us." Péguy, *Notes on Bergson and Descartes*, 144–45.

24. Péguy, *Notes on Bergson and Descartes*, 146.

truth. Polyeucte gives his entire being to God, but this is not enough. Out of love for his adversary, he also gives an image, an image of honor that is accessible to the adversary's consciousness: "A singular situation. The more does not suffice. The less must be added to it."[25]

Reversal: Dostoevsky

In turning now to Dostoevsky, we are again met with a "prodigious spiritual duel," but the ancient Roman pagan is replaced by the modern atheist. The ways in which Dostoevsky's great novels are a testing ground for the duel of thought between faith and atheism has long drawn the attention of those interpreters who regard him as a modern religious-philosophical thinker on a par with Friedrich Nietzsche. Yet the polyphonic manner in which Dostoevsky dramatizes the collision of ideas has led to serious misreadings; for instance, that his atheists, such as Ivan Karamazov in his "Rebellion," have "all the best arguments," or that his authorial intentions as a Christian were betrayed by characters who somehow slipped out of his control. Better readings note that a polyphonic orchestration of voices still requires a conductor, and that the duel of thought ultimately favors the Christian side, in all manner of ways that operate beyond the limits of rational argumentation. Nevertheless, it remains true that Dostoevsky is strictly careful about doing full justice to the other side, in all "its exactitude and its fullness." To express it in Bakhtinian terms, he renounces any authorial finalization of a character's consciousness, any imposed conversion to a way of thinking that is not a free possibility for the character.[26] It is clear that he understands this care to give the non-Christian side its due, not to elevate one side by debasing the other, as precisely what Christian faith requires. As Rowan Williams has it, this "dialogical principle" of Dostoevsky inevitably entails a certain risk: "To state a position and stake one's fidelity to it requires as complete an honesty as possible about the circumstances and ideas that would most severely test its credibility. Stating it honestly entails invoking its possible denial."[27] One might say that the risk run by the Christian author expressing the spiritual duel of thought is analogous to the risk run by God in creating human freedom.

25. Péguy, *Notes on Bergson and Descartes*, 148–49.
26. See Bakhtin, *Problems of Dostoevsky's Poetics*, 63.
27. Williams, *Dostoevsky*, 242.

Let us now, so to speak, add "the less to the more" by considering the *literal* duel in Dostoevsky, which has not received as much interpretive attention.[28] In his final masterpiece, the question of the duel arises, in one instance, from the public shaming of a father, the lowly Snegiryov, who is dragged by Dmitri Karamazov through the street by his beard. Snegiryov's son, the child Ilyusha, burns with a desire to vindicate his father's honor: "Papa,' he said, 'papa, I'll throw him down when I'm big, I'll knock the sword out of his hand with my sword . . . throw him down, hold my sword over him and say: I could kill you, but I forgive you, so there!'"[29] We encounter this fantasy of a vanquishing of the opponent followed by magnanimous forgiveness in earlier works, for instance in the feverish imaginings of the underground man.[30] However Ilyusha does not, like that character, remain mired in impotent *ressentiment*. With Alyosha's help he is able, before his death, to enter into the healing cycle of mutual forgiveness in the face of offense.

In the experience of Ilyusha, we can see how the question of a literal duel becomes integrated into one of the larger spiritual duels at work throughout the novel, in this case between two visions of justice, one rooted in retribution and the other in forgiveness. Such an integration of the literal and spiritual is given yet more compressed dramatic expression in one of the events "From the Life of the Elder Zosima," chronicled by Alyosha Karamazov. The Russian monk, Zosima, is the last in the long line of major characters in Dostoevsky's work to be caught up in the rituals of the duel: preceding him, we have the underground man's absurd fantasies, in *Notes from Underground*; Prince Myshkin's refusal to challenge a slap in the face, in *The Idiot*; Nikolai Stavrogin's entry into a duel only deliberately to violate its most sacrosanct conventions, in *Demons*; Andrei Versilov's failure to respond to a public slap and his son's aborted efforts to bring about a duel for the sake of his father's honor, in *The Adolescent*. We might see these as a series of attempts on Dostoevsky's part to arrive at a clarity he achieves finally in the Zosima episode.

Zosima's duel is the centerpiece of his "turning around" from a life according to the worldly power structures symbolized by the Lion to the

---

28. For two treatments of the duel in Dostoevsky, from historical and literary-critical perspectives, see Reyfman, *Ritualized Violence Russian Style*, ch. 6; and Holland, "Poetics of the Slap," 21–40.

29. Dostoevsky, *Brothers Karamazov*, 207. Further references to *Brothers Karamazov* will be cited parenthetically in the text.

30. See Dostoevsky, *Notes from Underground*, 123–25.

new life of the messianic community based on the Lamb. Indeed, this episode from Zosima's life constitutes the most detailed account in all of Dostoevsky of the *process* of Christian conversion. At the beginning of the process, Zosima is a newly minted young officer in an elite regiment: "We were ready to shed our blood for the injured honor of our regiment, but hardly one of us knew what real honor is" (296). During a regimental posting to a provincial town, he falls in love (or rather, convinces himself that he has) with a young woman who is already engaged to another man. Zosima's own self-regard makes him oblivious to this elemental fact. When he learns that she has married while he was away on a posting, surprise turns to anger as he suspects that she led him on for her amusement. In his desire for revenge, he concocts a pretext for publicly insulting his rival, thereby ensuring his challenge to a duel: "At that time, though duels were strictly forbidden, there was even a fashion for them, as it were, among the military—thus do barbaric prejudices sometimes spring up and thrive" (297).

The seeds of Zosima's turning around had been planted long before, in childhood memories, but it is the evening before the duel that they begin to sprout. The stages of the process are carefully delineated. (1) Returning home in a foul mood that evening, he takes out his anger on his orderly, Afanasy, striking him in the face "with all [his] might" (297). (2) After going to bed and sleeping briefly, he rises and gazes out the window at the garden, just as the sun is appearing and the birds "begin to chime" (297). In the face of the world's beauty, he feels shame and remorse, and then identifies the source of the feeling as he recalls his beating of Afanasy. (3) This memory and the feeling of guilt accompanying it triggers another memory, from his childhood, of his brother Markel's last days before an early death and especially Markel's words: "Truly each of us is guilty before everyone and for everyone, only people do not know it, and if they knew it, the world would at once become paradise" (298). These words, repeated like a mantra with slight variations at different points throughout the novel, encapsulate Dostoevsky's messianic vision (4). The feeling of guilt and subsequent childhood memory bring Zosima to the full realization of his present situation: "And suddenly the whole truth appeared to me in its full enlightenment: what was I setting out to do?" (298). (5) The feeling, the memory, and the realization do not remain at the level of sentiment or idea but issue immediately in actions. First, Zosima finds Afanasy, bows down before him, and asks for forgiveness. Then he jumps into the carriage brought by his second to take him to the duel. There he faces his adversary at twelve paces, each with loaded pistol. After the other man fires a shot that nearly kills him, Zosima throws his own pistol away, and asks for forgiveness: "Forgive a foolish young man, for it is my own fault that I offended you and have now made you shoot at me. I am ten times worse than you, if not more. Tell that to the person you honor most in the world" (299). The other man, after some hesitation, accepts Zosima's apology and agrees to end the duel there. Later that same day, Zosima announces to his scandalized fellow officers that he has resigned his commission in order to enter the monastery.

In what we might call the line of apostolic succession within *The Brothers Karamazov*, Zosima stands at the head, as the mentor and model for Alyosha, who in turn is the founder of the messianic community of children with which the novel ends. Zosima's own entry into the messianic community coincides with the drama of the literal duel, thus achieving the integration of the literal and spiritual duels at which Dostoevsky seemed to have been aiming throughout his works.

Concluding Questions

The duel that is formative for the Russian monk leaves us with certain questions. First, why does Dostoevsky have Zosima enter into the duel at all? It has been suggested that, despite the parodic twists and distortions he applies to the duel ritual throughout his works, he nevertheless upheld it finally as a worthy manifestation of the human need for dignity.[31] This interpretation, however, flies in the face of Zosima's own unambiguous condemnation of the duel as a "barbaric prejudice." Yet, still, he goes to the duel *after* the decisive moment of his conversion has taken place. The inconsistency might seem a regression to the ways of the "old Adam" and an unnecessary concession to the reigning structures of the world, in this case the honor ethic. Dostoevsky's point, however, is that Zosima enters into the duel *only in order to subvert it*, thereby showing in this concrete instance that a properly apocalyptic thinking entails not a rejection of history and its power structures from a stance "outside" or "above" it, but rather, an "*acceptance and reversal* of fallen history."[32] Such an entry into history reflects the incarnational nature of

31. This is the position taken by Reyfman, *Ritualized Violence Russian Style*, 260.
32. This phrasing is Thomas Merton's, inspired by his reading of William Blake. See Ward, "Apocalypse and Modernity," 55.

Christianity, the sense of a grace that penetrates and transfigures from inside what is already there in nature and culture.

This reversal, which turns the ritual inside out from within, is not only for Zosima but also *for others*. Zosima's own explanation of why he went to the duel at all, thereby risking his life and thus ending the story right there, makes this concern for *the others* clear:

> I ought to have confessed as soon as we arrived here, even before his shot, without leading him into great and mortal sin, but we have arranged everything in the world so repugnantly that to do so was nearly impossible, for only now that I have stood up to his shot from twelve paces can my words mean something for him, but had I done it before his shot . . . then people would simply say: "he's a coward, he's afraid of a pistol, there's no point in listening to him." (299)

Zosima then shares his apocalyptic message with those at the duel, that we are living in messianic time, that "life is paradise," realizable through mutual taking on of guilt and forgiveness. Zosima wants to be listened to, to be taken seriously, because, to refer back to Augustine, "he wishes them to be reformed so that he may have them as fellow-citizens, not of the earthly city, but of the heavenly." If he is to be listened to, he must demonstrate his courage, because only that will be appreciated by those held by the honor ethic. He must add "the less" to "the more," to refer back to Péguy. He must break apart the armor of habit encasing those within the honor code by placing a stumbling block in their way, a scandal "in the good sense." This seems to have its effect, as his comrades debate his actions at the duel: "'He did stand up to the shot . . . but he was afraid of the other shots and asked forgiveness in the middle of the duel.' 'But if he was afraid of the other shots,' my defenders objected, 'he would have fired his own pistol first, before asking forgiveness . . . no, there's something else here, something original'" (300). That sense of "something else" could become the decisive point of leverage against the sheer weight of worldly habits of mind, perhaps functioning with similar spiritual effect in their lives, as did Zosima's own memory of his brother Markel's strange behavior and words prior to his death.

The duel raises a second question, posed by the surprising parallelism between the actions of Stavrogin (in *Demons*) and Zosima during their duels. Surprising from the perspective of Christian faith, because Stavrogin is, of all Dostoevsky's characters, the very apotheosis of modern atheism. He too enters into the duel and its honor ethic only to subvert it. It might appear that Dostoevsky is here abolishing the apocalyptic contrast between conquering Lion and suffering Lamb. However, the actions of Stavrogin and Zosima, which are outwardly almost identical, have entirely different results. Stavrogin's risking of his life by deliberately shooting high merely exacerbates the vengeful anger of his opponent,[33] while Zosima brings about reconciliation. The difference lies primarily in what motivates the reversal of the duel structure. Stavrogin's is a *nihilistic reversal*, for which two possible explanations might be offered, neither of which seems finally decided by Dostoevsky. One is that it is undertaken out of prideful contempt for the value frameworks erected by human beings to shelter themselves from the chaos of existence; the other is that it is the desire for self-punishment on the part of a man who feels guilt for his actions but, again out of pride, cannot move further into the process of genuine repentance. Both explanations focus on a pride so all-consuming that Stavrogin can be taken as a harbinger of that "man-god" to be evoked later by Ivan Karamazov (649). He does not fear death because he has cut himself off from the transcendent sources of "living life" (*zhivaya zhizn'*), thereby becoming indifferent to life, so much so that he finally ends his own.[34] Zosima, on the other hand, does not fear death because fear has been cast out by the divine love that is the fruit of his repentance. Zosima's is an *apocalyptic reversal*, enacting a "revocation" of his soldierly vocation as an expression of humility before God and love for others. In Agamben's words, "the messianic vocation . . . at once voids and transforms every vocation and every condition so as to free them for a new usage."[35] In Zosima's case, the "new usage" of his military status is as a platform from which to preach the messianic truth, although he will soon enter the monastic life.

Despite his own final choice of the monastery, Zosima's advice to his "apostolic successor," Alyosha, is to "sojourn" as a monk "in the world" (363). While the apocalyptic reversal begins with an interior transformation, it entails a communal dimension and thus an entry into fallen history. But entry to just what degree and in just what way? This is our final question. While the best thought of Dostoevsky, Augustine, and Péguy is one thing, their own historical choices cannot be seen to provide

33. His enraged opponent exclaims "Another offense!" See Dostoevsky, *Demons*, 286–87.

34. For one of several evocations of the connection between "living life" and transcendent reality, which is so central to Dostoevsky's vision, see *Brothers Karamzov*, 320.

35. Agamben, *Church and the Kingdom*, 18.

ethically normative models. In his attempt to discern in current history "signs" and "portents" that atheist totalitarianism would be overcome by the messianic idea, Dostoevsky came to support a "just war" for the Russian conquest of Constantinople.[36] Augustine came to support judicial torture by the Roman authorities as one of the "necessities" of pilgrim life within the fallen earthly city.[37] And Péguy's own adding of "the less to the more" led to his early death leading a hopeless charge in the opening battle of World War I, a war he believed would establish a just peace that would end war itself.[38] It seems our final question must remain, perhaps inevitably, an open one, always subject to fallible human judgments as to the varying requirements of historical times and places.

Bibliography

Agamben, Giorgio. *The Church and the Kingdom.* Translated by Leland de la Durantye. London: Seagull, 2012.

———. *The Kingdom and the Glory: For a Genealogy of Economy and Government.* Translated by Lorenzo Chiesa, with Matteo Mandarini. Stanford, CA: Stanford University Press, 2011.

Augustine, Aurelius. *Concerning the City of God Against the Pagans.* Translated by David Knowles. Harmondsworth, UK: Penguin, 1972.

Bakhtin, Mikhail. *Problems of Dostoevsky's Poetics.* Translated by Caryl Emerson. Minneapolis: University of Minnesota Press, 1984.

Corneille, Pierre. *Polyeucte.* In *The Chief Plays of Corneille*, translated by Lacy Lockert, 219–74. Princeton, NJ: Princeton University Press, 1957.

Dostoevsky, Fyodor. *The Brothers Karamazov.* Translated by Richard Pevear and Larissa Volokhonsky. New York: Vintage, 1991.

———. *Demons.* Translated by Richard Pevear and Larissa Volokhonsky. New York: Vintage, 1994.

———. *Notes from Underground.* Translated by Andrew R. MacAndrew. New York: Signet, 2004.

Holland, Kate. "The Poetics of the Slap: Dostoevsky's Disintegrating Duel Plot." In *Dostoevsky at 200: The Novel in Modernity*, 21–40. Toronto: University of Toronto Press, 2021.

36. See Ward, *Dostoevsky's Critique of the West*, 182–90, for a discussion of this aspect of Dostoevsky's prophetic politics, a discussion which, in retrospect, I would now deem too much an *apologia*.

37. Kroeker argues convincingly that it "is hard to see how appeals to 'necessity' make any moral sense . . . with regard to the practice of judicial torture," even on the basis of Augustine's own messianic political vision. See Kroeker, *Messianic Political Theology*, 60–62.

38. When departing for the front and the first battle of the Marne, Péguy said to a friend, "I am going as a soldier . . . in the cause of disarmament, to the last of all wars." Quoted in Villiers, *Charles Péguy*, 373.

Huttunen, Niko. *Early Christians Adapting to the Roman Empire.* Leiden: Brill, 2020.

Kroeker, P. Travis. *Messianic Political Theology and Diaspora Ethics: Essays in Exile.* Eugene, OR: Cascade, 2017.

Kroeker, P. Travis, and Ward, Bruce K. *Remembering the End: Dostoevsky as Prophet to Modernity.* London: SCM, 2002.

Milbank, John. *Beyond Secular Order: The Representation of Being and the Representation of the People.* Malden, MA: Wiley-Blackwell, 2013.

Nietzsche, Friedrich. *Twilight of the Idols and The Anti-Christ.* Translated by R. J. Hollingdale. London: Penguin, 1990.

Péguy, Charles. *Notes on Bergson and Descartes: Philosophy, Christianity, and Modernity in Contestation.* Translated by Bruce K. Ward. Eugene, OR: Cascade, 2019.

Reyfman, Irina. *Ritualized Violence Russian Style: The Duel in Russian Culture and Literature.* Stanford, CA: Stanford University Press, 1999.

Taylor, Charles. *Sources of the Self: The Making of the Modern Identity.* Cambridge, MA: Harvard University Press, 1989.

Villiers, Marjorie. *Charles Péguy: A Study in Integrity.* London: Collins, 1965.

Ward, Bruce K. "Apocalypse and Modernity." In *Thomas Merton: Monk on the Edge*, edited by Ross Labrie and Angus Stewart, 45–63. North Vancouver, BC: Thomas Merton Society of Canada, 2012.

———. *Dostoevsky's Critique of the West: the Quest for the Earthly Paradise.* Waterloo, ON: Wilfrid Laurier University Press, 1986.

Weil, Simone. *The Need for Roots.* Translated by Arthur Wills. New York: Harper & Row, 1971.

Williams, Rowan. *Dostoevsky: Language, Faith, and Fiction.* Waco, TX: Baylor University Press, 2008.

14

Sex Unburdened
Augustine, Foucault, and the Transfiguration of Desire

SARAH STEWART-KROEKER

IN *CONFESSIONS OF THE Flesh*, Michel Foucault argues that Augustine reframes ancient attitudes toward sex and sexuality by emphasizing the quality of the desiring subject's will. For Foucault, Augustine's emphasis on the will transforms the ethical questions around sexual conduct into a question of the self's relationship to itself. While this captures certain aspects of Augustine's thought, I argue that Foucault's account misses a crucial piece: the relationality built into Augustine's ideal of sexuality. Augustine's discussion of pre-Fall sexuality in *City of God* expresses longing for a therapeutic restoration of a lost harmony to the human subject—a relational alignment within the subject. More importantly, however, with regards to sexual ethics, Augustine's discussion of Edenic sex focuses on how this harmony of the unperturbed subject coheres with a harmony between lovers. This is a profoundly relational ideal generated by an imaginative exercise, by contrast to the individualistic subjectivity Foucault emphasizes. In this essay, I discuss the limits of Foucault's account of Augustine's thought on sexuality as well as the possibilities and limitations of Augustine's writing about sexuality. Finally, I pick up this Augustinian imaginative exercise in transfigured desire and place it in conversation with contemporary feminist thought and (briefly) literature.

Foucault on Sexual Subjectivity in Augustine's Thought

In many regards, Foucault's interpretation of Augustine is compelling. Certainly, he rightly accentuates Augustine's strong emphasis on the state of the will—and more specifically, the gaps or ruptures that emerge in the postlapsarian human condition between mind, will, emotion, and body—gaps that are in thrown into especially sharp relief in the domain of sexuality. As Foucault writes, the "punishment-consequence of the fault [of the Fall] is not placed between the soul and the body, between matter and mind, but in the subject itself, henceforth in rebellion against itself (body and soul included)."[1] Foucault perceptively draws out a range of implications of Augustine's account of sex and sexuality, which hinges on the will: "[Libido] consists not in some substantial impurity, not in a certain exaggeration of their violence, but very precisely in the involuntary form of the urge. The decisive point, the one that, as concerns sexual relations, separates the Creation from the fall and through which consequently the moral line of division should pass, is the one where the involuntary suddenly usurps the place of the voluntary."[2] Thus, for Foucault's Augustine, "the involuntariness of concupiscence . . . is embedded, due to the fall, in the present structure of the subject."[3] This seems right to me: for Augustine, the structure of the postlapsarian will is necessarily marked by involuntary "perturbations" of body, mind, and will, as well as by a range of "lusts" or *libidines*, the most unruly (though not, even on Augustine's terms, the most noxious!) being sexual concupiscence.

And yet, Foucault seems to extend this characteristic of sexual concupiscence to the entire structure of the will and the subject as such; this is a point on which I think Foucault overstates his claims. For Foucault, Augustine makes concupiscence "very form of the will, which is to say, of that which makes the soul a subject. For him, it is not the involuntary as against the voluntary, but the involuntariness of volition itself: that without which the will cannot will, except precisely with the assistance of grace."[4] But there's reason to be skeptical of this move. Certainly, for Augustine, experiences of involuntariness remain a feature of the fallen human will, including its experience of itself, and thus human subjectivity. But this does not entail that this is "the very form of the will" as

---

1. Foucault, *Confessions*, 262–63.
2. Foucault, *Confessions*, 262.
3. Foucault, *Confessions*, 271.
4. Foucault, *Confessions*, 271.

such. If this were the case, there would be little sense in speaking of a will at all without grace.

More significantly, though, for what I want to draw out of this conversation between Augustine and Foucault, is that Foucault persistently interprets Augustine's account of sex, both pre- and post-Fall, through the lens of subjectivity—the will's relationship to itself, to its own willing, and thus fundamentally turned in upon itself: "Concupiscence for Augustine belongs to the very form of volition. . . . In consenting . . . the will takes itself for an object."[5]

While Foucault offers a compelling interpretation of one of the implications of Augustine's account of the will and sexual concupiscence, he does overlook other features of Augustine's account of sex, sexuality, and the will in Eden, and what its implications or stakes might be. And this is the sense in which Augustine is concerned not only with the voluntary and involuntary, but with relationality and harmony at multiple levels: self, other/lover, and God.

Augustine on Sexuality in *City of God*

Various passages in which Augustine addresses sexuality in *City of God* are fundamentally engaged with imagination; the passages I focus on reflect an exercise in imagining what life (and particularly, the emotional and sexual life) of Adam and Eve in the Garden would have been like. The function of imagination for Augustine is variable: it is, most basically, the way that the mind calls forth images, thoughts, memories, or sensations. The imagination is the function by which we represent various things within the mind—be they memories, the passage of time, mathematical concepts, fantastical creatures or worlds, anticipating some kind of prospect or construing some alternate state of affairs that has not (yet) been experienced. Augustine also notes that when we listen to a narrative, read a text, or hear a description, we engage through the imagination—sometimes we picture something we have never seen, on the basis of description, drawing on experience, for example. He notes that we cannot help doing this.[6] In this sense, imagination is

---

5. Foucault, *Confessions*, 279.

6. Augustine, *Trinity*, 8.7, 246. See these passages from *The Trinity*—especially 8.7 through 8.9—for a fairly condensed discussion of imagination.

fundamental and unavoidable: it is engaged in the essential functioning of how humans orient themselves in time and to the world.

It is also, for Augustine, a function that can lead in both good and bad directions, ethically speaking. Imagination and its products may be deceptive or noxious—or they may enhance, enlighten, and engage us in critically fruitful ways. Augustine draws a distinction between two kinds of products of the imagination: *phantasia* (images or sensations recalled in memory), and *phantasmata* (products of the power of the imagination to fabricate something by the power of thought alone).[7] While the latter is much more worrisome to him, it's critical to note that *phantasmata* are not in and of themselves problematic—but they are potentially more dangerous or misleading. Despite the linguistic cognate, there is no ready parallel to the contemporary English term "fantasy" in Augustine's usage. By contrast to how we use the term, *phantasia* are anchored in memories; similarly to how we tend to use the word, however, Augustine also appreciates that both *phantasia* and *phantasmata* may be harmless, harmful, or helpful and good. Regardless, for Augustine, imagination is essential to how he relates (and thinks believers do and must relate) to biblical texts, themes, and ideas. Whether it's imagining what the Garden of Eden might have been like, what heaven may be like, what Christ might have looked like, how biblical figures might have felt in various situations, and so on, imagination is involved in engaging with these texts and their stories or concepts. And this may require trying to imagine ourselves not only beyond our own context and circumstances but beyond our very existential condition as temporal, mortal, sinful creatures. Imagining what it might have been or felt like to be human before the Fall—and, more prominently in Augustine's writings, in the heavenly homeland—are perhaps the most morally significant forms of imaginative exercises that we find in his thought. But note that in this regard, the kinds of imaginative exercises he enters into are not simply random or arbitrary; they're engaged in and responsive to texts and traditions and they're reflective of our experiences and contexts, just as they push beyond the texts themselves in various regards and the present human condition. Yet there are multiple forms that these imaginative exercises may take. While all are theological in the sense that Augustine is guided by theological premises,

---

7. See the passages from *The Trinity* cited above; and Djuth, "Veiled and Unveiled Beauty." I discuss these elements of Augustine's thought in *Pilgrimage as Moral and Aesthetic Formation*, 95–99, and at significantly greater length on the specifically temporal aspects of imagination's function in "Scattered in Times."

some may be imbued with moral or normative stakes in a way that others aren't. For example, simply picturing a cityscape one hasn't seen (as Augustine describes[8]) is not particularly morally significant, whereas trying to imagine the prelapsarian protological state or the redeemed eschatological human condition certainly is, in that it involves representing a sinless state of which humans have no direct experience.

Augustine's most pressing aim in this vein, however, is to try to convey the beauty and goodness both of God's Creation and, more importantly for him, its ultimate healing and redemption. Why? Because for Augustine, the cultivation of good longing and desire—for truly good and beautiful things, which requires us to be oriented to God as the source of them all—requires this shift to imagining what is no longer and what is also yet to come. In this way, it is apocalyptic. That imagining is also deeply reflective of the present; what we long for reflects what is absent, lost, harmed, or tarnished in some way. In the realm of sexuality and the erotic, this is particularly acute on Augustine's terms, since he thinks that fallen human sexuality is ineradicably marked by lust or concupiscence, a force that frequently overwhelms the human will (though it's also worth noting that the central piece of his discussion in *City of God* concerns the ways in which post-Fall sexual desire and the body's response may be manifested in both involuntary erections and in involuntary impotence—the gaps between will, desire, and the body, most readily visible for him in sexuality, are paradigmatically representative of the fallen state).

For Augustine, as Foucault writes, to imagine sex before the Fall—and he does—means imagining "an act whose every element is placed under the exact and unfailing control of the will."[9] Adam would have been "a diligent sower—one without passion."[10] Foucault writes that for Augustine, "paradisiacal sex was obedient and reasonable like the fingers of the hand."[11] Though it is common practice to make fun of this feature of Augustine's account of sex (for good reason!), it's worth noting that fingers are themselves highly erotic implements in their own right, and compared to the male genitalia to which Foucault is himself eager to draw our attention, the obedience of fingers, uncomplicated most of the time, is a feature for which many a lover may be glad.

8. Augustine, *Trinity*, 8.9, 250.
9. Foucault, *Confessions*, 260.
10. Foucault, *Confessions*, 262.
11. Foucault, *Confessions*, 261.

But to be sure, Augustine's vision of pre-Fall sex may seem, as many more recent interpreters have pointed out, rather boring—the tranquility he imagines may seem unappealing given what we typically imagine good sex to involve. It's worth noting, in relation to Foucault's "without passion" remark, that it is not the intensity of feeling that defines "perverse" emotion in earthly life, which Augustine mostly refers to as *perturbationes* or *passiones* (but the latter in the ancient technical sense, that is, as naming emotions that are by definition problematic, not the current sense in which we typically use the word "passion" unambiguously and positively to name intense feeling or drive). "Tranquility" in the sense that Augustine is concerned about is not disrupted by ardor, not by intensity of feeling as such, but by various divisions: divisions in human will; between will and emotion; or between will and the body.[12] So it is certainly possible to imagine that this paradisiacal sex in Eden—while characterized by this perfect obedience and a kind of tranquility that results from the alignment of mind, will, and body—is compatible with deep and intense feeling (even if some of us might also still want to include the paroxysms of obliterative ecstasy that Augustine rules out[13]).

But for Augustine, after the Fall, it is impossible to have sex without concupiscence or "lust." Even for the devout Christian, this concupiscence can only be absorbed into a theology of sex insofar as one can "make use" of it toward the end of procreation within marriage. Concupiscence remains necessary to sex after the Fall; it resists the command of a reformed will and thus can only be instrumentalized toward a good end, not eliminated, even provisionally or occasionally.

On the whole, Augustine's account drastically restricts a range of goods and possible conditions for sex and sexuality that I, for one, would incorporate theologically. First of all, I reject the limit of marriage as the only context for sex that can be called good and can be included in a Christian vision of sexuality. Second, the various personal and relational

---

12. These two sentences closely follow my discussion of emotion in "Wordless Cry of Jubilation," 74.

13. Note that Augustine specifically refers to the way that "lust assumes power not only over the whole body, and not only from the outside, but also internally; it disturbs the whole man, when the mental emotion combines and mingles with the physical craving, resulting in a pleasure surpassing all physical delights. So intense is the pleasure that when it reaches its climax there is an almost total extinction of mental alertness; the intellectual sentries, as it were, are overwhelmed ... surely [any friend of wisdom and holy joys] would prefer, if possible, to beget children without lust of this kind." Augustine, *City of God*, 14.16, 577.

goods of sex and sexuality I would want to elaborate far exceed Augustine's: finding pleasure in one's own and another's body, mutual and consensual desire, intimacy both physical and emotional, to name but a few. Third, in my view, there is no necessary relationship between sex and procreation. Far beyond being the only good end of sex, in many peoples' lives it may be a minor, occasional, or entirely absent aim of sex, certainly over the course of a sexual lifetime.

Nevertheless, Augustine's vision for what this Edenic state may have entailed, not just in terms of subjectivity but in terms of relationality, is more expansive than Foucault's discussion captures. Consider these initial passages, discussing the emotions of the first humans: "The pair lived in a partnership of unalloyed felicity; their love for God and for each other was undisturbed. This love was a source of immense gladness, since the beloved object was always at hand for their enjoyment. . . . They were not distressed by any agitations of the mind, nor pained by any disorders of the body."[14] When Augustine returns again to the pair's condition in Eden in *City of God* 14.26, he reinforces this congruence or harmony: "He lived without any want . . . [he] enjoyed perfect health in the body, entire tranquillity in the soul. . . . But true joy flowed perpetually from God, and towards God there was a blaze of love. . . . Between man and wife there was a faithful partnership based on love and mutual respect; there was a harmony and a liveliness of mind and body."[15]

Augustine here describes multiple levels of an imagined seamless and integral harmony, first at the level of the subject, who is undistressed and undisturbed by agitations of mind or body—that is, not subject to the painful gaps that open up after the Fall between mind, will, and body. Perhaps more importantly, however, Augustine emphasizes a perfect mutuality in love between partners. Here too, there is a notable absence of a kind of gap, not in the subject but in a relationship: desire and enjoyment are united, resulting in an immense gladness. The partners share a congruence in liveliness of mind and body. Finally, there is reciprocity in joy and love between humanity and God: joy flows from God, and love flows from the subject to the partner and to God.

These aspects of Augustine's attempt to imagine the pre-Fall ideal reflect a profound interest in relationality freed from multiple levels of alienation. This is not a self turned in on itself or self-contained, unperturbed

14. Augustine, *City of God*, 14.10, 567.
15. Augustine, *City of God*, 14.26, 590.

by any intensity of feeling, but rather a subject bound to beloveds wherein no fear of loss, no threat of illness or death, no painful ruptures constrain or obstruct the flow of love, joy, enjoyment.

This tension between paradise and the present is central to Augustine's complicated attitude toward sex and sexuality. One may not like or endorse the specific contents of his vision of sexuality, before or after the Fall, but the exercise in imagining desire, sexuality, and sex itself freed from the forces that constrain and bind but also sever, rupture, and alienate us—from ourselves, from others, from God—strikes me as one that we might do well to pick up, even if radically altered in its terms. The exercise in imagining what our most intimate, most exposing, most vulnerable aspects of ourselves and our encounters with others might look like, unburdened by the things that burden us now, seems to me a kind of aperture that opens onto possibilities for exercising moral-theological imagination—and possibilities that I would want to claim are important for feminist theology.

John Cavadini has suggested that Augustine's rather pessimistic view of sex may perhaps nevertheless get at something recognizably difficult about human sexuality after the Fall.[16] Drawing on the work of radical feminist Andrea Dworkin, he traces a possible resonance with her concern that sex under patriarchy is inherently wrapped up with power dynamics, domination, and violence, and as such, often (always for Dworkin?) not great for women (to put it in much milder terms than she does!). We might add that it is often not great for any number of people and groups who are subject to the various intersectional biases and exercises of power and privilege that characterize our culture, however progressive we might consider it to be relative to Dworkin's context, let alone Augustine's. Certainly, this also reflects the ways in which we are profoundly formed and shaped by the norms of our context, not only in our attitudes toward ourselves but also to others. The formation of desire is a force both powerful and often subterranean—and one that, yes, often exceeds the strictly voluntary.

Contemporary Feminist Critique and Politics of Desire

Extending this move to connect to feminist discourse, I turn to two contemporary pieces that focus on this difficulty. As the feminist philosopher

---

16. Cavadini, "Feeling Right."

Amia Srinivasan notes in her widely read essay and book, contemporary feminist discourse about sex and sexual ethics has had little to say "about desire: men's desire, women's desire, and the ideological shaping of both."[17] She notes that it "used to be the case that if you wanted a political critique of desire, feminism was where you would turn. A few decades ago feminists were nearly one in thinking about the way sexual desire—its objects and expressions, fetishes and fantasies—is shaped by oppression."[18] But Srinivasan claims that the turn toward intersectionality has (rightly) "made feminists reluctant to prescribe universal policies, including universal sexual policies."[19] The turn to intersectionality, claims Srinivasan, "has also deepened feminist discomfort with thinking in terms of false consciousness."[20] This reflects an epistemic worry tied to trusting women's testimonies about their experience as well as an ethical one: "a feminism that trades too freely in notions of self-deception is a feminism that risks dominating the subjects it wants to liberate."[21]

Srinivasan claims, however, that it is worth interrogating the convergence "between sex positivity and liberalism in their shared reluctance to interrogate the formation of our desires."[22] Srinivasan notes that per the feminist writer Ellen Willis in her 1981 essay "Lust Horizons," feminism needs to "treat as axiomatic our free sexual choice, while also seeing why, as 'anti-sex' and lesbian feminists have always said, such choices, under patriarchy, are rarely free."[23] Srinivasan argues, picking up from Willis, that "in our rush to do the former, feminists risk forgetting to do the latter."[24] There's a risk of naturalizing and neutralizing sexual preference, making it pre-political, as if it is not subject to the forces of cultural-political pressure and production. Personal preferences are

---

17. Srinivasan, "Does Anyone Have the Right to Sex?"; Srinivasan, *Right to Sex*, 76.
18. Srinivasan, *Right to Sex*, 76.
19. Srinivasan, *Right to Sex*, 81.
20. Srinivasan, *Right to Sex*, 82. Notably, in the *London Review of Books* essay, Srinivasan defines this accordingly: "that's to say, with the idea that women often act against their own interests, even when they take themselves to be doing what they wanted to do." Srinivasan, "Does Anyone Have the Right to Sex?" In the book version, she defines it more narrowly (in my opinion less powerfully): "that's to say, with the idea that women who have sex with and marry men have internalised the patriarchy." Srinivasan, *Right to Sex*, 82.
21. Srinivasan, *Right to Sex*, 82.
22. Srinivasan, *Right to Sex*, 83.
23. Srinivasan, *Right to Sex*, 84; citing Willis, "Lust Horizons."
24. Srinivasan, *Right to Sex*, 84.

never "merely" personal, which isn't to say that political critique of desire doesn't carry its own risks (notably, policing identity and desire in potentially repressive ways). Yet if it is important to feminism to critique the hetero-patriarchal sexist, racist, transphobic, fatphobic, ableist, ageist forces that shape desire in ways that constrain, limit, and harm not only our sexual encounters or partnerships but our relationships to ourselves and our own bodies, then it seems there needs to be some kind of tension that requires holding in place—one that has to do with a possible reshaping or even transfiguration (Srinivasan's term![25]) of desire.

Kathy Chow responds to this point in particular in her article "On Loving White Boys," wherein she writes: "On the one hand, Srinivasan holds that our desires are mutable and products of political rather than metaphysical forces; on the other, that our desires can also surprise us, and, if we are so lucky, 'desire can cut against what politics has chosen for us, and choose for itself.'"[26] Chow goes on to say that while she doesn't disagree with Srinivasan, "it's worth pointing out where she doesn't explicitly go, which is to the original question: Should we try to discipline our desires? No! No!! There is a duty to work, to the best of our abilities, toward the transformation of the political, economic and cultural forces that shape our desires. But to discipline desire itself? I think not."[27]

The Transfiguration of Desire

Returning to the point that introduced this segue, as I stated above, the formation of desire is a force both powerful and often subterranean—and one that, yes, often exceeds the strictly voluntary. In this regard, one might ask: To what extent can "desire . . . choose for itself" under the conditions of bias, discrimination, domination, and the misshapen forces that shape our desire? Can transformation and some form of "discipline" (it matters what we mean by that) be disentangled? Certainly, Foucault was precisely worried about the matter of discipline, including in Augustine's thought, which he ties to the progressive *juridification* of sexual moral codes, and rightly so. But might critique count as a form of discipline? I'm inclined to say that it does, under an expansive definition of what one may mean

25. "The question posed by radical self-love movements is not whether there is a right to sex (there isn't) but whether there is a duty to transfigure, as best we can, our desires." Srinivasan, *Right to Sex*, 90.
26. Chow, "On Loving White Boys."
27. Chow, "On Loving White Boys."

by "discipline," one that leans on the Latin sense of instruction or training that shapes, molds, and ameliorates, rather than the (historically later) sense of punishment. Of course, critique as discipline must be rightly bounded by epistemic humility, anti-triumphalism, anti-authoritarianism. It needs to acknowledge the limits of what the will can accomplish while remaining open to contestations that nonconformity and radical moral imagination may offer for expanding the possibilities for creative affirmations of our bodies and agencies. But articulated as such, it seems that some kind of difficult (and never perfectly accomplished) tension between the real and the ideal is essential to how we think and talk about sex and sexuality. But it is notably something that cannot be done simply on one's own, nor something that only concerns oneself: it is relational, which is to say, social, cultural, and political as well.

It seems important to me to explore, examine, and yes, perhaps challenge or strive to reshape desires at least to some degree, insofar as our desires are shaped in contexts and cultures that are (and will ever be this side of the eschaton) marked by inherited and unjust or misshapen biases. At the same time, this reality—one from which we cannot fully escape—does not preclude the possibility of genuinely good sexual pleasure and erotic connection.

All of this is to say that while I do not subscribe to the Augustinian theology of sex and sexuality, I think there remains something fruitful to engage in his imaginative exercise of sex unburdened by anxiety, agitation, alienation, and domination—which importantly opens up the relational dimensions of sexuality. It's also worth noting that Augustine himself was sensitive to the cultural-political formation of desires. In various regards, detailing how this functions, for good and for ill, is the overarching aim of *City of God* as a work. And that's where the imaginative exercise takes its place.

Might we imagine what it would be like to be so fully and unselfconsciously at home in our own skins—where no fear, shame, insecurity, anxiety, self-loathing, or problematic dynamics disrupt the inhabiting of our body and its interactions with another's body, no uncertainty, worry, suspicion of another's feelings or perceptions—as to allow for erotic desire and its fulfillment both ardent and integral? Might this give us some critical purchase on the ruptures and alienations, dominations and discriminations laden by cultural forces that constrain, suppress, and shame bodies and sexualities in our present? And thus constitute a form of discipline as critique of the cultural and political formation of desire, and also an opening to a longed-for transfiguration that might orient us to alternatives?

To conclude, I shift slightly on two fronts: first, from sexuality to gender (though these are often profoundly intertwined in terms of how they affect our relationships to our own bodies as sexual and erotic, and to others in those same registers); and second, from theory and theology to literature, specifically to a novel by Casey Plett called *Little Fish*.[28] Set in Winnipeg, Manitoba, the central character, Wendy, is a transwoman who was raised Mennonite (Casey Plett herself is a trans Mennonite Winnipegger). Over the course of the novel, Wendy is slowly drawn into a mystery surrounding the gender identity and sexuality of her recently deceased grandfather, Henry. Her probing of this mystery eventually takes her to an old friend of Henry's in rural Manitoba, an old Mennonite woman named Anna who was a friend of Henry's and whom she suspects might know something more of this side of Henry. Anna, she discovers, is not exactly welcoming, or rather, she's ambivalent: responsive to Wendy and yet wary of her; surprisingly open to her in certain moments but also quickly turning back to conservative Christian tenets. Here's how a key portion of their conversation goes:

> [Anna] looked heavy for a moment, staring at Wendy, then said, "I know you had this idea that Henry. Wanted to be a woman. Do you still think that?"
>
> "I don't know," Wendy said, surprised. "Maybe. I wonder if there is a possibility if he had that desire, and he wasn't aware . . ."
>
> "There is much he didn't tell me," Anna said. "Won't presume to tell you that you are wrong."
>
> Wendy finished her sandwich and looked at Anna with gratitude.
>
> "Henry might even be a woman in heaven for all eternity," said Anna. "Perhaps that's his Godly reward for enduring on Earth. I don't think it's inappropriate to say that's a possibility. I don't think it's sinful or wrong to consider. If you feel sad for him, maybe you can think on that."
>
> "Do you think that?"
>
> "I think," she said eager and grey, "that it would be as presumptuous to assume that he is not, as it would be presumptuous to assume that he is."
>
> It dawned on Wendy like a bird settling into a tree.

---

28. Plett, *Little Fish*.

"You're gay."
"I've never touched a woman!" Anna said immediately.[29]

The encounter doesn't end on a particularly happy note, but this moment is the moment where Anna opens herself most decisively—and most counter to the Christianity to which she otherwise clings—in a dramatic and surprising way.

A little later, Wendy has a dream:

> Wendy dreamed of herself and Henry. They were sitting on a couch, and Henry was swaddled in long billowy clothing. Henry had a baby in her arms, and its face leaned against Henry's chest. Her hair was thinning and grey like it'd always been when Wendy was a kid, but her fingers were long and smooth and lotioned. The lawn outside was growing fast, and someone needed to cut it. Everyone else was yelling and there was chaos and smoke everywhere, but Henry just stayed there and smiled at Wendy, and her smile got bigger and bigger with joy pouring out of her face, and as the couch grew scratchy and the air under it whirled and screamed, Henry pulled her feet onto the couch with the baby still in both arms and leaned forward on her knees in her long billowy clothing looking at Wendy, and she laughed with her radiant, pure lit-up smile getting bigger and bigger until both of their faces were almost touching with light light light shining from all of Henry's soft lotioned body, until they were so close, Henry now silent and smiling at Wendy deep and big and light, and neither of them moved. Wendy woke up thrashing and sitting up in the same motion with her eyes scanning every part of the room and her heart beating fast.[30]

In this dream, it seems that Wendy is visited by that heavenly Henry, the same and yet transfigured (notably indicated by the use of "she" pronouns).

These two interactions in Plett's novel capture something of what I'm interested in lifting out of Augustine that I do not find in Foucault's focus on self and subjectivity. It's a piece of what this kind of theological imaginative horizon may offer: Anna, for all of her own homophobic and transphobic views, fueled by her Christianity, nevertheless can hold open this possibility that Henry may be a woman in heaven—but this is significant not just for the sake of Henry or Henry's memory but for

29. Plett, *Little Fish*, 262.
30. Plett, *Little Fish*, 289.

Wendy in her relationship to Henry and to herself. I take Anna's suggestion and Wendy's dream as a pair: Wendy's dream responding in some way to Anna's suggestion but also moving further, shining light and joy onto Wendy herself, as she struggles to navigate her way as a transwoman in a world that is often by turns violently hostile toward her or fascinated by her or by some fetishization of her. In this regard, her bodily gendered and sexual identity and experiences of sex are deeply reciprocally implicated (as the novel's frequent explicit sex scenes illustrate). Who is the baby? The novel doesn't say, but I think there's reason to imagine that it is Wendy herself: Wendy the infant and Wendy the woman meet this radiant Henry, who bathes them in her light. It is a gift this heavenly Henry gives Wendy in her dream.

Our desires are never only our own, nor detached from our varied relationships; and yet precisely in this sense, there is perhaps something to glean from Augustine's ventures into protological and eschatological imaginings that show us a different side of this cluster of themes in his thought than Foucault's discussion draws out. Augustine undertakes a relationally situated exercise in moral and erotic imagination, relative to our own self and will, our relationships with others, and to God. Perhaps we can pick up that exercise with a different set of aims to probe, critique, and perhaps transfigure some of the ways our desire and sexuality is formed and embodied.

Bibliography

Augustine. *City of God*. Translated by Henry Bettenson. New York: Penguin, 1972.

———. *The Trinity*. 2nd ed. Edited by John E. Rotelle. Translated by Edmund Hill. Part 1, vol. 5 of *The Works of Saint Augustine*. New York: New City, 1991.

Cavadini, John. "Feeling Right: Augustine on the Passions and Sexual Desire." *Augustinian Studies* 36 (2005) 195–217.

Chow, Kathy. "On Loving White Boys: Eros and Identification." *The Point* 29 (February 22, 2023). https://thepointmag.com/examined-life/on-loving-white-boys/.

Djuth, Marianne. "Veiled and Unveiled Beauty: The Role of the Imagination in Augustine's Esthetics." *Theological Studies* 68 (2007) 77–91.

Foucault, Michel. *Confessions of the Flesh*. Edited by Frédéric Gros. Translated by Robert Hurley. The History of Sexuality 4. New York: Penguin Random House, 2022.

Plett, Casey. *Little Fish*. Vancouver: Arsenal Pulp, 2018.

Srinivasan, Amia. "Does Anyone Have the Right to Sex?" *London Review of Books* 40, no. 6 (March 22, 2018). https://www.lrb.co.uk/the-paper/v40/n06/amia-srinivasan/does-anyone-have-the-right-to-sex.

———. *The Right to Sex*. London: Bloomsbury, 2021.

Stewart-Kroeker, Sarah. *Pilgrimage as Moral and Aesthetic Formation in Augustine's Thought.* Oxford: Oxford University Press, 2017.

———. "'Scattered in Times': An Augustinian Meditation on Temporal Fragmentation, Imagination, and Climate Change." *Journal of Religious Ethics* 48 (2020) 45–73.

———. "A Wordless Cry of Jubilation: Joy and the Ordering of the Emotions." *Augustinian Studies* 50 (2019) 65–86.

Willis, Ellen. "Lust Horizons: Is the Women's Movement Pro-Sex?" In *No More Nice Girls: Countercultural Essays*, 3–14. Minneapolis: University of Minnesota Press, 2012. First published in 1992 by University Press of New England for Wesleyan University Press.

15

Unveiling Beauty
Seeking the Messianic Measure in Elaine Scarry
and Dostoevsky's *The Idiot*

GRANT POETTCKER

APOCALYPTICISM IS FREQUENTLY VIEWED with suspicion because it invites an all-too-enthusiastic embrace of a hermeneutical key that is, in principle, unratifiable. The authenticity of the revealed measure that apocalyptic discourse provides only seems knowable somehow in the visionary experience itself or in the unmasking it performs. Yet here too, the apocalyptic faces obstacles. Visionary experience is defined by its unrepeatable, oracular character, hence it is judged to be spurious and unreliable. As a result, apocalypticism has historically been marginalized in Christian theology, and particularly so after the project of stipulating the limits of possible experience became central for modern philosophical method.

Yet a dissatisfaction with those limits has been voiced from many corners. Moderns tend to dismiss spiritual experiences out of hand and often offer deflationary accounts of truth, goodness, and beauty. Yet the visionary mode of experience enabled by apocalyptic discourse is profoundly orienting and perhaps essential to genuine discussion of meaningful and fulfilled life, much more so redeemed or sanctified life. As a result, many recognize the reductionist imperative as a cause of moral inarticulacy[1] and a source of aesthetic impoverishment.[2] More problematic yet is that the very swagger and confidence the would-be debunker displays when dismissing the apocalyptic can accurately be described as an appropriation of the gesture of apocalypse.[3] It is a peculiar form of apocalypticism indeed that does not reveal a hitherto unseen presence but posits and even *insists upon* an absence.

One may therefore ask, what—beyond a typically modern preoccupation with epistemological rigorism and a fear of heteronomy—licenses this *inverse* apocalypticism?[4] In fact, the latter fear drives the former preoccupation with the limits of knowledge toward a dangerous, form-dissolving pitch of intensity. Immanuel Kant's philosophy of the noumena differs from apophatic theology in its insistence that the deliverances of reason cannot suffice to move the will; for Kant, enlightenment demands eschewal of obedience in faith. Nonetheless, from Kant through Jacques Derrida, the problem of epistemological closure haunts modern philosophy. "The center is not the center."[5] The moral law binds but cannot be said to motivate.[6] The aesthetic measure is awaited yet cannot be conjured forth.

If visionary experience could justify embrace of a positive vision of beauty, finitude sets a challenge for those who would defend beauty or celebrate the way it graces human life. Indeed, human finitude and the non-absolute character of finite being render human judgments of beauty fragile. Particularly vulnerable are the judgments rendered by those who claim a messianic faith that history itself is somehow beautiful as the dramatic apocalypse of divine love, and who would therefore bear witness to the presence of that love within time.

---

1. Taylor, *Sources of the Self*; see especially pt. 1, ch. 3.

2. Shusterman, "End of Aesthetic Experience," 39. Shusterman reflects near the conclusion (rather wistfully, it must be noted) that "it may seem very 'retro' to suggest that aesthetic experience can function something like an empathy box, restoring both our ability and inclination for the sorts of vivid, moving, shared experience that one once sought in art. Perhaps our informational evolution has already gone too far."

3. Leithart, *Solomon Among the Postmoderns*.

4. Although he does not put it in terms of an inverse apocalypticism, Cyril O'Regan argues that the habits of mind that characterize it stem from the Enlightenment. "The Enlightenment frustrates opposition because its determinacy is indeterminate, and induces sputter, since the only game in which it is willing to participate is one in which it is player, referee, and rules committee." See O'Regan, *Anatomy of Misremembering*, 1:3.

5. Derrida, "Structure, Sign, and Play," 279.

6. Kant, *Groundwork for the Metaphysics of Morals*.

Perhaps, however, as John's messianic logic holds, the aesthetic measure is present within this age but has neither been understood nor overcome despite being unrecognized.[7] The question-begging character of secular inverse apocalypticism has given philosophers, theologians, and novelists reason to voice dissatisfaction with the myriad attempts to banish beauty in particular. This essay will focus upon Elaine Scarry's *On Beauty and Being Just*, which defends beauty against its cultured despisers, and Fyodor Dostoevsky's novel *The Idiot*, which famously springs from its author's effort "to portray a perfectly beautiful man."[8] Both works reckon with the defeasibility of aesthetic judgments and make claims about the unity of truth, goodness, and beauty without falling back into a medieval philosophy of the transcendentals. They differ, however, in their willingness to situate beauty within a messianic or apocalyptic frame.

To anticipate the argument, Scarry claims that although beauty's detractors voice various concerns, their arguments are sometimes contradictory; further, the axiological costs they incur are too high to carry conviction. Scarry's defense of beauty rightly considers the problem posed by the lack of an aesthetic measure. In addressing it, she frequently refers to and relies upon the arguments of thinkers who are open to the transcendent; she sympathetically cites the medieval dictum "beauty is a call."[9] Nonetheless, and unlike her sources (notably Iris Murdoch and Simone Weil, whose work will also be considered here),[10] Scarry studiously avoids referring to a source of beauty; the source of that call remains nameless. Fascinatingly, Dostoevsky's *Idiot* is similarly indirect in its handling of the origin and status of beauty and seems similarly to consign the fulfillment of the promise of beauty to an unreachable beyond. The "beautiful man," Prince Myshkin, is ineffectual. Dostoevsky also ties the visions that define Myshkin's personality uncomfortably to his epilepsy; the materialist reduction hovers over beauty much like Rogozhin's villainous presence. Nonetheless, bursts of light permeate the novel. Indeed, in it, beauty is mysterious and even paradoxical. Dostoevsky thus offers entry into an apocalyptic framing

---

7. John 1:5. "Understanding" and "overcoming" are the two main translations of the Greek term κατέλαβεν in v. 5.

8. Frank, *Dostoevsky: The Miraculous Years, 1865–1871*, 271.

9. Scarry, *On Beauty and Being Just*, 109. Further references to Scarry's text will be cited parenthetically by page number.

10. Others whom Scarry cites include Plato, Augustine, Dante, Gerard Manley Hopkins, and Emily Dickinson.

of beauty that can lead one into a vision of Johannine "light" and of the divine glory that permeates existence. Understanding this apocalyptic framing will clarify the meaning of *The Idiot*'s most famous but most enigmatic line, "beauty will save the world,"[11] and will show how the novel registers as a response to reductionistic approaches to beauty yet more profound than that offered by Scarry.

Elaine Scarry's Defense of Beauty

On Beauty and Being Just addresses recent scholarship that addresses beauty critically. Scarry considers the anti-enthusiastic, epistemological objection, which runs as follows: beauty overwhelms reason and leads to error, thus beauty should be avoided. In response, Scarry admits that beauty does decenter the self and induces enthusiastic over-claims that lack a proper sense of measure. However, she denies that the experience of having one's previous judgment overcome by a new one always involves an overcoming of reason. Scarry delineates two different errors that later induce what could be called moments of aesthetic repentance (12, 15): in the first, an object formerly regarded as beautiful loses its luster; in the second, an object once held in low regard is recognized as having been beautiful all along (14). What begins by appearing as an enthusiastic over-claim may mark the ascent toward a higher rationality. Hence, Scarry argues, while beauty may induce errors, it also incites the sort of attentive devotion that leads to the correction of those errors. Beauty invites artists who create beautiful things and those who behold them to adopt postures of humility, wonder, and even reverence.

Scarry illustrates these claims by finding in Odysseus's encounter with Nausicaa (in book 6 of Homer's *Odyssey*[12]) a nearly paradigmatic phenomenology of aesthetic perception. Scarry sees four qualities emerging in this phenomenology that are essential to aesthetic perception. First, she argues that beauty is *sacred*, that is, capable of raising

---

11. Dostoevsky, *Idiot*, 383. Further references to Dostoevsky's text will be cited parenthetically by part (in Roman numerals) and chapter (in Arabic numerals). This quotation appears three times in the novel, twice by Ipollit (in III.6), and once by Aglaya (IV.6), although each time the speaker attributes it to Myshkin. This enigmatic statement receives no commentary in Kroeker and Ward, *Remembering the End*, which focuses much more on *The Brothers Karamazov*. If the conclusions of this essay are correct, it will show that Dostoevsky's *Idiot* registers prophetically even against Scarry's strong critiques of much contemporary aesthetic commentary.

12. Scarry uses Homer, *Odyssey*, translated by Robert Fagles.

human life up so that it partakes of the eternal and divine. This makes a worshipful attitude fitting: Odysseus says he is "too struck with awe to grasp [Nausicaa] by the knees" (22). Second, beauty is *unprecedented*, yet it "incites deliberation" (28), since beauty demands truthfulness about itself of the beholder. Beauty's unprecedented and truth-demanding character remains consistent across Odysseus's first and second perceptions of Nausicaa; Odysseus will have no reason to repent of his eulogy. This aesthetic judgment differs from others made of merely apparent beauties, which turn out to be unstable because the object in question possesses only borrowed glory. Third, beauty is *lifesaving*. Scarry says that beauty "makes life more vivid, animated, living, worth living" (24–25). Escape from a watery grave would be sufficient cause for celebration, but beauty banishes the cynical pride that might have set in. Fourth, and vividly in Odysseus's case, beauty is *humanizing* (25). His encounter with Nausicaa invites him to fit himself into an ordered, beautiful society (the Phaeacian assembly). Wily Odysseus recognizes that losing contact with lifesaving beauty is the true threat; successful strategy could confer only a lower sort of advantage.

This point about higher and lower advantages raises the question of how rationality itself ought to be understood. In Odysseus's case, beauty grants a "wordless certainty" (29) that unifies aesthetic, moral, and political judgment. This sort of certainty differs decisively from the desiccated and joyless deliberation fetishized by post-Cartesians. As beauty is effulgent, reason must be self-transcending. Nonetheless, Scarry reckons with the way the beholder's "wordless certainty" may seem unsatisfying: With reference to what measure are such beauties judged? Scarry asks, "Does the plenitude and aspiration for truth stay stable, even if the metaphysical referent is in doubt?" (33).

Yet in a deft turn, Scarry notices that when scientists or mathematicians denigrate aesthetic judgments by confidently appealing to the certainty-granting criteria that justify the judgments they make in their own fields, they routinely fall back into the vocabulary of beauty: scientists "speak of problems that are 'nice,' theories that are 'pretty,' solutions that are 'beautiful,' approaches that are 'elegant,' 'simple'" (52). Though Scarry does not draw this point out explicitly, the smuggling in of substitute criteria can also be noticed in the objections fueling contemporary political arguments against beauty. In response, Scarry argues that the enthusiast does justice to the beautiful thing by attending to and acknowledging its beauty. Hence her title, *On Beauty and Being Just*.

Scarry's attention to the persistent use of aesthetic language strengthens her argument that (a) beauty remains a live concern of those who would disavow reference to it; and (b) beauty even naturally forms a unity with justice or goodness for those who voice political or other objections to it. In fact, she argues, this is unsurprising. Scarry writes,

> Over the last several decades many people have either actively advocated a taboo on beauty or passively omitted it from their vocabulary even when thinking and writing about beautiful objects... but if one [were to ask] 'is it your wish for [subsequent humans] that they be beauty-loving?'—the answer seems to be 'Yes'... delivered with speed and without hesitation. (117–18)

This argument is followed by a similar Rawlsian argument, which considers whether persons situated behind a veil of ignorance regarding their ability to enjoy the sky "would wish there to be beautiful sky" (120). These concluding arguments, which Scarry regards as decisive (she remarks, "the evidence is in" [124]), have a worrying *ad populum* quality. This accords with Scarry's concerted effort to avoid realist claims about a transcendent source for beauty; the criteria she invokes are at most social or intersubjective. When she considers whether the aspiration toward aesthetic plenitude *and* truth are justified if the metaphysical referent (i.e., beauty itself) is in doubt, she offers a digressive answer; she explains how the artist Henri Matisse came to see palm trees as beautiful and narrates the way this led her also to appreciate them. Instead of a metaphysical referent, she offers a micro-consensus and invites reader participation.

The disjunction between the very strong claims that Scarry makes about beauty and the metaphysically minimalist base upon which she stands them is striking. She seems aware that this basis may be insufficient: "If the metaphysical realm has vanished... the girl, the bird, the vase, the book now seem unable in their solitude to justify ... the weight of their own beauty" (47). Although Scarry's argument does much to restore the good conscience of beauty enthusiasts, her approach to beauty is deliberately piecemeal, individualist, egalitarian (110), and pacific (107). It is not apocalyptic; this would require that it reveal not only different aesthetic criteria but a different synthetic order. Scarry's anti-apocalypticism would be less obvious if some of her own sources—Murdoch and Weil particularly—did not directly insist upon a transcendent framing of beauty.

Murdoch and Weil on Beauty and Transcendence

Though Scarry appropriates much from Murdoch in her philosophy of the "unselfing" caused by beauty and much from Weil in her philosophy of "attention," much in their work scandalizes the account Scarry develops. Scarry exhibits a deference to the protean movements of the evaluating will that Murdoch and Weil refuse. Murdoch directly critiques moral philosophers who assert that "good is indefinable because judgments of value depend upon the will and choice of the individual."[13] Instead, Murdoch focuses on the idea of perfection, which does not *relatively improve* vision but rather *grants* and *orients* vision, despite not being rationally fathomable.[14] Somewhat surprisingly for a Platonist, Murdoch states that "the argument for looking outward at Christ and not inward at Reason is that self is such a dazzling object that if one looks *there* one may see nothing else."[15] Because the ego distorts human judgment, Murdoch inveighs against egocentrism and calls not for deflationary realism but for realism that requires elevated attention to the world. Scarry seeks to appropriate this point about the displacement of the self: she writes, citing Murdoch, "It is precisely the ethical alchemy of beauty that what might in another context seem like a demotion is no longer recognizable as such.... It is our own adjacency that is pleasure-bearing" (113–14).[16] So far, so good. But notice that Scarry prefers "adjacent" and "lateral" rather than the more natural "subordinate," which she mentions only hypothetically and parenthetically (113). Here one detects the modern anxiety about heteronomy. Murdoch would worry that Scarry falls into the longing for the egocentric consolation of the "pretty" rather than the unselfing beauty uniquely prompts. For unselfing borders on the tragic, even the grotesque, that is, experiences within which the human is oriented even in being overmastered.

Weil, Scarry's other source, explores these themes profitably and provocatively—but in ways that cut against the grain of Scarry's argument. Weil's discussion of "attention" unfolds within a human teleology that culminates in the opening of the self to God in prayer.[17] Like Scarry,

---

13. Murdoch, *Sovereignty of Good*, 3.
14. Murdoch, *Sovereignty of Good*, 30.
15. Murdoch, *Sovereignty of Good*, 30.
16. The quotation is from Murdoch, *Sovereignty of Good*, 82.
17. Weil, *Waiting for God*, 57.

Weil urges her readers to dwell upon the phenomenology of error,[18] but for Weil, the revelation that error *is* readies the mind for something beyond it: "Attention consists of suspending our thought, leaving it detached, empty, and ready to be penetrated by the object."[19] Further, Weil does not approach objects in piecemeal fashion, as Scarry does when she writes about flowers, poems, birds, and so forth. For Weil, attention requires a kenotic movement wherein the perceiver renounces their cosmically central position. This movement imitates God's own "creative renunciation" of the right to command creation.[20] Once made, all created beings can bear their testimony. Even the solution to a geometry problem, "being a little fragment of particular truth . . . is a pure image of the unique, eternal, and living truth, the very Truth that once in a human voice declared: 'I am the Truth.'"[21]

By shearing off the incarnational metaphysics that permeates Weil's writing, Scarry also limits the range of experiences that may testify to divine beauty. Weil can find beauty in suffering because she sees affliction, "an uprooting of life,"[22] as falling perfectly *within* divine providence. Weil writes that "extreme affliction . . . is a nail whose point is applied at the very center of the soul . . . Affliction is a marvel of divine technique . . . which introduces into the soul of the finite creature the immensity of force, blind, brutal, and cold."[23] One might think that this introduction could take place simply through the twin passions of joy and suffering; the former delights the mind and the latter disciplines the body.[24] But to think this would be to sell short the divine self-revelation that takes place in affliction.

Weil thus sees God in all things, yet also notices how God gives things over to be ruled by mechanical causality or "gravity."[25] Because the power of vertical ascent does not lie in human hands,[26] material becomes spiritual only by becoming obedient. Weil writes, "For us, this obedience of things in relation to God is what the transparency of a window pane

18. Weil, *Waiting for God*, 60.
19. Weil, *Waiting for God*, 62.
20. Weil, *Waiting for God*, 99.
21. Weil, *Waiting for God*, 62.
22. Weil, *Waiting for God*, 81.
23. Weil, *Waiting for God*, 81.
24. Weil, *Waiting for God*, 79.
25. Weil, *Waiting for God*, 75–76.
26. Weil, *Waiting for God*, 79.

is in relation to light. As soon as we feel this obedience with our whole being, we see God."[27] Weil uses a variety of metaphors to capture this obedience, including "apprenticeship"[28] and even the consumption of the obedient one by God.[29] But Weil relies heavily on nuptial imagery; implicit forms of love of God (neighbor love, love of the order of creation, love of religious practices, and friendship) grow into explicit forms only "when God comes in person to take the hand of his future bride."[30] This messianic imagery involves a uniting of human and divine by way of human passivity, nudity, and exposure before God, and a divine movement of descent and a supernatural filling that purifies the soul. These positive accounts both of God's activity and of human consent to divine heteronomy enable Weil to denounce an error that completely escapes mention in Scarry's otherwise admirable defense of beauty: idolatry.

Dostoevsky on a Messianic Measure for Beauty

Beauty always betokens a beyond. Thus, Dostoevsky's *Idiot* can comment powerfully upon beauty's tendency both to induce idolatry and to elevate the soul because of the beyond that Dostoevsky keeps in view. His measure for the beautiful is neither Scarry's social consensus nor even the Platonic One celebrated by Murdoch, but the *apokalypsis* of the incarnate Christ, who appears in the form of a servant.

The question of appropriate measures for various kinds of value dominates the novel. Dostoevsky stages countless scenes where something of surpassing worth is threatened by the modern materialistic drive to reduce higher unities, such as beauty itself, to quantity or to mere material. Roger Anderson thus aptly remarks, "The objectification of man, by money or in nature, poses fundamental problems that Dostoevsky seeks to overcome through the influence of his 'truly good man.'"[31] For Dostoevsky, the appropriate response to modern objectification is neither

---

27. Weil, *Waiting for God*, 77.

28. Weil, *Waiting for God*, 78.

29. In a daring image, Weil pictures God as creating beauty as a labyrinth in which God waits at the center for one who wanders in: "there God is waiting to eat him. Later [the one who wandered in] will go out again, but he will be changed, he will have become different, after being eaten and digested by God." Weil, *Waiting for God*, 103.

30. Weil, *Waiting for God*, 83.

31. Anderson, "Idiot and the Subtext of Modern Materialism," 77.

the despair voiced by Ippolit and his crew of "pseudo-nihilists"[32] (II.8) nor an appeal to the traditional values of the Russian aristocracy (whose bankruptcy the narrator describes with dripping irony at the conclusion of IV.6). Yet Dostoevsky allows his alternative, messianic measure to appear indirectly. Dostoevsky invites the reader to consider the claim "beauty will save the world" (III.5)—and has Ippolit and Aglaya attribute this statement, without commentary, to Myshkin. This attribution is in one way fitting, since Myshkin is the character that most seems to embody the apocalypse of divine love. Nonetheless, "beauty will save the world" is a nearly esoteric doctrine within the novel; Myshkin's existence is marked not by obvious beauty or salvific efficacy but by failure and humiliation. Likewise, Myshkin exercises his potentially saving influence not primarily through polemical invective but through subversion of the conventions of propriety that govern social interactions. By embodying divine love, Myshkin shines a light that *distinguishes* the true and false glories that other characters seek and *invites* others into the broader space that opens when their competitive reputation seeking gives way to a properly glorious human humility and consent to divine heteronomy.

Myshkin's distinguishing and inviting activity is on display during Nastasya's early visit to the Ivolgin household and at her birthday party, two incidents that reveal the central conflict fragmenting her personality. Though Nastasya's astonishing physical beauty does much to define society's reception of her, she cultivates an "original" attitude (I.12), a personal style and social circle that augment her power; simply by appearing in public (I.1) she brings others into her thrall. Her beauty interacts in a toxic way with her "maidenly dishonor" (I.4). Nastasya names the grounds of this dishonor explicitly: Totsky, her guardian, would "stay for two months a year, dishonor me, offend me, debauch me, leave me" (I.16). Nastasya alternately seeks to outrun her reputation as "Totsky's kept woman" (I.16), to believe herself truly sullied by it, to dream of liberation from it, and to embrace it in sheer defiance.

Nastasya arrives at the Ivolgin household in I.9 with ambiguous motives. She may be there to assess whether Ganya's family hates her, to needle Ganya (since his relationship with his family is a point of vulnerability), or for the purpose she states: "I came like a fool to invite [the Ivolgins] to my party" (I.10). When Rogozhin bargains with Ganya for Nastasya's hand, progressively raising his bid from one hundred to one

---

32. This term from Anderson, "*Idiot* and the Subtext of Modern Materialism," 79.

hundred thousand rubles, Nastasya affectedly and purposefully draws out the ugly scene. She glories not in being an inviolate beauty like Nausicaa but in being the object of competition and the master manipulator of the scene, which embarrasses Ganya and his family. Indeed, Nastasya is delighted when Ganya's father and sister denounce Ganya for allowing it to continue. Their wrath at being humiliated enrages Ganya, who even attempts to strike his sister Varya.

At this point, Myshkin intervenes in two crucial ways. First, he stops the blow Ganya has aimed at Varya and himself suffers an intentional slap from Ganya. Second, Myshkin reproaches Nastasya: "You can't be the way you pretended to be just now. It's not possible!" (I.10). Myshkin senses the falseness of the posture Nastasya has adopted and appeals to her subterranean knowledge that she is glorying in powers that she may possess but which are out of tune with her true beauty. The narrator reports Nastasya's responses to Myshkin's interventions. After witnessing Myshkin stop Ganya's strike, "[Nastasya,] now visibly animated by a new feeling . . . seemed unwilling to show it . . . the mockery remained as if forcedly on her face." Nastasya quizzically remarks, "Really, I've seen [Myshkin's] face somewhere!" Nastasya's response to Myshkin's direct reproach of her is as telling: "'He guessed right, in fact, I'm not like that,' she whispered quickly, fervently, suddenly flushing and becoming all red" (I.10). Myshkin calls forth from Nastasya an incomplete repentance, the significance of which only becomes evident later. Myshkin's interventions thus lead Nastasya radically to reconsider the criteria by which she judges herself beautiful.

Nastasya's birthday party vividly displays Nastasya's cultivated originality. She invites a set of guests so varied as to be "impossible to imagine" (I.13) and capriciously indulges the buffoon Ferdyschenko's request that a disgraceful *petit jeu* be played: Ferdyshchenko says, "It's the simplest of tasks, to tell the worst thing you've done in your life." Although women are exempt, Nastasya promises to "[tell] a deed from [her own] life" (I.14). Rather than speaking of her past, however, she participates by forcing Prince Myshkin to decide whether she should keep her word to Totsky and formally accept Ganya's proposal of marriage. This is another ambiguous gesture. Given the context of the game, however, and her stated intention to prove to Myshkin that his judgment that she is "perfection" is mistaken, she intends her act to be her own worst deed. Nastasya glories in the recklessness of knowing that her "whole life [is] hanging by a hair," and in her power to implicate Myshkin in social machinations that degrade all parties involved. When Myshkin proves himself trustworthy by insisting that she not marry Ganya (who does not love her), Myshkin is immediately slandered by Totsky; the latter assumes that Myshkin must be angling for her dowry.

Despite Nastasya's "worst deed," and even after she admits Rogozhin's motley crew to her party, brandishes the one-hundred-thousand-ruble packet Rogozhin has brought to pay for her hand, and declares herself "Rogozhin's kind of woman" (I.15)—Myshkin proclaims his willingness to take Nastasya as an "honest woman." Myshkin says, "You have suffered and have emerged pure from such a hell. . . . Why do you feel ashamed and want to go with Rogozhin? You've given Mr. Totsky back his seventy thousand and say you will abandon everything you have here, which no one else here would do. . . . I . . . love you . . . Nastasya Filippovna" (I.15). Though Myshkin seems to speak out of infatuation with Nastasya's beauty, he enthuses instead about the nobility of her soul. Initially, a marriage seems highly unlikely, but when it is revealed that Myshkin has come into an enormous inheritance, Nastasya abruptly speaks of their marriage as a *fait accompli*: "I'm a princess now. . . . Only now does real life begin!" (I.16). The anticipated union is quickly undone when the gap between the grounds for Myshkin's offer of marriage and Nastasya's acceptance of it is revealed. Myshkin sees that Nastasya would ruin herself by marrying Rogozhin. With a pitying love, he invites her into freedom from the tyrannical gaze of social morality—though only through repentance and a renunciation of the false glories that have thus far defined her existence. Nastasya speaks of having had a vision that someone "good" like Myshkin "would suddenly come and say, 'You're not guilty, Nastasya Filippovna, and I adore you!' And I sometimes dreamed so much that I'd go out of my mind" (I.15). This quotation reveals the meaning of Nastasya's previous incomplete repentance and her strange remark about having seen Myshkin's face before (I.10). Now (in I.15), Nastasya's tears testify that she longs to trust this vision. However, she renounces the apocalyptic beauty she sees in the divine love and forgiveness Myshkin bears and instead believes the tale told her in her victimization. Only Myshkin sees the beauty with which she would shine were she to believe herself guiltless for Totsky's offense and to accept the Christ-formed love Myshkin bears.

Myshkin, then, appears in the form of a servant and bears an all-suffering love that unmasks the criteria by which others judge Nastasya as bankrupt. This love issues from Myshkin's obedience to the sense for measure that is given him in the mystical visions that accompany his illness. These visions may seem an uncertain basis for such momentous judgments. But Dostoevsky dramatizes what failing to embrace this messianic measure looks like by having Nastasya refuse to be oriented by her own apocalyptic visions and their concrete manifestation in Myshkin's pitying love. Her fate threatens to make entropy the novel's ultimate message. But the dictum ascribed to Myshkin, "beauty will save the world," points in the opposite direction. Myshkin emphasizes that his sensations, when "remembered and examined in a healthy state, [turn] out to be the highest degree of harmony, beauty, [they give] a hitherto unheard-of and unknown feeling of fullness, measure, reconciliation, and an ecstatic, prayerful merging with the highest synthesis of life" (II.5). Though fleeting, these moments provide a basis for a proper evaluation and love of all phenomena precisely in time's own fleetingness.

Dostoevsky explores the eternal dimension of fleeting beauties and the higher synthetic order that lies behind them in the late, fateful party scene during which the Epanchins intend to introduce Myshkin into polite society. Prior to the party, Aglaya predicts that Myshkin will "start discussing some 'topic,' something serious, learned, lofty... [like] capital punishment or... that 'beauty will save the world.'" She predicts he will "make some gesture... hit [the family's prized Chinese vase] and break it" (IV.6). Sure enough, during the party Myshkin bursts into an enthusiastic speech that is alternately prophetic, triumphalist, and ridiculous. Despite his efforts to distance himself from it, Myshkin ends up bumping into the vase, which smashes upon the floor. Myshkin is struck dumb: "It was not the shame... not the unexpectedness that struck him most of all, but the fulfilled prophecy!... instead of horror there was light, joy, rapture" (IV.7). This folding together of past prophecy and present fulfillment betokens an eschatological breakthrough and the presence of a synthetic order beyond Myshkin himself and beyond time, a breakthrough for which his moments of epileptic *ecstasis* prepare him. In these moments Myshkin is "able to understand the extraordinary phrase that *time shall be no more*"[33] (II.5). Myshkin's trust of this eschatological vision enables him to perceive that his apparently time-bound activity unfolds within a deeper eternity.

In response to Myshkin's destruction of the vase, the party's hostess Lizaveta Prokofyevna compassionately remarks, "A man, too, comes to an end, and this was just a clay pot" (IV.7). This line recalls 2 Cor 4:6–7:

---

33. Rev 10:6.

the "light of the knowledge of God's glory" is a treasure held in "jars of clay to show that this all-surpassing power is from God, not from us" (NIV). This passage testifies that fragile human beings are insufficient as sources of light. Its quotation is fitting, since Myshkin's party speech inveighs against Jesuitical Catholicism, atheism, and socialism, all of which represent Promethean attempts to appropriate the divine prerogative to enlighten humankind. Against this Prometheanism, Myshkin opposes the urgency of witness to Christ in hope of "the future renewal of all mankind and its resurrection" (IV.7). His speech suggests that human beings, as clay pots, can bear a light not their own only if they will consent to receive it as empty vessels. As Travis Kroeker puts it, "the 'perfectly good' person illuminates the surrounding darkness so that those living within that darkness can see it and judge themselves."[34] In the novel, Myshkin appears ineffective because he recognizes that bearing a higher light requires that he be an empty vessel. Thus, paradoxically, it is Myshkin's Christ-imitating kenosis that is beautiful. In this way Dostoevsky elaborates the criteria by which beauty may be judged and points to the Messiah who alone completes them.

Conclusion

Scarry's key claims—that beauty graces human life, and that beauty is sacred, unprecedented, lifesaving, and humanizing—are important and carefully argued in *On Beauty and Being Just*. Moreover, they have an intuitive appeal that makes one wonder why they require the subtle defense she provides. Her claim that beauty "saves" by making our own non-ultimacy "pleasure-bearing" (113) invites further and deeper reflection on how salvation may be defined, and on the transcendent or ultimate dimension that beauty opens. One finds this sort of reflection in Scarry's own sources, Murdoch and Weil, who are more willing than Scarry to pass beyond the personal, piecemeal, or intersubjective frames for beauty Scarry prefers, and to speak in realist terms about the transcendent and divine. In *The Idiot*, Dostoevsky displays the way saving beauty—the beauty that will save the world—is paradigmatically present in the apocalypse of divine love. This love must be borne, concretely, into the very situations that bring it most under threat. And those who consent to bear it will suffer for it, for it registers with a paradoxical

34. Kroeker and Ward, *Remembering the End*, 248.

authority as it collides with lesser beauties. Hoping to evade this suffering or to align oneself with authorities deemed more rational or otherwise trustworthy is understandable, especially if the claims made on behalf of divine love seem defeasible—as they inevitably will within this age. Yet just as the truth is no less true for not being believed, so true beauty is no less beautiful for not being recognized.

Bibliography

Anderson, Roger. "*The Idiot* and the Subtext of Modern Materialism." *Dostoevsky Studies* 9 (1988) 77–89.

Derrida, Jacques. "Structure, Sign, and Play in the Discourse of the Human Sciences." In *Writing and Difference*, translated by Alan Bass, 278–93. Chicago: University of Chicago Press, 1978.

Dostoevsky, Fyodor. *The Idiot*. Translated by Richard Pevear and Larissa Volokhonsky. New York: Vintage, 2003.

Frank, Joseph. *Dostoevsky: The Miraculous Years, 1865–1871*. Princeton, NJ: Princeton University Press, 1995.

Homer. *The Odyssey*. Translated by Robert Fagles. New York: Penguin, 1996.

Kant, Immanuel. *Groundwork for the Metaphysics of Morals*. Edited and translated by Allen W. Wood. New Haven, CT: Yale University Press, 2002.

Kroeker, P. Travis, and Bruce K. Ward. *Remembering the End: Dostoevsky as Prophet to Modernity*. Boulder, CO: Westview, 2001.

Leithart, Peter J. *Solomon Among the Postmoderns*. Grand Rapids: Brazos, 2008.

Murdoch, Iris. *The Sovereignty of Good*. London: Routledge, 2006.

O'Regan, Cyril. *The Anatomy of Misremembering: Von Balthasar's Response to Philosophical Modernity*. Vol. 1, *Hegel*. Chestnut Ridge, NY: Crossroad, 2013.

Scarry, Elaine. *On Beauty and Being Just*. Princeton, NJ: Princeton University Press, 2010.

Shusterman, Richard. "The End of Aesthetic Experience." *Journal of Aesthetics and Art Criticism* 55 (1997) 29–41.

Taylor, Charles. *Sources of the Self: The Making of the Modern Identity*. Cambridge, MA: Harvard University Press, 1989.

Weil, Simone. *Waiting for God*. Translated by Emma Craufurd. New York: Harper Perennial Modern Classics, 2009.

16

Kissing, Killing, and the Epistemological Significance of Faith
A Reading of *Othello* and *Sapientia*

CHRIS K. HUEBNER

THIS ESSAY OFFERS A reading of two dramas that share remarkably similar scenes of kissing and killing: Hrotsvit of Gandersheim's *Sapientia*, and Shakespeare's *Othello*. Drawing on the work of the American philosopher Stanley Cavell, I will suggest that these scenes of kissing and killing present divergent but complementary readings of the theological virtue of faith. They do so, moreover, in ways that feature an intertwining of ethical and epistemological themes. By developing these themes, I demonstrate how these plays point to an understanding of faith as a kind of epistemological virtue. But before getting there, let me open with a short summary of the two key scenes of that suggest a linking of these plays in the first place.

In the final act and scene of Shakespeare's play, Othello enters the darkened bedroom with a light to find his bride already asleep in the bed which has just been made with their wedding sheets. He is lost within his thoughts. He flounders about in anguished interior conversation, interrogating himself about how he feels he must deal with Desdemona. He reassures himself that he is not capable of shedding her blood, and yet he also knows that she has to die. If she does not, he reasons, she will no doubt betray other men in the same manner he thinks she has betrayed him. He marvels at the whiteness of her skin, which he describes as being whiter than snow and as "smooth as monumental alabaster" (5.2.4–5).[1] He leans down to give her a kiss. And he quickly returns to kiss her once more, acknowledging that it will be "the last" (5.2.19). He weeps what he calls "cruel tears," noting that "this sorrow's heavenly, / It strikes where it doth love" (5.2.21–22). Desdemona is roused from her sleep, and she invites Othello to join her in bed. We know where this is heading, that this closing scene will follow the murderous logic of tragedy. Unable to hear what she has to say in response to his accusations, Othello smothers Desdemona with a pillow. Her last words are uttered as a reply to her maidservant, Emelia, who asks, "Who hath done this deed?" (5.2.123). Desdemona lies, telling Emelia that she was herself responsible for committing the horrific act. Desdemona crumples into her sheets and takes her last breath.

Othello first denies any involvement in her killing but soon confesses to Emilia that he was responsible for his wife's death. He justifies his actions by condemning Desdemona as a "liar gone to burning hell" (5.2.129). And he recounts his suspicions about Desdemona's infidelity. Emilia responds by setting the record straight, demonstrating to Othello how he had misinterpreted the "evidence" when he saw the handkerchief he had given to Desdemona in the hands of Cassio. Emilia assures Othello that his wife was "chaste" and "innocent," before she is herself killed by her conniving husband, Iago, who had gleefully stoked the flames of Othello's doubts. Distraught, Othello impales himself with a dagger. His last words find him returning to the two kisses with which the scene opened: "I kissed thee ere I killed thee—no way but this: / Killing myself, to die upon a kiss" (5.2.57–58). He kisses Desdemona once more. And then he collapses onto the bed and dies beside her.

In the tenth-century martyrdom drama *Sapientia*, which is among other things an allegorical account of the theological virtues as epistemological virtues, the German canoness and dramatist Hrotsvit of Gandersheim provides an account of the martyrdom of a young virgin named Faith that is also punctuated by series of three kisses. This occurs at the end of Faith's earthly life. By the time we get there, Faith has already been pressed by the emperor Hadrian to worship the goddess Diana in a way

---

1. Unless otherwise specified, all quotes from Shakespeare's play are drawn from *Othello, the Moor of Venice*, and will be cited parenthetically in the text by act, scene, and line number.

that is far more thorough and intense than the demands he has placed on her two younger sisters, Hope and Charity. And she has twice decried the emperor's foolishness, addressing him much more forcefully than her sisters would and challenging his veneration of "base metal" (135).[2] Her strong words earn a rebuke from Hadrian's adviser, Antiochus, who takes them as signs of her "insanity" and "madness" (136). The kissing scene also takes place after Faith has been severely tortured and follows the miraculous event in which milk rather than blood flows from her wounded breasts. In the moments after Hadrian finally orders her to be put to death by the sword, Faith turns to her mother and says: "O, venerable mother, say your last farewell to your child; give a kiss to your firstborn; expel sadness from your heart because I am on my way to eternal rewards" (138). Her mother responds by saying, "I kiss your mouth and eyes with tears of joy praying that you preserve the holy mystery of your name" (138). Faith then turns to address her two younger sisters: "O my sisters, born of the same mother," she says, "give me a kiss of peace, and prepare yourselves to bear the impending strife" (138). After Faith succumbs to the blow of the executioner's sword, Wisdom once again takes her eldest daughter into her arms. "I embrace the severed head of my dead daughter," she says, "and keep kissing her lips. I thank thee, Christ, for granting victory to a little girl still in infancy" (138–39).

It is surely no mere coincidence that the deaths of Faith and Desdemona are both bracketed by a series of kisses. These kisses bind the characters of Faith and Desdemona together, and it is through the scenes of ritual kissing that the question of faith in the two plays both meets most directly and is split apart in the most dramatic fashion. In each case, there are three kisses—two that precede the loss of the recipient's earthly life and one that follows their death. But despite this formal similarity, these two sets of kisses belong to radically divergent forms of life. Indeed, they serve to frame a kind of antithesis. In one case, three kisses mark the comedic consummation of a heavenly marriage. In the other, they symbolize the tragic failure of an earthly one. It is between these two sets of kisses that the two dramas can be said to present an account of faith as a kind of epistemological virtue. If *Sapientia* depicts a vision of faith as inaugurating a transformation of knowledge into wisdom, *Othello* shows what it might look like when that vision is viciously distorted and turned inside out. Before turning to a discussion

2. All quotes from *Sapientia* are drawn from Hrotsvitha, *Plays of Hrotsvit of Gandersheim*, and will be cited parenthetically in the text by page number.

of how these plays explore the question of faith as an epistemological virtue, let me say a bit more about how the different angles they present are symbolized by the nature of a kiss.

When Hrotsvit incorporated three kisses into her presentation of the martyrdom of Faith, she was invoking an important Christian ritual that was central to the formation of the early church and a key practice of early Christian martyrdom piety. Recalling Paul's injunction to "greet one another with a holy kiss" (2 Cor 13:12; Rom 16:16; 1 Thess 5:26),[3] Christians kissed each other as a way of nourishing and sustaining the bonds of Christian community. Kissing one another in this way fostered a connection that was not grounded in anything the subjects could claim for themselves but was mediated by their joint devotion and loyalty to Christ. This spirit of dispossession, as we might call it, is reflected in the way the ritual both built upon and transformed the traditional Roman rhetoric of the family, which associated kissing with kinship. The ritual of early Christian kissing was oriented toward a redefinition of natural bonds, whether biological or social, knitting together its participants as brothers and sisters in Christ. This attempt to differentiate the relationships formed by the Christian kiss from other relational forms is nicely illustrated by John Chrysostom in his commentary on 2 Corinthians. "The kiss is given so that it may be the fuel of love, so that we may kindle the disposition, so that we may love each other as brothers [love] brothers, as children love parents, as parents [love] children." Notice how Chrysostom begins by pointing to standard familial bonds. But he quickly moves beyond them, claiming that the Christian kiss creates a bond that is "also far greater, because those are by nature, these by grace. Thus, our souls are bound to one another."[4] The centrality of kissing in the emergence of the early Christian church is helpfully documented by Michael Penn, who notes that the Christian kiss is "not a momentary action; it is a sacred prescription for an entire way of life."[5] By concluding her portrayal of Faith in this way, Hrotsvit points to the kiss as a symbol of the way the Christian life involves a relationship to knowledge that is informed by the theological virtue of faith.

If the kisses that Faith exchanged with her mother and sisters express their shared loyalty to Christ, Othello's kissing of Desdemona represents

---

3. All quotations from Scripture are from the NRSV.

4. John Chrysostom, *In epistulam II ad Corinthios* 30.2; as quoted in Penn, *Kissing Christians*, 34.

5. Penn, *Kissing Christians*, 29.

the complete undoing of this way of life. His kiss is not a gesture of fidelity but an act of treachery. Far from a dispossessive giving of himself over to another, it is an expression of the way he was consumed by a form of possessive jealousy. In this respect, it does not reflect the formation and kindling of bonds but their utter dissolution. That Othello's kissing of Desdemona enacts a radical inversion of the Christian kiss is helpfully demonstrated by Hannibal Hamlin in his study of Shakespeare's extensive use of biblical allusions.[6] Hamlin notes that when Othello says to the dead body of Desdemona "I kissed thee ere I killed thee" before he kisses her for the third and final time, he is alluding to the kiss by which Judas betrayed Jesus in the Garden of Gethsemane. Hamlin points out that this identification with the kiss of Judas is anticipated in the speech given by Othello in the moments before he turns a knife upon himself. Here, Othello describes himself as "one whose hand, / Like the base Judean, threw the pearl away / Richer than all his tribe" (5.2.344–46).[7] Not only is the pearl a clear reference to Jesus, whom Judas treated as a disowned possession when he offered him up in exchange for thirty pieces of silver; its milky white hue is one of many references to the traditional color of faith that are scattered throughout the play.[8] Hamlin notes further that the overall thematic structure of the play is based upon an allusion to the opening words of 2 Cor 11, where Paul appeals to the images of marriage and jealousy in order to provide an illustration of fidelity to Christ:

> I wish you would bear with me in a little foolishness. Do bear with me! I feel a divine jealousy for you, for I promised you in marriage to one husband, to present you as a chaste virgin to Christ. But I am afraid that as the serpent deceived Eve by its cunning, your thoughts will be led astray from a sincere and pure devotion to Christ. (2 Cor 11:1–3)[9]

---

6. Hamlin, *Bible in Shakespeare*.

7. As quoted in Hamlin, *Bible in Shakespeare*, 232.

8. Other notable references to the color white include the wedding sheets and handkerchief, Iago's punning on the word "wit" as meaning both witty and white, the character of Bianca, the white paper on which Othello imagined it being written down that Desdemona is a "whore," Othello's vision of Desdemona as monumental alabaster, the angel to whom Emilia compares Desdemona, not to mention the very color of Desdemona's skin, which contrasts with Othello's blackness. The color white is also prominent in Hrotsvit's depiction of the martyrdom of Faith, most notably in her depiction of the milk that flows from her chaste and wounded breasts.

9. See Hamlin, *Bible in Shakespeare*, 231.

Where Paul describes faith as a form of divine jealousy that nurtures thoughts that, like those of Hrotsvit's Faith and other chaste virgins, do not stray from devotion to Christ, Othello embodies a form of jealousy that destroys both his faith and his marriage. If Shakespeare's play is reflecting on the question of faith, it does so by means of a parodic inversion of Paul's nuptial analogy of faith. In this context, the concluding image of Othello's Judas-like kiss of betrayal invites a comparison between *Othello* and *Sapientia*. When read alongside the epistemological themes that are at the heart of Stanley Cavell's well-known reading of the play,[10] Othello's treacherous kiss stands as an emblem of his vicious distortion of faith and its relationship to knowledge, and suggests that Shakespeare's play can be read as a kind of commentary that deepens and extends the vision of Hrotsvit's *Sapientia*, in which faith is allegorized as a kind of epistemological virtue.[11]

Cavell may not have explicitly framed his reflections on Othello as an examination of faith as an epistemological virtue. But the relevance of his reading to such an approach is suggested by his discussion of Othello's vision of Desdemona as "monumental alabaster." Cavell takes this reference to be the pivotal image of the play and central to an understanding of its epistemological significance. Although he does not put it this way himself, I read Cavell's discussion of the appearance of Desdemona as a statue as an exploration of what we might call the epistemological regions of faith, and in particular a suggestion that faith is better understood as a virtue that disciplines and informs the human use of reason rather than as a distinct epistemological faculty that exists alongside of reason in a kind of complementary way.

Why does Cavell take Othello's imagination of his sleeping wife as a statue made of alabaster to be such a critical piece of the play's epistemological investigations, and what does this have to do with the question of faith? Cavell opens his reading by focusing on the petrification of Desdemona in *Othello* and of Hermione in *The Winter's Tale* and describes their stone-like appearance as the "imagination of the body's fate under skepticism."[12] He finds *Othello* and *The Winter's Tale* to contain important epistemological insights because they demonstrate the extent to

---

10. See Cavell, *Disowning Knowledge*.

11. This way of summarizing the relationship of *Othello* to *Sapientia* echoes the inverted relationship that exists between *Sapientia* and Shakespeare's *King Lear*, which I have examined in my essay "Absent Fathers, Invisible Mothers."

12. Cavell, *Disowning Knowledge*, 125.

which being viewed as stone is an effect of the particular form of skepticism represented by the jealous husbands, Othello and Leontes. "In both plays," Cavell contends, "the consequence for the man's refusal of knowledge of his other is an imagination of stone."[13] The general context for this claim is the way modern epistemology tends to construe knowledge in terms of the apprehension of generic material objects like stones or tables and chairs, or what J. L. Austin famously referred to as "moderate sized specimens of dry goods."[14] According to such an approach, we can be said to have knowledge about a given object just to the extent that we are capable of bringing it within our cognitive grasp. Cavell takes skepticism to represent an intensification of this need to grasp an object. It expresses a desire for knowledge that has become extreme. The skeptic yearns for a knowledge that is so complete and his standards for success are so high that he inevitably finds himself in a situation of disappointment. And so, he comes to inhabit a condition in which the very possibility of knowledge as such is irredeemably threatened.[15] No matter how much he may love them, the skeptic is forced to conclude that the objects of his love, of his knowledge, must be disowned.

This way of putting it should make it clear why Cavell takes the figure of Othello to be an embodiment of the condition of skepticism. That Othello embraces the skeptical need for the best case is reflected in his demand that Iago supply him with "the ocular proof."[16] "Be sure of it," he roars at Iago, "give me the ocular proof" (3.3.362). He continues: "Make me to see't; or at least, so prove it / That the probation bear no hinge nor loop / To hang a doubt on—or woe upon thy life!" (3.3.366–68). But why does Cavell invoke Shakespeare in order to make this point about skepticism and modern epistemology? Because he finds that Shakespearean tragedy captures something important that tends to remain obscured in more narrowly philosophical discussions of skepticism. The demand for ocular proof is only one side of the skeptical equation. The other side, Cavell maintains, is that this demand and the fascination with generic objects with which it is associated is a function of active denial. It is not simply that the skeptic sets unreasonably high standards for knowledge. Rather, Cavell maintains that the appearance of stone is an effect

13. Cavell, *Disowning Knowledge*, 125.

14. Austin, *Sense and Sensibilia*. For Cavell's discussion of the epistemologist's focus on generic objects, see Cavell, *Claim of Reason*, 135.

15. Cavell, *Claim of Reason*, 268.

16. Cavell, *Disowning Knowledge*, 128.

of a sort of de-animation, a rendering of objects that presents them as if they are stripped of any life they might have. As Cavell puts it, "Skepticism's 'doubt' is motivated not by (not even where it is expressed as) a (misguided) intellectual scrupulousness but by a (displaced) denial, by a self-consuming disappointment that seeks world-consuming revenge."[17] It is this aspect of skepticism as a denial of life that is captured so powerfully in Shakespeare's tragedies. They demonstrate that skepticism is not simply a failure of cognition. It is not merely the inability fully to grasp an object. It also involves a distorted conception of the very objects it seeks. This is what Cavell means when he opens his discussion of *Othello* by saying that it studies "the imagination of the body's fate under skepticism."[18] *Othello* shows how the body comes to be imagined as stone when it is approached through the skeptic's desire for a knowledge that is guaranteed by ocular proof. Desdemona and Hermione did not always appear as statues. To exist as stone is not their natural condition. Rather, they are turned into stone by virtue of the way they are viewed by Othello and Leontes. These two powerful men relate to their wives in such a way that their status as living beings whose existence is separate from that of their husbands is denied them.

It is not just the spouses of jealous husbands, of course, who suffer the fate of being imagined as stone. This is also the fate of God under the condition known as idolatry. It is important to recognize that the idolatrous portrayal of God as an object is the result of the same process of active denial that *Othello* exemplifies. Cavell recognizes this connection when he describes Othello's "self-interpretation to be that of an idolater."[19] Idols, we might say, don't just sit there tempting us to gravitate toward them while giving us enough room to avoid them if only we are strong enough. Rather, they are objects constructed by a distorted imagination. Natalie Carnes captures this dimension of idolatry well when she observes that the condition of being an idol does not "inhere in a thing," but "name[s] a relationship mediated by communities, institutions, histories, and desires."[20] More specifically, she suggests that "idolatry names a form of desire that is stuck, that terminates before it reaches God, sometimes because it mistakes God for an object in the world."[21] It is the inclination

17. Cavell, *Disowning Knowledge*, 6.
18. Cavell, *Disowning Knowledge*, 125.
19. Cavell, *Disowning Knowledge*, 134.
20. Carnes, *Image and Presence*, 5.
21. Carnes, *Image and Presence*, 154.

to speak of and to God as if God were a statue made of stone. This is why the primary grammatical rule for theological speech about God is the reminder that God is not an object.

That Othello's turning Desdemona into stone is an outworking of the same process that informs the inclination toward idolatry suggests that the question of knowledge being explored by the play is not merely a philosophical matter. It also contains an important theological dimension. *Othello* is not just a study of the way knowledge is envisioned under the condition of skepticism. It is also an exploration of how this approach to knowledge is an expression of the loss of faith. One of the tacit contributions of Cavell's reading of *Othello* is the way it points to the central biblical allusion that lies at the heart of the play, namely the classical definition of faith as the "conviction of things not seen" (Heb 11:1). Against the background of this description of faith, it becomes clear that Othello's demand for ocular proof is an expression of his faithlessness, his inability to comprehend anything that he cannot clearly see. The petrification of Desdemona is a tragic consequence of this vicious rejection of faith. If Othello's faithlessness is reflected in the way he approaches his relationship to Desdemona as if it was based upon the epistemological possession of an object, then the play is also suggesting that faith is a mode of understanding that counters this temptation. The person of faith should not be driven to pursue the knowledge of lifeless objects capable of being possessed. Rather, she seeks an engagement with complicated beings who are infused with life. Cavell interprets Othello's desire for knowledge and his demand for ocular proof as an attempt to bypass or short-circuit the difficulty of his relationship to Desdemona. He is threatened by what Cavell calls her separateness, the realization that she is other than him and does not straightforwardly conform to his desires for what she might be like. If this is what it looks like to be in the grip of a vicious distortion of faith, then faith can be understood as an epistemological virtue that enables one to persevere in the face of this difficulty, to refuse the very powerful inclination to deny the separateness of another.

Let me return to my intuition that Shakespeare's drama serves as a commentary on the vision of faith suggested by Hrotsvit's *Sapientia*. Where Cavell tends to emphasize the way *Othello* anticipates some of the developments associated with modern epistemology, I find that his reading of the play also helps to clarify the allegorical depiction of faith that is presented in Hrotsvit's martyrdom drama. When the two plays are read alongside each other, we are presented with a picture of faith that is framed by a contrast between the figures of Faith and Othello. By relating to Desdemona in such a way that she appears to him as an image of stone, Othello embodies precisely the kind of approach that Faith resists when she refuses Hadrian's request that she "look with respect upon the venerable image of great Diana and bring offerings to the holy goddess so that you may possess her favor" (*Sapientia*, 135). Othello's yearning for a knowledge grounded in ocular proof is so strong that Desdemona comes to be figured as a statue. His will to knowledge leads him to relate to another human being in such a way as to deny her life, treating her as nothing more than an object about which he might have a kind of possessive knowledge. It is in this way that he is presented as a figure who has abandoned his faith. By contrast, Faith describes Hadrian's attempt to direct her attention to the statue of Diana as a foolish command to "venerate base metal" and a show of "contempt for the Creator" (135). Hadrian presents Faith with what appears to be an ideal object of knowledge, something that was clearly available for her to see and whose favor she was told she could win as a possession. But she turns it down because the posture required could not possibly be reconciled with the way she understands her relationship to the living God. In this way she is presented as one whose life and whose understanding of knowledge has been informed by the theological virtue of faith. What is this conception of faith that Faith embodies and that Othello so tragically distorts? And how does it relate to the question of knowledge?

One popular way of understanding the role of faith in relation to "things unseen" is to think of it as a way of grasping a distinct type of object. This is to conceive of faith as a special sort of epistemic capacity that can be distinguished from other such capacities. In this context, the word "unseen" is treated as an adjective that is used to specify a particular class of entity. Faith is then understood to be uniquely suited to the comprehension of this type of thing. "Things not seen" is thus rendered as something rather like "unseen things," as a particular sort of object that is not capable of being seen and so must be grasped in some other way. The implication is that faith works not by seeing, as knowledge does, but is an entirely different form of comprehension. It suggests that there are things that escape our vision because of the kind of thing they are and presents faith as an alternative way of securing epistemological access to those things. On this view, it is only through faith that we are capable of grasping these unseen things. Here we have an epistemic distinction between knowledge and faith that is thought to correspond to a metaphysical distinction between material and immaterial objects. Faith is presented as a path that takes us up to the second story of a two-tiered universe and allows for a sort of epistemic "top-up" to the natural knowledge of things that reside on the material ground floor. In this way, faith is seen to complement our knowledge of the natural world, providing access to the supernatural order of things that cannot be seen in a straightforward way.

The juxtaposition of Shakespeare's Othello and Hrotsvit's Faith, when read through the eyes of Cavell, suggests a rather different way of understanding how faith works in relation to knowledge. This discussion does not emphasize a difference in kind between two radically different types of thing—or two realms or orders—and the corresponding epistemological processes through which they might be comprehended. It does not turn, in other words, upon a sharp distinction between what can be seen and what cannot be seen. Rather, it is an attempt to elaborate a qualitative distinction between different ways of seeing. The primary concern in these discussions of faith is something more like an elaboration of the difference between seeing well and seeing poorly. This suggests that the question of faith is not so much, or not only, about the *what* of our understanding as it is about the *how*. Faith is not a means of comprehending something in a special way that somehow does not involve seeing. Rather, it describes a particular manner of seeing. It is not a special kind of epistemological capacity but a virtue that disciplines and gives shape to a range of human capacities, including that of reason.

Bibliography

Austin, J. L. *Sense and Sensibilia*. Edited by G. J. Warnock. Oxford: Oxford University Press, 1964.

Carnes, Natalie. *Image and Presence: A Christological Reflection on Iconoclasm and Iconophilia*. Stanford, CA: Stanford University Press, 2018.

Cavell, Stanley. *The Claim of Reason: Wittgenstein, Skepticism, Morality, and Tragedy*. New ed. Oxford: Oxford University Press, 1999.

———. *Disowning Knowledge: In Seven Plays of Shakespeare*. Updated ed. Cambridge: Cambridge University Press, 2003.

Hamlin, Hannibal. *The Bible in Shakespeare*. Oxford: Oxford University Press, 2013.

Hrotsvitha. *Sapientia*. In *The Plays of Hrotsvit of Gandersheim*, translated by Katharina Wilson, 81–97. New York: Garland, 1989.

Huebner, Chris K. "Absent Fathers, Invisible Mothers, and the Theological Dance of Knowledge and Love." *Conrad Grebel Review* 39 (2021) 192–213.

Penn, Michael Philip. *Kissing Christians: Ritual and Community in the Late Ancient Church*. Philadelphia: University of Pennsylvania Press, 2005.

Shakespeare, William. *Othello: The Moor of Venice*. Edited by Michael Neill. Oxford: Oxford University Press, 2006.

17

Enough
Casey Plett on Everyday Trouble and Love

GRACE KEHLER

CASEY PLETT, A CANADIAN author of diverse genres, features the everyday lives of transwomen in her writing. Not infrequently, she also includes the Mennonites, her relatives and ancestors who came out of the Radical Protestant Reformation of the sixteenth century. In a 2016 *Journal of Mennonite Studies* article titled "Natural Links of Queer and Mennonite Literature," Plett avers that

> in both [queer and Mennonite] literatures, there remains a persistent promise of a new community that accepts whatever fucked-up-ness the old community deemed sinful or improper—but of course it turns out the new community rarely lives up to its promises, that what the queer or Menno left behind held some kindnesses and goodnesses the new fails to match. The old, established ways didn't work [particularly well], but neither did assimilation towards what many in the larger world would've viewed as normal, and so they have to figure out something else.[1]

Here as well as in her fiction, Plett resists purity narratives, observing the inherent limits of those that promise inclusion of all peoples into the normative or suggest that things inevitably get better when one

---

1. Plett, "Natural Links of Queer and Mennonite Literature," 289.

acknowledges that prior models of care or recognition were fucked up and hierarchical. She calls attention to the utopian, progressivist notion that haunts both Menno-Christian and queer narratives—that notion of getting it right. Not only does the assumption of rightness tend to cast aspersions on the sites and people whose experiences or affects differ from one's own, it also adheres to a teleological narrative of arrival and achievement. The implication is that one should be able to attain happiness and fulfillment. Plett, like trans theorist Hil Malatino and theologian Linn Marie Tonstad, demonstrates that such idealist narratives and politics of inclusion and attainment all too often run up against their own limits.[2] However well intentioned, they tend to replicate hegemonic power structures that gatekeep the boundaries of inside/outside, authentic/inauthentic, fulfilled/unfulfilled. In both religious and queer contexts, divisions arise regarding who genuinely stands for progression and inclusion—and who should be included. If, for example, in religious circles divisions often arise from contests to define righteous behavior, in queer circles divisions arise from questions about gender credentials. Who represents trans subjectivity, and does one representation supersede another? As is all too familiar and dispiriting, the right sets itself up against the wrong.

Equally problematic, as Plett indicates, is the failure to recognize that goodness, kindness, and at-homeness manifest not in a sanitized space of arrival or achievement but within the mess and flux of relationality. To return to my opening quotation from Plett, Christians *and* queers need "something else," something more than the tyrannies of inclusion and recognition. That something else in her fiction—which eschews linear time and singular origin stories—takes form as a compassionate witness to everyday troubles and loves, both queer and Mennonite. In this essay, I look in particular at how Plett's aesthetics resonate with the book of Matthew and more particularly Matt 6:34, offering a vision of creative, emergent loves while remaining attuned to the "enough trouble" of the day. Plett uses this biblical verse as an epigraph and as a title for her penultimate short story in *A Dream of a Woman*, yet the verse applies equally to her 2018 novel *Little Fish*, the primary focus of this essay.[3] Both fictions feature a transwoman struggling with addiction and scant employment opportunities. *Little Fish* also takes on more extensively the challenges of

2. This is a frequent topic in Malatino's criticism. See in particular "Future Fatigue" in *Side Affects*.

3. All page references to Plett, *Dream of a Woman* and Plett, *Little Fish* will be cited parenthetically in the text.

navigating—and of staying alive in—often hostile societies in which transwomen experience multiplied forms of social and physical precarity.

Yet the sufficiently troubled days of many of Plett's characters also hold the potential for life-giving loves, for recoveries of the lost, and for beginnings not in spite of but within difficult lives. Only in staying with the trouble do they find possibilities. Or to rephrase, beginning is a perpetual becoming. That holds true for physical transformations and social positioning as well. Trans theorist Dina Georgis attests that gender/sex transition signals not an end in itself but one beginning or transition among many.[4] Transitioning in whatever form—aesthetic, hormonal, surgical—does not necessarily provide a clear experiential or narrative arc to fulfillment.[5] As Wendy Reimer, the protagonist of *Little Fish*, observes, not only does her sex keep "changing on her" (278), but her public interactions within secular and Mennonite communities also remain unpredictable. Kindnesses and cruelties, both unexpected and intentional, recur. Thus the novel, like Plett's nonfiction, calls for Mennonites and queers to attend to unfinished histories and to the inherently uneven ways in which goodnesses, kindnesses, *and* hurts manifest within community, whether new or old. Compassionate living takes place (or not) only in the everyday.

The version of Matt 6:34 that Plett cites in *A Dream of a Woman* is as follows:

> *Therefore do not worry about tomorrow;*
> *for tomorrow will worry about itself.*
> *Each day has enough trouble of its own.* (185)

What, we might ask, is enough trouble? Taken from Jesus's Sermon on the Mount, the verse suggests that there's a sense in which oversolicitousness takes one nowhere, while still acknowledging the doubled feelings of worry and hope in lives that necessarily entail struggle. To commit to the everyday, to this day, means acknowledging needs—spiritual and physical—while allowing for the possibility of care and grace. If the troubles are enough for the day (and, truly, they are), then so too is the grace for the day, or at least for some days. This is the countercultural perspective Jesus espouses, inviting his hearers to turn away from competitive, self-interested striving for individual success and material comforts (the

---

4. Georgis, "Gender Transitions and Aesthetic Possibilities," 55.

5. Georgis, "Gender Transitions and Aesthetic Possibilities," 55; Malatino, *Side Effects*, 3, 20, 24.

kinds of trouble we habitually indulge in the West) in order to open to flickers of the possible: notably, the gifts of connection or eros that one cannot possess or even deserve but that one can offer and receive. Plett's fiction also embraces the countercultural and, arguably, the counterintuitive, subversively imagining loves that may be practiced in the quotidian even by those who have been harmed or silenced. These loves may cross generations as well as the traditionally held boundaries between the living and the dead. These loves, significantly, offer the gift of reconceiving the possible.

Little Fish features Wendy Reimer, a Mennonite transwoman, precariously employed and therefore a sometime sex worker, who comes to learn that her late paternal grandfather, Henry, was definitely queer and possibly trans. Initially, Wendy resists revisioning the past, musing, "She'd had a boy life. It was shitty and murky. So her grandfather probably had too and just never got out. So her Opa'd been a woman. Fine. Closed" (24). But shortly thereafter she mentally apologizes for not taking Henry "seriously" and vows to "find" her Opa (82). This retrospective seeking for her queer Mennonite ancestor connects with the novel's format, which begins not at section 1 but at 0, a brief scene in which Wendy and three trans friends discuss temporality. They explore their beginnings as transwomen (such as their first dress in public, hormone therapy, and surgery) as well as their divergences from cis timelines. Those on hormones look younger than their cis counterparts, but they also seem to die earlier. They also don't really know what their life markers should be. What should they aspire to? They feel estranged from many typical narratives of the nuclear family and stability. Yet 0 denotes not emptiness but natalities—fraught natalities, yes, but also inquiries into the possible, both past and present. The 0 suggests (to repurpose Jack Halberstam's definition of queer time) "the potential to open up new life narratives and *alternative* relations to time and space."[6] In *Little Fish*, these narratives include repeatedly renewed affective orientations toward loves that are simultaneously costly and generative. In 0 time, the time of now, the time of being and beginning, both queer persons and Mennonites might choose to open effectively to one another precisely while contending with unresolved trouble and dissonance.

If the close third-person perspective of Wendy anchors the novel, Henry arguably serves as one of its most powerful figures of

---

6. Halberstam, *In a Queer Time and Place*, 2; emphasis added.

multidirectional time and of generative loves that defy easy categorization. Significantly, he first appears in the novel not in terms of Wendy's warm memories of her reputable, kind Mennonite grandfather (and these are ample), but as an unexpected queer progenitor who disrupts heteronormative time and affects. Wendy, along with her father, Ben, are in her late grandparents' home on the day after the funeral of her grandmother, Nettie, when Anna Penner, an old Mennonite friend of Henry's, calls to unburden herself about Henry's long-ago hidden life. Nettie, one suspects, might not have welcomed this belated and likely inopportune witness after twenty years of widowhood and whatever their marriage with children and grandchildren actually entailed. Yet it *is* opportune for Wendy, who takes the phone call and becomes the unintended recipient of the secret that Henry was "like" Ben's son (21)—that is, like Wendy herself. It's never entirely clear whether Anna actually anticipated Henry as a possible transwoman (more on this later). But her belated revelation enables Wendy, along with her Mennonite transwoman friend Sophie, to speculate about Mennonite trans-ancestors and to rescue from oblivion desires and loves that, in the past, were categorically denied or consigned to rumor and scandal. Recovering Henry as a transwoman, Wendy and Sophie perform retrospective witness of an ancestor, opening up queer and Christian loves to one another in the past and the present.

In his small-town Manitoba community, Henry was a committed church member and family man. In the city of Winnipeg, he was queer. For Wendy, he was one who exemplified caring relations in the everyday. From her childhood, she adored—or, in Plett's words, "loved the shit out of" (86)—her gentle, forbearing Opa, who along with her Oma raises Wendy at times when her father, Ben, is unable to do so. She recalls Henry modeling for her a commitment to expansive Christian loves. He not only resists religious dogma and blinkered prioritization of the nuclear family; as importantly, he queries the sources and manifestations of love. For Henry, love is not the provenance of those who appear stable, a matter of reciprocal exchanges, or a conferment on psychosomatic supplicants. Rather he envisions love as a part of a gift economy that has nothing to do with merit and everything to do with receptivity to others in the midst inevitably flawed relationships. He impresses on Wendy: "Your father loves you. He is imperfect [. . .]. [Still] Love is not attached to our human foibles because if we are truly loving, it comes from god. Love withstands our sins; love is higher than all the . . . crud we might inflict on those we love" (81).[7] Wendy notes that her Opa iterates his belief in love enacted in difficult times and by fallible people. Like the author of the book of Matthew, Henry acknowledges the struggle of addressing spiritual and physical frailties, while allowing for the possibility of beauty and generosity. His is the enactment of queer and Christian love at its best.

Impelled by her Opa's example and the sustaining memory of his love, Wendy, struggling with alcohol dependency, job loss, and the suicide of a close friend, recurrently seeks to find the "enough" goodness in the everyday to keep herself alive and available to her transwomen friends. She also undertakes the emotionally wrenching task of returning to the past to bear witness to Henry's life, a life she suspects was one of sacrifice and renunciation: a shitty, un-exitable boy life. Re-envisioning Henry's past, however, entails repeated encounters with intersubjective narratives and bonds not based on the easily recognizable and the normative. His past of radical loves provides her with alternative imaginations of his history and her everyday.

Before turning to the struggles of Wendy and her intimate friends, I linger on her complex inheritances from Henry, notably his long-term friendship with Anna Penner. Anna, an ostensibly pious, conservative Mennonite, vacillates between compassionating Henry (and, for that matter, Wendy) and voicing extreme denunciation of the "selfishness" of acting on one's nonnormative desires. Anna certainly inflicts "crud" on Wendy, yet also gifts the younger woman with the knowledge of Henry's queerness and, surprisingly, even takes up Wendy's speculation that Henry might have been trans rather than gay. "Won't presume to tell you that you are wrong," Anna says. "Henry might even be a woman in heaven for all eternity. Perhaps that's his Godly reward for enduring on Earth" (262). At first glance, this familiar Menno-Christian idea of earthly deferral to a compensatory afterworld seems an especially disappointing promissory narrative of arrival. In the context of the novel, however, it is much more than that. It is a moment of grace for Anna as much as for Wendy, a moment when the God of extravagant loves as envisioned by Henry touches Anna precisely as she wrestles with her human foibles and prejudices. However fleetingly, Anna puts aside her dominant narrative about Henry, in which he successfully "overcame" his queer desires and lived repentantly in his later years, to one in which he experiences a God who eternally affirms his desires (259). Eternity does not simply supersede historical time;

---

7. Ellipses are original to Plett's text except for those in square brackets.

rather the divine that makes human love possible in the first place opens up an infinity of loves both within and outside of historical time, adjacent to and disruptive of the cruelties of the everyday.

The odd, triangulated relationship among Anna, Henry, and Wendy—possibly all three queer people—brings the "enough" of love, trouble, and conflict into focus. Anna remarks the unusualness of her connection with Henry. Rural, married, Mennonite people of the opposite sex typically did not become close in the mid-twentieth century, yet these two spoke of and corresponded about spirituality and to an extent about sexuality and gender. Their exchanges, Wendy discerns, relied as much on partial revelations and listening to silences as on direct speech. Their shared communal prohibitions against acting on or even conversing frankly about sexual desire in their somewhat isolated towns suggests that Anna likely had to make surmises about Henry's male friend in the city and about Henry's grief after the friend dies. In her fittingly halting, clipped speech, Anna replicates with Wendy this pattern of revelation-concealment, claiming, for example, not to know if the city friend whose death Henry mourned was his lover. Wendy, frustrated with this reticence, presses for answers about how the friend died. "Was it AIDS? Oh, holy shit, did Henry die of AIDS too?" "No!" Anna said. "Henry never got it. I mean . . ." (260). Anna trails off, goes quiet again. What I'm getting at here (in my own circuitous and halting way!) are the kindnesses and goodnesses that emerge and re-emerge in the most unpropitious of circumstances. Anna, clearly burdened by what she understands as Henry's religiously unsanctioned desires and possibly by her own queer longings, has listened to Henry's words and silences; two decades after his death she still grapples with how to acknowledge their unique friendship and what she terms his "Various. Desires. And Things" (71). Her care coexists with her anxiety and moralistic judgments, a *productive* conflict that makes possible the witnessing and begetting of previously unknown, unwanted histories: more specifically, a witnessing of the desires of Henry beyond scandal and rumor.

Let me elaborate these claims by touching briefly on Walter Benjamin's theses "On the Concept of History," in which such atemporality and difficult witness figure prominently. Benjamin postulates that each age "has been endowed with a *weak* messianic power, a power on which the past has a claim. Such a claim cannot be settled cheaply."[8] The weak

---

8. Benjamin, "On the Concept of History," 390.

messianic power concerns itself with (disavowed) peripheral histories that complicate the dominant cultural narratives as well as with histories that could have been, in both cases histories that call for realization in the present. This power is weak, in Benjamin's transvalued use of the term, because it derives exclusively from mutual begettings and from receptivity to ethical obligations. The past expects or desires a redeemer/witness, but of course, one might refuse the solicitation of the past. In turn, the power of the receptive witness to beget a nonconformist image of the historically possible depends on affectively risking oneself by opening to and taking on responsibility for other subjects and other eras. While I want to be clear that Benjamin's concept of a weak messianic power does not fully align with Plett's novel, his attention to the difficulty and to the *multidirectional* work of witnessing fits well with *Little Fish*. Anna struggles with shame and queerphobia, Wendy with fears that Henry lived in pain and that the Mennonite community wishes that she, like him, stayed hidden. Still Henry bequeaths to them an ethical present of expansive, difficult loves that enables the two women to stay with the trouble of witnessing him long enough to recover him as lovable in his queerness. Witnessing him, they affirm queer and Christian potentialities of love—past, present, future, and atemporal.

For Wendy, Henry has always been her "guide" for godliness and goodness both in childhood and womanhood (61); notably, she strives to treat others with generosity and love beyond normative ledgers of merit in spite of the verbal and physical abuse she and her transwomen friends experience. These women all too often find themselves reviled in public, called out as offenses to and blights on heteronormative culture, as deceivers who attempt to pass themselves off as women.[9] "You're not fooling anyone, boys," shouts "one lone huge man" (44). Often the language is far more violent: "Are you a fuckin' man?" Wendy gets asked (96). The women also experience attacks on their bodies, such as when a "rough" trick traps Sophie in a hotel room (118), or when an elderly man, over protests by Wendy, thrusts his hand down her clothes to ascertain that she really has a vagina (122). As Malatino asserts, the panopticon is real and it is gendered:[10] those who do not scan readily as "born" women and men will be made to bear the antagonism of those who fear disorder or complexities.[11] Rather than risking themselves ethically and

9. See Malatino, *Trans Care*, 12.
10. Malatino, *Trans Care*, 27.
11. Gozlan, Introduction to *Current Critical Debates*, 6.

compassionately, rigid defenders of the heteronormative falsely divide questions of gender and sex from the inevitable difficulties of caring relationships.[12] Wendy, at times, responds to such violations with the extremes of numb dissociation (often accompanied by drinking) or rage—the former a survival mechanism in the face of countless aggressions, the latter an impassioned response to injustice and outright inhumanity.[13] Yet Wendy, like Henry before her, continues to enact care for both intimates and strangers, friends and aggressors. She stays with the trouble.

To be clear, among Wendy and her transwomen friends, care is mutual. But, as I've been arguing, figurally speaking, Henry informs the entire novel's ethics of expansive queer and Christian loves—loves that are multiple and generous. He affirms love as a gift that is not subject to an economy of scarcity or merit. As he explains to Wendy when she is a child, people misunderstand care as self-referential and limited. Hence, Henry despairs, they pray in solipsistic ways: "Protect my wife, my children, protect me" (39). To such petitions he prefers the questions: What might one give, and what is one given? He calls for queer and Christian lovers to liberate themselves from boundaried and hierarchical forms of care, undertaking instead unpredictable, yet generative, forms of relationality. Such gifted and giving loves typify the t4t (trans for trans) care Plett's protagonists show for one another. However harmed they are by their treatment in the cisnormative public sphere, they celebrate the beauties of their bodies and persons; they celebrate embodiment as a possible site of resurgence. Their verbal and text messages are replete with love emojis (<3) and statements as well as testaments to each other's physical attractiveness. If, as Wendy discerns, in public, their reception as women "could always be taken away" (101), she and her friends open erotically and affectively to one another, reciprocally affirming their embodied beings as lovely and lovable, and feminine beauty as capacious and open to diversity. Often, such affirmations include intimate touch—cuddling, holding, hugging, kissing—that bespeaks chosen family, but never a closed one. Their eros extends nonpossessively to each other's friendships and sexual lives. To select a few instances, Sophie sets up Wendy with a man with whom Sophie has had sex; Wendy enjoys the sounds of her roommate Raina and her girlfriend in the grip of passion (40); and Wendy and Raina both become lovers of the visiting

---

12. Georgis, "Gender Transitions and Aesthetic Possibilities," 52.
13. Malatino, *Side Affects*, 67–69, 107.

transwoman Aileen, while devastated by the loss of Sophie, who has died by suicide. In any of these instances, jealousies or refusals could have divided them. Especially after the death of Sophie, the women could have become withdrawn and self-protective, wary of loves that expose them to nearly unbearable losses and to the reality of how "fucking hard [it is] for [transwomen] to stay alive" (241). They, however, continue to risk themselves affectively and erotically. Their cares extend to people and situations Henry may or may not have imagined. Significantly, their cares, like his, begin where the normative often ends.

One especially affecting scene in the novel entails Wendy caring for a trick, a recently discharged military boy who identifies as Kaitlyn. For the most part, Wendy is matter-of-fact about returning to ho-ing and encounters with tricks, even unpleasant ones. She is deeply shaken, though, by her encounter with the coke-addled and isolated girl wannabe who literally lives on the periphery of the city of Winnipeg in a mostly unfurnished house in a shoddily built suburb. Kaitlyn wants to experience the vulnerability of being penetrated, and Wendy, very drunk and without a penis, manages to attend both sexually and affectively to the "quivering" (217) girl, while choking back tears of pained recognition for this "*Sweetie*" who has no community (216)—no intimates with whom she might be able to explore what her desires mean. It's a fairly extended scene in the novel, with Wendy silently recalling the difficulties of her own transition and surgery (including a transphobic assault) and then offering instead what Kaitlyn likely needs most: information about the Winnipeg Klinic with a "K," where those who want to talk about or begin transitioning will be supported. Wendy, whose "hearts breaks for the girl" (233), hopes that, like her, Kaitlyn will find "enough" (224) in gender transitioning to meet the trouble of the day, whether or not this brings happiness. As Malatino writes in another context, "transitioning does not have to be happy-making in order for it to be imperative," and trans narratives do not necessarily provide harmonious resolutions.[14] Wendy is acutely aware of urgent needs *and* of the instabilities that transwomen continue to experience. Still, she leads with her heart, following it to the point of her own breakage, her own limits, to witness this girl in her vulnerability and questioning. Queerly, Christianly, Wendy offers love at the very limits of the self. Here I am, for you. I am not sure of what I'm being asked or even if I can do this. But here I am.

14. Malatino, *Side Affects*, 3, 7.

Similar generosities inform Wendy's relations to the Mennonites, with whom Wendy practices compassion in the most inauspicious situations, repeatedly overcoming rage and numbness in the face of their many microaggressions. At her grandmother's funeral, in the present of the novel, she gets left out of the obituary, and the relatives who deign to speak with her misgender her or reject her offer to help with the food, firmly excluding her from domesticity and femininity. In stark contrast, she permits herself to feel "warm and blessed" in the company of others who loved her Oma (14), gifting them with the very Christian care they refuse to her, the care beyond the normative and self-referential. With the stranger Anna, Wendy, too, reaches across differences and past recriminations. Even before they meet, Wendy realizes that in spite of their miscommunications, she "want[s] to love this old woman. She was so, so tired of loving her people and them not loving her back" (150). In this will to love, to act counterculturally, Wendy finds herself capable of putting aside her anger, sadness, and tremendous weariness and of following her late Opa's example, treating others with generosity and love beyond what they could possibly deserve. She puts aside questions of fairness and rights, extending to the noninclusive other a prevenient compassion—what theologian Linn Tonstad terms "redemption in reverse."[15] This is not an offering by those comfortably positioned in society, the ones who typically get to decide whom to include or exclude from their affections. Rather, this is love at its most queer and most Christian, originating from one who cannot count on being recognized, let alone receiving compassion. This is love offered in response to hatred, antagonisms, and disgust. Loving those who query her lovability, Wendy redeems love itself from the framework of progressiveness and supersessionism.

Prevenient and extravagant love, as presented by Plett, enables a relay of witnessing that occurs both within and outside of historical time, through embodied encounters and spiritual heritability. Notably, Wendy's ability to channel Henry's love effects an opening for the old and the young Mennonite women to allow difficult truths to emerge, including Anna's own unacted queer desires and the possibility of Henry as a transwoman. I return to Anna's grace-given vision of Henry that moves her briefly out of her transphobia, because that vision in turn gifts Wendy with the capacity to retrospectively imagine Henry—along with a Christian trans story—as he and it could be. Anna glimpses a

---

15. Tonstad, "Limits of Inclusion," 14.

Christian heaven welcoming of a female Henry. Wendy subsequently dreams of Henry as an angel, the bearer of life-affirming news, who invites her into a mutual witnessing of trans bodies and of loving natalities. I quote part of Wendy's dream:

> Henry had a baby in her arms, and its face leaned against Henry's chest. [. . .] Outside [. . .] there was chaos and smoke everywhere [. . .]. [But] Henry pulled her [Wendy's] feet onto the couch with the baby still in both arms and leaned forward on her knees in her long billowy clothing looking at Wendy, and she laughed with her radiant, pure lit-up smile getting bigger and bigger [. . .] light light light shining from all of Henry's soft lotioned body, until they were so close. (289)

Recovering Henry as both a maternal figure and an angelic witness, Wendy posthumously confirms that her Opa has always fostered radical corporeal and spiritual compassion while staying alert to all that threatens them. Wendy envisions him shutting out the atmospheric menaces (presumably those chaotic, destructive forces common to Mennonite and secular cultures) and intentionally nurturing both the infant and Wendy, all three of them partaking of o time that allows for bodily beginnings and new relational possibilities. The dream, thus, embraces trans time with its multiple firsts as well as elements of t4t care. For Wendy and the infant, Henry provides physical touch and cherishing in a manner reminiscent of Wendy's living community of transwomen, affirming the child and adult bodies as sites of unpredictable but always lovable becomings. As the visitor who arrives out of linear time, Henry additionally symbolizes multidirectional memory and witnessing. The past (in Benjamin's configuration) calls for a present witness to beget a nonconformist image of the historically possible: that is to say, the witness in the present must vulnerably open to lost, peripheral, or unwanted histories that complicate dominant cultural narratives.[16] Wendy heeds this costly call of the past, finding Henry in his feminine and Christian incarnation and daring to see him, once again, as an annunciation of enough grace for the difficult days in the life of a transwoman.

Prior to the dream of Henry, Wendy sums up her life, musing that she "was a pissy, alcoholic tranny hooker, for better and for worse, and probably always would be" (280). Following the dream, Wendy prepares to take on a ho job at the Fort Gary Hotel, where "some guy [. . .] badly

---

16. Benjamin, "On the Concept of History," 391.

wanted her ass" (288). She drinks and puts "Violet" on repeat, Hole's song in which lead singer Courtney Love rages against a gendered system of violence, ironically screaming, "Go on take everything, take everything, I want you to." But leaving the job, Wendy affirms her belief that she "would have love," that she "felt okay about where her life was headed" (293). From Henry, Wendy learns to embrace love that begins in and engages the trouble of the everyday. She attests not only to her lovability but more radically to her ability to love in an often exclusive, judgmental society, in a society wants the asses and other bodily parts of people without wanting the person. Wendy recalls Henry saying, "Love withstands our sins" (81). As *Little Fish* manifests, this includes the sins of transphobia and of the assumption that we've already arrived at a socio-cultural-religious site of inclusion. We are never there. But, if we are susceptible and attentive, we might have enough love to extend to one another.

Bibliography

Benjamin, Walter. "On the Concept of History." In *Selected Writings, 1938–1940*, translated by Harry Zohn, edited by Howard Eiland and Michael W. Jennings, 4:389–400. Cambridge, MA: Harvard University Press, 2003.

Georgis, Dina. "Gender Transitions and Aesthetic Possibilities." In *Current Critical Debates in the Field of Transsexual Studies: In Transition*, edited by Oren Gozlan, 48–58. Abingdon, UK: Routledge, 2018.

Gozlan, Oren. Introduction to *Current Critical Debates in the Field of Transsexual Studies: In Transition*, edited by Oren Gozlan, 1–12. Abingdon, UK: Routledge, 2018.

Halberstam, J. Jack. *In a Queer Time and Place: Transgender Bodies, Subcultural Lives*. New York: New York University Press, 2005.

Malatino, Hil. *Side Affects: On Being Trans and Feeling Bad*. Minneapolis: University of Minnesota Press, 2022.

———. *Trans Care*. Minneapolis: University of Minnesota Press, 2020.

Plett, Casey. *A Dream of a Woman*. Vancouver: Aresenal Pulp, 2021.

———. *Little Fish*. Vancouver: Arsenal Pulp, 2018.

———. "Natural Links of Queer and Mennonite Literature." *Journal of Mennonite Studies* 34 (2016) 286–90.

Tonstad, Linn Marie. "The Limits of Inclusion: Queer Theology and Its Others." *Theology and Sexuality* 21 (2015) 1–19.

Major Publications of P. Travis Kroeker

Books

Christian Ethics and Political Economy in North America: A Critical Analysis. Montreal: McGill-Queen's University Press, 1995.

and Bruce K. Ward. *Remembering the End: Dostoevsky as Prophet to Modernity.* Boulder, CO: Westview, 2001.

Messianic Political Theology and Diaspora Ethics: Essays in Exile. Theopolitical Traditions 23. Eugene, OR: Cascade, 2017.

Empire Erotics and Messianic Economies of Desire. J. J. Thiessen Lectures. Canadian Mennonite University Press, 2013.

Articles

"Canada's Catholic Bishops and the Economy: A Theological Ethical Analysis." *Toronto Journal of Theology* 2 (1986) 3–18.

"Ethics, Economics, and Christian Realism: Religious Social Theories of Reinhold Niebuhr and Gregory Vlastos." *Annual of the Society of Christian Ethics* (1988) 77–89.

"Pluralism and Policy Monism: The Political Irrelevance of Theology." *Toronto Journal of Theology* 7 (1991) 35–43.

"Theology, Ethics and Social Theory: The Social Gospel Quest for a Public Morality." *Studies in Religion/Sciences Religieuses* 20 (1991) 180–99.

"The Ironic Cage of Positivism and the Nature of Philosophical Theology." *Studies in Religion/Sciences Religieuses* 22 (1993) 93–103.

"The Humanization of Production: A Critique of *Economic Justice for All.*" *Église et Théologie* 25 (1994) 65–83.

"Reply to Donald Wiebe." *Studies in Religion/Sciences Religieuses* 23 (1994) 81–82.

"The Peaceable Creation: Stanley Hauerwas and the Mennonites." *Conrad Grebel Review* 13 (1995) 136–41.

"Spirituality and Therapy in Secular Culture." *Canadian Journal of Occupational Therapy* 64 (1997) 122–26.

"Theocentric Ethics and Politics." *Annual of the Society of Christian Ethics* 17 (1997) 19–27.
"Anabaptists and Existential Theology." *Conrad Grebel Review* 17 (1999) 69–88.
"The War of the Lamb: Postmodernity and John Howard Yoder's Eschatological Genealogy of Morals." *Mennonite Quarterly Review* 74 (2000) 295–310.
"Why O'Donovan's Christendom Is Not Constantinian and Yoder's Voluntariety Is Not Hobbesian: A Debate in Theological Politics Redefined." *Annual of the Society of Christian Ethics* 20 (2000) 41–64.
"Eschatology and Ethics: Luther and the Radical Reformers." *Consensus* 27 (2001) 9–25.
"Educative Violence or Suffering Love? Radical Orthodoxy and the Radical Reformation." *Conrad Grebel Review* 23 (2005) 19–24.
"Is a Messianic Political Ethic Possible? Recent Work by and about John Howard Yoder." *Journal of Religious Ethics* 33 (2005) 141–74.
"Whither Messianic Ethics? Paul as Postmodern Political Theorist." *Journal of the Society of Christian Ethics* 25 (2005) 37–58.
"Messianic Freedom and the Secular Academy: Educating the Affections in a Technological Culture." *Consensus* 32 (2006) 41–57.
"Messianic Political Theology: Yoder *contra* Redekop." *Direction* 38 (2009) 67–78.
"Rich Mennonites in an Age of Mammon: Is a Messianic Political Economy Possible?" *Journal of Mennonite Studies* 27 (2009) 168–78.
and Carole Leclair. "Mennonite and Métis: Adjacent Histories, Adjacent Truths?" *Journal of Mennonite Studies* 28 (2010) 187–202.
and Bruce Ward. "Gulag Ethics: Russian and Mennonite Prison Memoirs from Siberia." In JMS Forum: "Mennonites in Siberia," edited by Royden Loewen and Paul Toews. *Journal of Mennonite Studies* 30 (2012) 249–66.
"Technology as Principality: The Elimination of Incarnation." *Pro Ecclesia* 24 (2015) 162–77.
"Saint Paul at Sea: A Mystical-Political Reading of *Moby Dick* via Stanislaus Breton." *Pro Ecclesia* 26 (2017) 111–18.
"Scandalous Displacements: 'Word' and 'Silent Light' in Miriam Toews' *Irma Voth*." In JMS Forum: "Mennonite/s Writing VIII: Personal Narratives of Place and Displacement," edited by Robert Zacharias. *Journal of Mennonite Studies* 36 (2018) 89–100.
"The Scandalous Drama of Trinitarian Theology for a Radical Church." *Conrad Grebel Review* 37 (2019) 146–53.
"Apocalyptic Political Theology: Response to Philip Ziegler's *Militant Grace*." *International Journal of Systematic Theology* 22 (2020) 313–26.
"Postsecular History or Figural Messianism?" *Political Theology* 24 (2023) 342–46.

Book Chapters

"Sexuality and the Sacramental Imagination: It All Turns on Affection." In *Wendell Berry: Life and Work*, edited by Jason Peters, 119–37. Lexington: University of Kentucky Press, 2007.
"Messianic Ethics and Diaspora Communities: Upbuilding the Secular Theologically from Below." In *Religious Voices in Public Places: Religion and Liberal Reason*, edited by Nigel Biggar and Linda Hogan, 110–30. Oxford: Oxford University Press, 2009.

"Living 'As If Not': Messianic Becoming or the Practice of Nihilism?" In *Paul, Philosophy and the Theopolitical Vision*, edited by Douglas Harink, 37–63. Eugene, OR: Cascade, 2010.

"The War of the Lamb: Postmodernity and Yoder's Eschatological Genealogy of Morals." In *The New Yoder*, edited by Peter Dula and Chris Huebner, 70–89. Eugene, OR: Cascade, 2010.

"Making Strange: Harry Huebner's Church-World Distinction." In *The Church Made Strange for the Nations: Essays in Ecclesiology and Political Theology*, edited by Paul Doerksen and Karl Koop, 92–99. Eugene, OR: Pickwick, 2011.

"A Contemporary Perspective on Spirituality." In *Spirituality and Occupational Therapy*, edited by Mary Ann McColl, 81–89. Ottawa: CAOT, 2011.

"On the Difference Between Torture and Punishment: Theology, Liturgy and Human Rights." In *Theology, University, Humanities: Initium Sapientiae Timor Dominis*, edited by Christopher Brittain and Francesca Murphy, 19–38. Eugene, OR: Cascade, 2011.

"Recent Continental Philosophers." In *The Blackwell Companion to Paul*, edited by Stephen Westerholm, 440–54. Chichester, UK: Wiley-Blackwell, 2011.

"Jesus Is the Bread of Life: Johannine Sign and Deed in *The Violent Bear It Away*." In *Dark Faith: New Essays on Flannery O'Connor's "The Violent Bear It Away,"* edited by Susan Srigley, 136–56. South Bend, IN: University of Notre Dame Press, 2012.

"Augustine's Messianic Political Theology: An Apocalyptic Critique of Political Augustinianism." In *Augustine and Apocalyptic*, edited by John Doody et al., 129–49. Lanham, MD: Lexington, 2014.

"Technology as Principality: The Elimination of Incarnation." In *Life amid the Principalities*, edited by Michael Root and James J. Buckley, 99–116. Eugene, OR: Cascade, 2016.

"The Secular—The Political: Augustine and Political Augustinianism in Twentieth-Century Political Theology." In *The Edinburgh Critical History of Twentieth-Century Christian Theology*, edited by Philip Ziegler, 237–61. Edinburgh University Press, 2022.

"'The Word Became Flesh': What Are the Implications of an Augustinian Incarnational Economy for Biotechnology?" In *The Ethics of Grace: Engaging Gerald McKenny*, edited by Michael Mawson and Paul Martens, 87–104. London: T. & T. Clark, 2022.

Rachel Matheson and Travis Kroeker. "Eros, Eating, Attention: The Ethics of Incarnation in Augustine and Simone Weil." In *Augustine and Ethics*, edited by Kim Paffenroth and Sean Hannan, ch. 20. Lanham, MD: Lexington, 2023.

Other Publications

"Doubting Thology: Wisdom—Divine and Human." *Christian Century* (June 29, 2004) 27–30.

"Living 'As If Not': Pauline Messianism and Continental Political Philosophy." *Arc: The Journal of the Faculty of Religious Studies, McGill University* 38 (2010) 59–68.

"Overcoming Historicism: Weak Messianic Apocalpyticism." Symposium on *The Heterodox Yoder*, by Paul Martens. Syndicate, June 2014. *Syndicate: A New Forum for Theology* 1 (2014) 87–93. https://syndicate.network/symposia/theology/the-heterodox-yoder/.

"Preface." In *Toward an Anabaptist Political Theology*, by James Reimer, edited by Paul Doerksen. Eugene, OR: Cascade, 2014.

and Kyle Gingerich Hiebert, eds. "Political Theology and Apocalyptic." Symposium on P. Travis Kroeker, *Messianic Political Theology and Diaspora Ethics*, and Kyle Gingerich Hiebert, *The Architectonics of Hope: Violence, Apocalyptic and the Transformation of Political Theology*. *Conrad Grebel Review* 36 (2018) 274–306.

Symposium on *Messianic Political Theology and Diaspora Ethics*, by P. Travis Kroeker. Syndicate, July 2019. https://syndicate.network/symposia/theology/messianic-political-theology-and-diaspora-ethics/.

Subject Index

aesthetics, xxiii, 42, 209–13, 209n2, 235–36
affection, xviii, 84, 244
agon, 178–84
Anabaptism, x, 12, 18, 20, 32, 38, 50, 57, 68, 82, 94, 97, 104, 145
angels, 16, 51, 57, 227n8, 245
antichrist, 42–43
apocalypticism, xxiii-vii, 15–17, 26–33, 38–59, 64–75, 79, 81, 87, 94, 107–20, 123, 131, 133, 163–73, 177–79, 182, 188–91, 197, 208–20; and eschatology, 26–33, 43; Jewish, 26, 27, 34; messianic, 38, 87
Augustine: *City of God*, 13–16, 50–60, 180–83, 193–200, 203; *Confessions*, xxiii, 16, 82, 96–99; *De Doctrina Christiana*, 163–64; *On Grace and Free Choice*, 97; and Plato, 16–17; and sexuality, 193–200. See also Augustinianism.
Augustinianism, xi, xxvi, 13–17, 50, 94, 97; political, 13–16

Barth, Karl, 42, 57, 112n13, 133–34, 136, 136n1
beauty, 95–96, 99–103, 115, 123, 153, 166, 187, 197 208–22, 239, 242
Benjamin, Walter, 41–42, 52, 81, 240
Berry, Malinda, xxi

Berry, Wendell, 12–13; *Remembering*, 22
Boff, Leonardo, 100, 102–4
Bonhoeffer, Dietrich, 69–71
Buell, Kimber, 59–60

Canada, 21, 53–54
Catholicism, 12–15, 56, 113n15, 182, 221
Christian nationalism, 32–33
Christology, 31, 51, 65–66, 74, 96, 108, 110n8; kenotic, 65; pneumatological, 95–96
climate change, 112n12, 123. See also ecocrisis.
colonialism, xxii, 21, 51, 83, 87, 130–31, 139n36; and the environment, 130; and Mennonites, 21. See also decolonization.
community, 11, 15, 19–23, 40, 54, 57–58, 68, 93, 234, 241–45; messianic, xxvii, 10–11, 19, 23, 46, 53, 178, 187–88; political, 55
conversion, 11, 20–21, 57, 94, 100, 185–88
Corneille, Pierre, xxvii, 179, 182–85
creation, 10, 12, 23, 29, 53, 67, 70–73, 100, 110–18, 122–34, 136–37, 165–72, 194–99, 215–16; Messianic, 109–10
crucifixion, 64, 70, 108–9, 117n22, 120, 154

Davies, W. D., 44–46
death, 3, 27, 33, 65–66, 70–71, 75, 103, 108–10, 115, 126, 134, 145, 153–57, 168–73, 183
decolonization, 93–104
decreation, 150–51, 153, 154n13, 155–62
delayed parousia, 26n2, 29–31
desire: possessive, xxi, xxvi, 10, 78–88; sexual, 22–23, 197, 201, 240; transfiguration of 202–4
diaspora, 33, 53, 87; ethics of, 50
Dostoevsky, Fyodor, *The Brothers Karamazov*, 178–91; and the concept of the duel, 178–91; *The Idiot*, 210–22

ecocrisis, 123–28. See also climate change
economism, 128–29, 133; political, 10, 22–23
education, xviii, xx, xxiv, 11, 22
equity, 73–74
eros, xi, xxii, xxiv, 9–11, 237, 242; divine, 23; and memory, 22–23; Messianic, 11, 22;
erotics. See eros
eschatology, 64, 66; apocalyptic, 26–33, 72; Jewish, 39–40
ethics: Christian, x; diaspora, 50; honor, 179–80, 189–90; kenotic, 65; messianic, 21, 72, 94, 123–26, 130, 133; queer, 242; theological, xxvii, 11, 22, 31–32
ethnoculture, 55, 57
existentialism, 15, 53, 59, 82–84, 87

Fall, the, 153–56, 193–200; and sexuality, 193–200
Foucault, Michel, xxiii, 193–207
friendship, xi, 123, 139, 216, 239–42

Gelassenheit, 34, 85
Genesis story, 111, 141, 153–56
gnostic, xi, 53
Good, the, xix, 14

grace, 69, 72–73, 117, 137, 146, 169, 17–73, 184, 189, 194–95, 226, 236; and decolonization, 93–104
greatness, 150, 153, 158–62, 183
Gustafson, James, ix, xxii–iii, 81n5

Han, Byung-Chul, 44–45
Hauerwas, Stanley, ix, 52–53, 57, 109n7
Hobbes, Thomas, 52, 61, 83
Holy Spirit, 13, 17, 23, 47, 68, 72, 77, 94–104, 108–11, 117, 120, 163–64
honor, Roman, 180–82
hos me, 34, 46–47, 52
Hrostsvit of Gandersheim. See *Sapientia*

idolatry, 52, 216, 230–31
imagination, 51–52, 56, 195–96, 101, 115, 161, 195–96, 200, 203, 206, 228–30, 239; Christian, 121–23; messianic, xix, xxvii, 9–24, 133
incarnation, xxiv, xxvi, 10–11, 16, 58, 64, 70–71, 75, 94–95, 99, 108–9, 117, 120, 136, 154, 188. 215, 245
Israel, 51, 53, 58–59

Jesus: movement, 27, 29, 32; of Nazareth, 17, 45, 102, 117 politics of, 45
John, Apostle, 28
Judaism, 26, 37, 59–60; messianic, 37–38; rabbinical, 38
judicial system, 69–74, 82

Käsemann, Ernst, 26, 34
katechon, 42, 42n21, 47
kenosis, 46–47, 65–66, 69–74, 87, 150–62, 215
kenotic hymn, 154, 156, 158, 160–61
Kingdom of God, 27–28, 32, 34
Kohák, Ezrahim, 131–33, 163n1
Kroeker, Travis: "Augustine's Messianic Political Theology", 13, 94; "An Apocalyptic Critique of Political Augustinianism", 13–14; *Christian Ethics and Political*

Economy in North America: A Critical Analysis for the Journal of Mennonite Studies, xxiv, 13; "The Ironic Cage of Positivism and the Nature of Philosophical Theology", xvi; "Making Strange", 77; "Mennonite and Métis", 20–21 ; *Messianic Political Theology and Diaspora Ethics: Essays in Exile*, xx, 30–34, 50, 78–83

labour. *See* spirituality of work
Leclair, Carole, 20–21, 83
liberalism, xi, 50, 54, 61, 201
logos, 71, 73–74, 111, 129, 134
Luther, Martin, 30, 32, 68–73

Markus, Robert, 15–16
martyr, 17, 70, 182–83, 224–26, 227n8, 231
memory, xxii, 11, 22–23, 54, 187, 189, 196
Mennonite, ix–xii, xxi, 9–12, 18–21, 32, 34, 35n4, 52–53, 77, 81, 204, 234–46; and colonialism, 21; and ethnicity, 18; experiences in gulag, 19; and queerness, 234–46; relationality, 19
Merchant, Carolyn, 129–30
mercy, 14, 74, 95n5
messianism, xxi, xxvi, 11, 17–18, 23, 37–47, 124; Jewish, 37–41; and politics, xxvii, 41, 50, 61, 77–78, 80–83, 94, 106, 123–26, 177
Métis, 20–21
Milbank, John, xi, 11, 15, 116n20, 182n13
miracle, 130–33; empirical, 131–33; scandal of, 133
morality, xxiii, 127–28, 219
Murdoch, Iris, 210, 213–16, 221
mysticism, xxvi, 37–38

nationalism, xxii, xxvi, 54–59, 62; Christian, 33; religious, 57; white, 103n34

nature: divine, 97–99; human, 53, 109, 110n8, 153, 157; laws of, 114–15, 130, 133
Nietzsche, Friedrich, xviii, 185
nihilism, 41, 124, 190, 217
Nixon, Rob, 144–45
nomos, xxvi, 64–75, 134

O'Donovan, Joan Lockwood, 32
O'Donovan, Oliver, 30, 32, 52, 53n7, 72–74
obedience, 72, 137, 141, 153–58, 162, 165
Odyssey, 211–12
oikonomia, 40, 77, 181n11
ontology, xxiii, 67, 83, 87, 129
Othello, xxvii, 223–33

patience: Christian, 136–48; urgent, 147–48
Paul, Apostle, xxvi, 17, 23, 26–30, 33–34, 39–42, 45–46, 50–54, 59, 77, 87, 95–96, 106n1, 107–8, 163–73
Peabody, Francis Greenwood, 33
pedagogy, xxi, 15
Pelagius, 96–99
penitence, 10, 16–17, 20–21
penultimate, the, 69–70, 100
Plato, xi, xvii–iii, xix, 10, 16, 20, 52–61, 116n21; and Augustine, 16–17, 20
Plett, Casey, xxvii, 204–6, 234–46
power, xxv, xxvii, 10, 13, 27, 32, 41–42, 46–47, 61, 77–81, 87, 95–69, 100, 107–20, 129–34, 142n23, 144–45, 153–62, 164, 167, 178–80, 188, 198n13, 200, 235, 240–41; messianic, xxv, 42, 240–41
Protestantism, 12, 18, 50, 59, 103n34, 125, 234

queerness, 324–46

Radical Reformation, x, 12, 50
Ratzinger, Joseph, 69–73
realism, cosmic, 113–14, 118

relationality, 19–21, 193, 195, 199, 235, 242; and Mennonites, 19;
religious studies, x, xv, xviii–xx, 79
ressentiment, xxi–ii, 81, 83, 186
resurrection, 13, 29–30, 64–70, 75, 108–9, 117, 120, 130, 154, 221
Rosa, Hartmut, 79, 142–43; *The Uncontrollability of the World*, 84

Sabbati, 37, 40, 44–45
Sapientia (Hrotsvit of Gandersheim), xxvii, 223–33
Scarry, Elaine, *On Beauty and Being Just*, 210, 208–22
Schleitheim Articles, 68–69
Scholem, Gershom, 37-4, 44–46
Schürmann, Reiner, 79, 84–86
Schweitzer, Albert, 26n2, 28n7, 29, 31, 33
science, 106–20, 127–29
sentimentality, xi, 13
sexuality, xxvii, 193–206, 240; Augustinian, 193–97
social acceleration, 142–43
soul, xi, xvi–xx, 10–13, 15–16, 18–19, 50–62, 112–13, 119, 151, 179, 194, 215–16, 219
sovereignty, 10, 17, 21, 34, 46, 52–53, 61, 81–82, 123–34, 150–1, 154, 158–61
spiritual causality, 11, 16–17
spirituality of work, 150–62
Swinton, John, 138–40

Taubes, Jacob, 39–46, 52, 65n5
Taylor, Charles, xi, 41–44, 11, 14–15, 179, 182
theology: Anabaptist, 12; decolonial, 94–95, 100; and ethics, xxvii, 11, 22, 31–32; kenotic, 150–54, 160; Mennonite, 18; messianic, 106–20; negative, 116–17; philosophical xv–xviv; political, xxiv, 13–15, 26–34, 40, 43n24, 50–53, 61, 65–66, 72–74, 77–81, 94, 106–7, 123–23, 133, 177; of science, xxvi, 106–20
time, 131–32, 136–48, 173
transcendence, xi, 108n4, 126–28, 190, 152, 210–16
Trinity, 82, 108, 110–11
Trump, Donald, 54, 59
truth, xvi, xix, xxiii–iv, 16, 20, 38, 43, 83, 113–15, 118–20, 131–32, 146–47, 153, 166–67, 183–85, 208–15, 222

United States, 33, 54–55, 57, 59, 74
utopianism, 37–38, 235

Vico, Giamattista, xix
violence, xxi–ii, 3, 67, 80, 82–83, 97, 124, 126, 133 140–46, 153, 157, 194, 200, 246; slow, 144–47

Weil, Simone, xxvi, 51, 79, 94, 150–62, 179, 210, 213–16, 221
Weiss, Johannes, *Die Predigt Jesu von Reiche Gottes*, 27
Wiebe, Donald: *The Irony of Theology and the Nature of Religious Thought*, xvi; "Argument or Authority in the Academy", xvii
Wright, N. T., 30, 168n9

Yoder, John Howard, xxi, 30, 52, 53n7, 54, 61n32, 65n4, 73, 109n7

Scripture Index

Genesis

1:1–3	111
3:1–6	115
15:6	171

Psalms

33:5	167
90:4	29

Isaiah

6:3	167

Habakkuk

2:4	165

Zechariah

9:7	59

Matthew

5:1–20	88
7:16	101
7:21	95
10:23	28
10:34–35	165
11:25	171
16:28	27, 161
24:43	31

Mark

9:1	27
10:43–44	77
12:17	47
13	107
13:30	28
13:32	28

Luke

4	92
9:27	27
	24:21

John

14:25–26	95
15:5	96
16:12–15	95
21:22	28

Acts

3:14	166
7:52	166
17	58
2:14	166

Romans

1:15—3:26	163-73
4:6-8	164
4:24	165, 173
5:5	98, 164
5:9	164
6:8	165
7:15-18	96
8:15	164
8:21	100
9:30	170
10:9-10	165, 170
11:36a	167
13:11-12	29
16:16	226

1 Corinthians

1:18, 21	173
2:15	173
4:3	173
7	52
7:12-13	165
7:29-31	29, 34, 46, 59, 65, 77
8:1	77-78
9:17	77-78
9:19-22	173
10:11	29, 32
10:23	78
15:1-3	172
15:11	165
15:28	34

2 Corinthians

2:15-16	165
3:17	104
5:17	165
5:19	165
5:21	173
11:1-3	227
13:12	226

Galatians

1:12	107
2:15-16	173
2:19-20	107
3:6	171
3:23-28	171
3:28	59
6:14-15	107

1 Thessalonians

1:8	165
4:17	28
5:2	30, 31
5:26	226
15:51-52	29

2 Thessalonians

1:10	172
5:9	172
2:2	29
2:6	42

1 Timothy

6:1-2	165

Philemon

2:2-11	65
2:6-11	154
2:13	96

Hebrews

5:8-9	156
11:1	231

1 Peter

1:5	172
1:12	171
2:9	51

2 Peter	
1:4	98
3:8–9	139
3:4	29
3:8	29, 139
3:10	30
3:11–12	31

1 John	
4:13	98

Revelation	
5:1–14	65
22:2	59

www.ingramcontent.com/pod-product-compliance
Lightning Source LLC
Chambersburg PA
CBHW022002220426
43663CB00007B/919